SOLVING THE PROFESSIONAL DEVELOPMENT PUZZLE

101 Solutions for Career and Life Planning

ROBERT M. SHERFIELD
The College of Southern Nevada

PATRICIA G. MOODY
University of South Carolina

PEARSON

Prentice
Hall

UPPER SADDLE RIVER, NEW JERSEY 07458
COLUMBUS, OHIO

Library of Congress Cataloging-in-Publication Data

Sherfield, Robert M.
Solving the professional development puzzle: 101 solutions for career and life planning/
    Robert M. Sherfield, Patricia G. Moody.
        p. cm.
    Includes bibliographical references and index.
    ISBN-13: 978-0-13-500365-7 (pbk.)
    ISBN-10: 0-13-500365-2 (pbk.)
    1. Career development.   2. Vocational guidance.   3. Job hunting.   4. Self-actualization (Psychology)
I. Moody, Patricia G.   II. Title.
HF5381.S5429 2009
650.14—dc22

2008022389

Vice President and Executive Publisher: Jeffery W. Johnston
Executive Editor: Sande Johnson
Development Editor: Jennifer Gessner
Editorial Assistant: Lynda Cramer
Senior Managing Editor: Pamela D. Bennett
Project Manager: Kerry J. Rubadue
Production Coordination: Thistle Hill Publishing Services, LLC
Design Coordinator: Diane C. Lorenzo
Photo Coordinator: Valerie Schultz
Cover Design: Diane C. Lorenzo
Cover Image: iStockphoto
Operations Specialist: Susan W. Hannahs
Director of Marketing: Quinn Perkson
Marketing Manager: Amy Judd
Marketing Coordinator: Brian Mounts

This book was set in AGaramond by Integra Software Services. It was printed and bound by Edwards Brothers. The cover was printed by Phoenix Color Corp./Hagerstown.

Chapter-Opening and Additional Interior Photo Credits: Michal Heron/PH College, pp. 1, 202; courtesy of the Library of Congress, p. 17 (top); Michael Evstafiev/Getty Images Inc.–Hulton Archive Photos, p. 17 (bottom); Robert Voets/CBS/ Picture Desk, Inc./Kobal Collection, p. 18; Mira.com/John Stuart, p. 25; CBS Photo Archive/Getty Images Inc.–Hulton Archive Photos, p. 35; © Louie Psihoyos/CORBIS All Rights Reserved, p. 36; Spencer Platt/Getty Images, Inc.–Getty News, p. 39; Pearson Learning Photo Studio, p. 69; Ron Chapple/Getty Images, Inc.–Taxi, p. 97; Photolibrary.com, p. 116; Francis Miller/Getty Images/Time Life Pictures, p. 133; Superstock, Inc., p. 157; Peter Chadwick © Dorling Kindersley, p. 179. All individual photos for Graduate Quote features were provided by the photo subjects.

Pearson® is a registered trademark of Pearson plc

Pearson Education Ltd., London
Pearson Education Singapore Pte. Ltd.
Pearson Education Canada, Inc.
Pearson Education–Japan
Pearson Education Australia PTY, Limited

Pearson Education North Asia, Ltd., Hong Kong
Pearson Educación de Mexico, S.A. de C.V.
Pearson Education Malaysia Pte. Ltd.
Pearson Education Upper Saddle River, New Jersey

10 9 8 7 6 5 4 3 2 1
ISBN-13: 978-0-13-500365-7
ISBN-10:   0-13-500365-2

BRIEF CONTENTS

CONTENTS

v

CHAPTER 3

Designing Your Job Search, Writing Your Cover Letter, and Selling Yourself through Your Résumé   *Selling Yourself* 39

CHAPTER 7

Leading with Passion, Power, and Promise
Finding the Leader in You **133**

CHAPTER 8

Taking Care of Business   *Manage Your Personal Finances Wisely* **157**

CHAPTER 9

CHAPTER 10

To
Sande Johnson,
Amy Judd, Robin Balaszewski,
and Nancy Forsyth

Your support, advice, and guidance over the years have been

paramount to our success. Words will never be able

to express how thankful we are that you came into our lives,

believed in us, guided us, and nurtured us.

ROBERT M. SHERFIELD, PH.D.

Robert Sherfield has been teaching public speaking, theater, and student success as well as working with first-year orientation programs for over twenty-five years. Currently, he is a professor at the College of Southern Nevada, where he teaches student success, professional communication, public speaking, and drama. He is also an adjunct faculty member at the University of Nevada-Las Vegas in the William F. Harrah College of Hotel Administration, where he teaches classes in professional and career development.

An award-winning educator, Robb was named Educator of the Year at the College of Southern Nevada. He twice received the Distinguished Teacher of the Year Award from the University of South Carolina Union and has received numerous other awards and nominations for outstanding classroom instruction and advisement.

Robb's extensive work with student success programs includes experience with the design and implementation of these programs, including one program presented at the International Conference on the First-Year Experience in Newcastle upon Tyne, England. He has conducted faculty development keynotes and workshops at over 250 institutions of higher education across America and has presented workshops in forty-six states and several foreign countries.

In addition to his coauthorship of *Solving the Professional Development Puzzle*, he has authored or co-authored *Cornerstone: Discovering Your Potential, Learning Actively, and Living Well* (Prentice Hall, 2008); *Roadways to Success* (Prentice Hall, 2001), the trade book *365 Things I Learned in College* (Allyn & Bacon, 1996), *Capstone: Succeeding Beyond College* (Prentice Hall, 2001), *Case Studies for the First Year: An Odyssey into Critical Thinking and Problem Solving* (Prentice Hall, 2004), *The Everything® Self-Esteem Book* (Adams Media, 2004), and *Cornerstone: Building on Your Best for Career Success* (Prentice Hall, 2006).

Robb's interest in student success began with his own first year in college. Low SAT scores and high school ranking denied him entrance into college. With the help of a success program, Robb was granted entrance into college, and he went on to earn five college degrees, including a doctorate. He has always been interested in the social, academic, and cultural development of students, and he sees this book as his way to help students enter the world of work and establish lasting, rewarding careers. Visit **www.robertsherfield.com.**

PATRICIA G. MOODY, PH.D.

Patricia G. Moody is dean emeritus of the College of Hospitality, Retail, and Sport Management at the University of South Carolina, where she served on the faculty and in administration for over thirty years. An award-winning educator, Pat was honored as Distinguished

Educator of the Year at her college and as Collegiate Teacher of the Year by the National Business Education Association. She was also a top-five finalist for the Amoco Teaching Award at the University of South Carolina. She received the prestigious John Robert Gregg Award, the highest honor in her field of over 100,000 educators.

A nationally known motivational speaker, consultant, and author, Pat has spoken in almost every state, has been invited to speak in several foreign countries, and she frequently keynotes national and regional conventions. She has presented her signature motivational keynote address, "Fly Like an Eagle" to tens of thousands of people, from Olympic athletes to corporate executives to high school students.

An avid sports fan, she follows Gamecock athletics and chaired the University of South Carolina Athletics Advisory Committee. As the dean of her college, Pat led international trips to build relationships and establish joint research projects in hospitality. Pat now travels the country delivering workshops, keynotes, and presentations on topics such as how to motivate students, the emotional intelligence factor, the leader as a coach, time and stress management, and working in the new global community.

PROFESSIONAL ACKNOWLEDGMENTS AND GRATITUDE

Our sincere and grateful thanks to our insightful reviewers: Theresa Green-Ervin, Indiana University–Bloomington; Deborah Iturralde, Virginia College; Kate Sawyer, Lincoln Education; and Eric Wormsley, PIMA Medical Institute.

We would like to thank the following individuals for their support: Dr. Michael Richards, President, College of Southern Nevada; Dr. Darren Divine, Interim Vice President, College of Southern Nevada; Dr. Hyla Winters, Interim Associate Vice President, College of Southern Nevada; Professor Rose Hawkins, Interim Dean, College of Arts and Letters; Professor John Ziebell, Interim Department Chair–English; Professor Kathy Baker, Assistant Chair–English; Kate Sawyer, Lincoln Educational Services; Curtis Love, University of Nevada–Las Vegas; Sheri Hurd, Empire College; Karen McGrath, PIMA Medical Institute; Deborah Burleigh, Colorado Mountain College; Brad Waltman, The College of Southern Nevada; Al Dornbach, ITT Bensalem, PA; and Marty Flynn, Greenville Technical College.

Our Creative and Supportive Team at Pearson/Prentice Hall

Without the support and encouragement of the following people at Prentice Hall, this book would not be possible. Our sincere thanks to Nancy Forsyth, Jeff Johnston, Sande Johnson, Amy Judd, and Jenny Gessner. Your continuing faith in us over the years has been a most precious gift.

We also faithfully recognize the following Pearson professionals who have helped us with their advice, hard work, dedication, and determination. We are lucky to know you and are better people because of you. Thank you to Brenda Rock, Lynda Cramer, Walt Kirby, Debbie Ogilvie, Alan Hensley, Toni Payne, Pam Jeffries, Barbara Donlon, Cathy Bennett, Meredith Chandler, Jeff McIlroy, Steve Foster, Meghan McCauley, Connie James, and Matt Mesaros.

YOUR GOLDEN POTENTIAL FOR PERSONAL AND PROFESSIONAL SUCCESS

Chen Chao © Dorling Kindersley

Have you ever thought of yourself as "golden"? More importantly, have you ever treated yourself as if you are "golden"? We wanted to begin your professional development journey with a true story about discovering your golden self.

In 1957, a massive statue of Buddha was being moved from a temple in Thailand that had been abandoned in the early 1930s. The Buddha stands over 15 feet tall and measures over 12 feet in diameter. A crane had to be used to move the massive statue, but when the crane began to lift the Buddha, the weight of it was so great that the statue began to crack. To make matters even worse, it began to rain. Concerned with the condition of the Buddha, the head monk decided to have the statue lowered so it could be covered with a canvas until the rain stopped.

As nightfall came, the head monk took his flashlight outside to peer under the canvas to see if the statue had begun to dry. As he moved the light from area to area, he noticed something shining beneath one of the cracks. He began to wonder if something was under the clay. As he hammered and chiseled away at the crack, he found that the clay Buddha was *not* made of clay after all. The Monk found that the 15-foot-statue was really made of pure 18-carat gold.

Many scholars and historians believe the Buddha was cast sometime in the mid-1200s. It is suggested that in the 1700s the Siamese monks knew the Burmese army planned to attack them and, hoping to protect their statue, they covered it in 8 inches of clay, which dried and hardened much like concrete. When the army attacked, all of the monks in the village were killed, leaving no one who knew the truth about the Buddha. The clay remained intact until the statue was moved on a rainy day in 1957.

Today, the Golden Buddha, which was once covered with clay and abandoned, is said to be valued at almost $200 million.

YOUR GOLDEN OPPORTUNITY

We all have incredible talents, skills, and experiences that are all too often covered, underdeveloped, or simply never discussed. We move through life hiding our radiance, our golden self. As you begin to read and work through *Solving the Professional Development Puzzle*, we want you to think about how you are best going to let potential employers know about your talents, educations, experiences, and tenacity. We want you to begin to chip away at the clay that for years has been covering your brilliance. We want you to explore who you really are, what you have to offer to the world, and how best to use your talents and skills in the world of work—and beyond.

IN DISCOVERING YOUR POTENTIAL, WE ALSO INVITE YOU TO:

DISCOVER your *open-mindedness*

A truly educated person learns to consider a person's character rather than the color of one's skin, religion, sexual orientation, or ethnic background. As you enter the professional world of work, you will become more open-minded and better able to understand the need to learn before judging, reason before reacting, and to delve deeper before condemning. As you work to discover your potential and make your mark in today's workforce, strive hard to develop a habit of practicing open-mindedness.

DISCOVER your *competence and ability to question*

You have already established a certain level of competence or you wouldn't be here. Now is the time to push yourself to learn more than you ever have before. Your future depends on the knowledge you are gaining today. As you move through the coming months and years, don't be afraid to ask questions of others, especially your professors, mentors, and peers. Asking the right questions and listening will help you become a valuable member of any team.

DISCOVER your need to be *challenged*

The *easy road* will not lead to greatness, help you discover your true potential, or garner you success at work. Winston Churchill said, "It is from adversity that we gain greatness." When you are struggling, remember you are getting stronger. You are preparing for becoming the person you were meant to be. As you consider potential employers, look for positions that will benefit your professional progress, stretch you, and make you grow as a person.

DISCOVER your ability to *balance*

No *single* thing will ever bring you joy, peace, or prosperity. Include family, friends, cultural events, social activities, work, and service to others in your daily life. Seek balance between work and play. You will endlessly search for happiness unless you have a sense of balance in your life. Harmony and balance help you reduce stress, have more time for what you love, and live well.

DISCOVER your *success and true potential*

You need to define exactly what success means to you so you know what you are working toward. Whatever success is for you, pursue it with all of the passion and

Tony Souter @ Dorling Kindersley

energy you have. Set your goals high and work hard to create a life that you can ultimately look back on with pride, satisfaction, and joy. Create a life so that at the end of the road, you will be able to look back and say, ***"I did my best. I have no regrets."***

And so your golden journey to career and personal success begins . . .

Discovering Who You Are

Setting Yourself Apart and Finding Your Direction

WHY?

read and work through this chapter? Why will information on self-discovery help me with my life, an internship, my studies, or with my career? Why do I have to know where I'm going at this point in my life? Why is this stuff such a big deal?

College graduates are a dime a dozen, which does not mean, however, that *you* are. Herein lies the challenge. How do you distinguish yourself from the countless job seekers out there? What are you going to do that sets you apart from your competition—and yes, there is competition, strong competition. What do you have to offer that no one else can possibly offer to an employer? What unique skills do you have to help you thrive and survive in an ever-changing world gone crazy with outsourcing and technology? Answering these questions is the primary focus of this chapter, and indeed, this book and the course in which you are presently enrolled.

In his book *The 2010 Meltdown*, Edward Gordon (2005) writes, "Simply stated, today in America, there are just too many people trained for the wrong jobs. Many jobs have become unnecessary, technically obsolete . . . or worse yet, the job/career aspirations of too many current and future workers are at serious odds with the changing needs of the U.S. labor market" (p. 17). However, you can still have a very bright future, if you are well prepared. People who are highly skilled, possess superb oral and written communication skills, know how to solve problems, and can work well with others will be in high demand for many years to come.

Careers in the following areas are projected for high growth in the coming decade. *Health sciences* (dental and medical assistants, home health aides, physician assistants, medical assistants, occupational therapists, physical therapists, etc.); *aviation* (airplane mechanics and air traffic controllers); *skilled trades* (plumbers, electricians, mechanics, etc.); *teaching* (K-12 and college); *technology* (aerospace and GPS engineers, water and sanitation engineers, personnel in transportation services, systems analysts, programmers, interactive media designers, software engineers, desktop publishers, etc.); and *management, marketing, and public relations* (business managers, human resource directors, personnel in advertising and public relations, etc.).

This chapter will help you discover your unique qualities and characteristics that can give you the competitive edge in today's workplace. We offer 101 solutions to the career and life development puzzle in this book. Ten solutions are discussed here to get you on your way. More specifically, these ten tips will help you understand more about yourself, your personality, your challenges, your emotions, your strengths, your belief system, and, maybe most importantly, challenge you to write your own personal Guiding Statement for your personal and professional life. Welcome to *Solving the Career Development Puzzle*.

SOLUTION 1   KNOW WHO YOU ARE AND WHERE YOU'RE GOING

When asked, "Who are you?" so many people answer with "I'm a student," or "I'm a mom," or "I'm a teacher." Often we answer this question with *what* we are and not *who* we are. The difference between the two is huge. *What* you are is your work, your position, your family standing. *Who you are* is much deeper. Yes, who you are involves your work and relationships, but it is also the basis for your core, your foundation. Who you are involves much more than your title as a brother, a mother, a nurse, a mechanic, or a friend. Who you are involves your morality, your intellect, your spirituality, your emotions, your beliefs, your culture, your choices, and your dreams.

By understanding the difference between *what* you are and *who* you are, you can truly begin to understand yourself on a distinctive and higher level. Few people are willing to take this journey. Fear, time pressures, or lack of motivation may cause people to avoid finding the answer, but finding out who you are can be one of the most rewarding puzzle solutions in your life, and it can give you one of the competitive edges you need to survive and thrive in today's world of work.

Consider the puzzle in Figure 1.1. As you can see, *you* involves nine different pieces. Understanding how each piece affects your actions, goals, relationships, work ethic, and motivation can mean the difference between success and failure in work—and in life. As you study the puzzle, consider your strengths and challenges in each area. How does each piece drive your choices, and how does each piece help you understand more about who you are? Are there pieces of the puzzle you have never considered? If so, how has this affected your life in the past? At this time and place in your life, which piece is the most or least important? Which pieces can you use to gain a competitive edge, and which pieces need improvement?

As you look at each piece of the me puzzle, think about *one strength* you have to offer in the workplace and how it will help you in the future. Then think about *one challenge* you will have to overcome for each piece of the me puzzle and how you plan to do so.

> **QUOTE**
>
> Self-knowledge is the beginning of self-improvement.
>
> Spanish Proverb

EXAMPLE

Moral Me

Strength: *I am very grounded in my work ethic. I consider myself a loyal and dedicated employee and will do my best every day.*

The Future: *This strength will help me gain the trust of my superiors and peers. They will know that I am a person to whom they can turn in times of turmoil. They will know I can make ethical and honest decisions.*

Challenge: *I sometimes judge others too harshly when they do not have the same work ethic as I do. This can become a problem when I move up the ladder and begin supervising people.*

Overcome: *I plan to begin listening more and try to understand others' backgrounds before making judgments.*

Intellectual Me

Strength: _____

_____

_____

The Future: _____

_____

_____

Challenge: _____

_____

_____

Overcome: _____

_____

_____

FIGURE 1.1 Solving the Me Puzzle

Intellectual Me	Moral Me	Cultural Me

☑ What I know
☑ Common sense
☑ Skills I possess
☑ Critical thinking
☑ Reasoning
☑ Problem solving
	☑ Character
	☑ Ethics
	☑ Values
	☑ Choices and decisions
	☑ Reactions
	☑ Principles
		☑ How I interact
		  with others
		☑ Knowledge of my own
		  culture, norms, heritage,
		  environment, race, etc.

Visionary Me	**Physical Me**	**Emotional Me**

☑ Where am I going
☑ What do I want
☑ What are my goals
  and dreams for the future
☑ What skills will I need
  in the future to be
  successful
	☑ My health
	☑ My appearance and
	  grooming
	☑ My body
	☑ My habits such as
	  drinking, smoking,
	  eating, etc.
		☑ What I feel
		☑ How am I guided by
		  emotions
		☑ My heart versus my head
		☑ How I manage conflicts
		  and challenges

Spiritual Me	**Social Me**	**Material Me**
☑ What I believe ☑ My religion ☑ Wisdom gained ☑ Meditation ☑ Altruistic notions ☑ My "grounding"	☑ My relationships ☑ My activities ☑ My associations ☑ My involvement ☑ Introvert versus extrovert	☑ What I have ☑ What I want ☑ What I need to survive ☑ Economic background

SOURCE: Based, in part, on the work of psychologist William James (1842–1910).

Moral Me

Strength: _____

_____

_____

The Future: _____

_____

_____

Challenge: _____

_____

_____

Overcome: _____

_____

_____

Cultural Me

Strength: _____

_____

_____

The Future: _____

_____

_____

Challenge: _____

_____

_____

Overcome: _____

_____

_____

Visionary Me

Strength: _____

_____

_____

The Future: _____

_____

_____

(*continued*)

SUCCESS NOTES:

_____
_____
_____
_____
_____
_____
_____
_____
_____
_____
_____
_____
_____
_____
_____
_____
_____
_____
_____
_____
_____
_____

Challenge: _____
_____
_____

Overcome: _____
_____
_____

Physical Me

Strength: _____
_____
_____

The Future: _____
_____
_____

Challenge: _____
_____
_____

Overcome: _____
_____
_____

Emotional Me

Strength: _____
_____
_____

The Future: _____
_____
_____

Challenge: _____
_____
_____

Overcome: _____
_____
_____

Spiritual Me

Strength: _____

_____

_____

The Future: _____

_____

_____

Challenge: _____

_____

_____

Overcome: _____

_____

_____

Social Me

Strength: _____

_____

_____

The Future: _____

_____

_____

Challenge: _____

_____

_____

Overcome: _____

_____

_____

Materialistic Me

Strength: _____

_____

_____

The Future: _____

_____

_____

(continued)

Challenge: _____

_____

_____

Overcome: _____

_____

_____

SOLUTION 2 RECOGNIZE AND OWN YOUR STRENGTHS

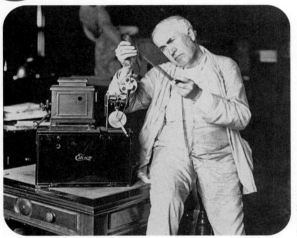

Library of Congress

"I am super organized."
"I can't find a thing on this desk."

"I am extremely good at my profession."
"I feel so stupid at work."

"I know I can solve that problem."
"I don't even know where to begin."

Notice the difference among these perspectives? One person seems optimistic and to know his or her abilities and strengths, and the other is unsure, timid, and pessimistic. Which one would you hire? Which one would you like working on your team?

Knowing what you're good at and owning those strengths can be an enormously positive attribute and can give you another competitive instrument in your toolbox.

Basically, you must answer this question: *What do I have going for me?* Writer, professor, and motivational speaker Leo Buscaglia (1982) wrote,

> You want to be the most educated, the most brilliant, the most exciting, the most versatile, the most creative individual in the world, because then you can give it away; and the only reason you have anything is to give it away. You are all you have. Therefore, make yourself the most beautiful, tender, wonderful fantastic person in the world.

If you don't know your strengths, it will be impossible to convey them to an employer. It is also impossible to use the strengths you don't even know you have. Perhaps you've never thought of yourself as a problem solver, but think again. Don't you do this daily with your personal budget? Your children? Your studies? Juggling schedules with work and classes? You solve problems every day, and acknowledging this skill can only make it stronger.

Writer and educator Abe Arkoff (1995) suggests that the old saying, "Anything worth doing is worth doing well," is outdated and needs to be junked. He suggests that by doing a lot of things (and yes, experiencing failure and setbacks), we find a way to identify our strengths. "Having to do things perfectly can keep you from trying and finding out what we like and what we can do well" (p. 176).

Thomas Edison, inventor of the light bulb, was once asked, "Sir, how do you feel about failing 2,000 times to make the light bulb work?" His response was this: "I have *never* failed at making the light bulb work. I have successfully identified 1,999 ways that it will *not* work." Think of the positive message in that statement.

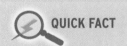

QUICK FACT

Eight million U.S. workers speak English so poorly that they cannot hold high-paying jobs.

Center for Law and Social Policy, 2003

You probably have strengths you have never thoroughly identified. Consider the following list. Circle your strengths. Add any of your strengths that are not listed. You will need to reference this list later in the chapter.

accountable	budget-minded	coaching skills
decision-making skills	problem-solving skills	negotiating skills
writing skills	speaking skills	editing skills
time management	organized	planner
research abilities	team building ability	analyzing
critical thinking skills	positive attitude	integrity
intuitive	stable	punctual
inquisitive	rational	ethical
reliable	tolerant	resourceful
humorous	compassion	hopeful
self-reliant	decisive	courageous
competent	grateful	loyal
loving	sincere	fun loving
open minded	stylish	helpful
friendly	optimistic	respectful
conviction	involved	trusting
well groomed	neat	prepared
planner	supportive	honest
strong	reserved	coping skills
logical	spiritual	warm
giving	helpful	versatile
motivated	grounded	trustworthy
creative	modest	imaginative
fair	leader	flexible
forgiving	persuasive	yielding

_____   _____   _____

_____   _____   _____

_____   _____   _____

 SOLUTION 3 **IDENTIFY YOUR PERSONALITY TYPE AND USE IT TO BEST ADVANTAGE**

TAKE THE PAP

The Personality Assessment Profile

© Robert M. Sherfield, Ph.D., 1999, 2002, 2005, 2008 from *Cornerstone: Your Foundation for Discovering Your Potential, Learning Actively and Living Well*, 2008. Sherfield, R., Montgomery, R., Moody, P., Prentice Hall.

DIRECTIONS: Read each statement carefully and thoroughly. After reading the statement, rate your response using the scale provided. There are no right or wrong answers. This is not a timed survey. The PAP is based, in part, on the Myers-Briggs Type Indicator (MBTI) by Katharine Briggs and Isabel Briggs-Myers.

(continued)

3 = Often applies

2 = Sometimes applies

1 = Never or almost never applies

_____   **1a.** I am a very talkative person.

_____   **1b.** I am a more reflective person than a verbal person.

_____   **2a.** I am a very factual and literal person.

_____   **2b.** I look to the future and I can see possibilities.

_____   **3a.** I value truth and justice over tact and emotion.

_____   **3b.** I find it easy to empathize with other people.

_____   **4a.** I am very ordered and efficient.

_____   **4b.** I enjoy having freedom from control.

_____   **5a.** I am a very friendly and social person.

_____   **5b.** I enjoy listening to others more than talking.

_____   **6a.** I enjoy being around and working with people who have a great deal of common sense.

_____   **6b.** I enjoy being around and working with people who are dreamers and have a great deal of imagination.

_____   **7a.** One of my motivating forces is to do a job very well.

_____   **7b.** I like to be recognized for, and I am motivated by, my accomplishments and awards.

_____   **8a.** I like to plan out my day before I go to bed.

_____   **8b.** When I get up on a non-school or non-work day, I just like to let the day "plan itself."

_____   **9a.** I like to express my feelings and thoughts.

_____   **9b.** I enjoy a great deal of tranquility and quiet time to myself.

_____   **10a.** I am a very pragmatic and realistic person.

_____   **10b.** I like to create new ideas, methods, or ways of doing things.

_____   **11a.** I make decisions with my brain.

_____   **11b.** I make decisions with my heart.

_____   **12a.** I am a very disciplined and orderly person.

_____   **12b.** I don't make a lot of plans.

_____   **13a.** I like to work with a group of people.

_____   **13b.** I would rather work independently.

_____   **14a.** I learn best if I can see it, touch it, smell it, taste it, or hear it.

_____   **14b.** I learn best by relying on my gut feelings or intuition.

_____   **15a.** I am quick to criticize others.

_____   **15b.** I compliment others very easily and quickly.

_____   **16a.** My life is systematic and organized.

_____   **16b.** I don't really pay attention to deadlines.

_____   **17a.** I can be myself when I am around others.

_____ **17b.** I can be myself when I am alone.

_____ **18a.** I live in the here and now, in the present.

_____ **18b.** I live in the future, planning and dreaming.

_____ **19a.** I think that if someone breaks the rules, the person should be punished.

_____ **19b.** I think that if someone breaks the rules, we should look at the person who broke the rules, examine the rules, and look at the situation at hand before a decision is made.

_____ **20a.** I do my work, then I play.

_____ **20b.** I play, then do my work.

Refer to your score on each individual question. Place that score beside the appropriate question number. Then tally each line at the side.

SCORE					TOTAL ACROSS	CODE
1a _____	5a _____	9a _____	13a _____	17a _____	_____	**E** Extrovert
1b _____	5b _____	9b _____	13b _____	17b _____	_____	**I** Introvert
2a _____	6a _____	10a _____	14a _____	18a _____	_____	**S** Sensing
2b _____	6b _____	10b _____	14b _____	18b _____	_____	**N** Intuition
3a _____	7a _____	11a _____	15a _____	19a _____	_____	**T** Thinking
3b _____	7b _____	11b _____	15b _____	19b _____	_____	**F** Feeling
4a _____	8a _____	12a _____	16a _____	20a _____	_____	**J** Judging
4b _____	8b _____	12b _____	16b _____	20b _____	_____	**P** Perceiving

PAP SCORES

Personality Indicator

Look at the scores on your PAP. Is your score higher in the E or I line? Is your score higher in the S or N line? Is your score higher in the T or F line? Is your score higher in the J or P line? Write the code to the side of each section.

Is your higher score E or I?   Code _____

Is your higher score S or N?   Code _____

Is your higher score T or F?   Code _____

Is your higher score J or P?   Code _____

Understanding Personality Typing (Typology)

The questions on the PAP helped you discover whether you are extroverted or introverted (E or I), sensing or intuitive (S or N), thinking or feeling (T or F), and judging or perceiving (J or P). These questions were based, in part, on work done by Carl Jung, Katharine Briggs, and Isabel Briggs-Myers.

In 1921, Swiss psychologist Carl Jung (1875–1961) published his work *Psychological Types.* Jung suggested that human behavior is not random. He felt that behavior follows patterns, and these patterns are caused by differences in the way people use their minds. In 1942, Isabel Briggs-Myers and her mother, Katharine Briggs, began to put Jung's theory into practice. They developed the Myers-Briggs Type Indicator, which after more than fifty years of research and refinement has become the most widely used instrument for identifying and studying personality.

Keep in mind that no part of this assessment measures your worth, your success factors, how smart you are, or your value as a human being. The questions on the PAP assisted you in identifying your type, but neither the PAP nor your authors want you to assume that one personality type is better or worse, more valuable or less valuable, or more likely to be successful. What personality typing can do is to "help us discover what best motivates and energizes each of us as individuals" (Tieger & Tieger, 2001).

Why Personality Matters

When all of the combinations of E/I, S/N, T/F, and J/P are combined, there are sixteen personality types. Everyone will fit into one of the following categories:

ISTJ	ISFJ	INFJ	INTJ
ISTP	ISFP	INFP	INTP
ESTP	ESFP	ENFP	ENTP
ESTJ	ESFJ	ENFJ	ENTJ

> **QUOTE**
>
> Many people go fishing all of their lives without ever knowing that it is not fish they are after.
>
> H. D. Thoreau

Let's take a look at the four major categories of typing. Notice that the higher your score in one area, the stronger your personality type is for that area. For instance, if you scored 15 on the E (extroversion) questions, you are a strong extrovert. If you scored 15 on the I (introversion) questions, you are a strong introvert. However, if you scored 7 on the E questions and 8 on the I questions, your score indicates you possess almost the same amount of extroverted and introverted qualities. The same is true for every category on the PAP.

E Versus I (Extroversion/Introversion)

This category deals with the way we *interact with others and the world around us.*

Extroverts prefer to live in the outside world, drawing their strength from other people. They are outgoing and love interaction. They usually make decisions with others in mind. They enjoy being the center of attention. There are usually few secrets about extroverts.

Introverts draw their strength from the inner world. They need to spend time alone to think and ponder. They are usually quiet and reflective. They typically make decisions by themselves. They do not like being the center of attention. They are private.

S Versus N (Sensing/Intuition)

This category deals with the way we *learn and deal with information.*

Sensing types gather information through their five senses. They have a hard time believing something if it cannot be seen, touched, smelled, tasted, or heard. They like concrete facts and details. They do not rely on intuition or gut feelings. They usually have a great deal of common sense.

Intuitive types are not very detail oriented. They can see possibilities, and they rely on their gut feelings. Usually, they are very innovative people. They tend to live in the future and often get bored once they have mastered a task.

T Versus F (Thinking/Feeling)

This category deals with the way we *make decisions.*

Thinkers are very logical people. They do not make decisions based on feelings or emotion. They are analytical and sometimes do not take others' values into consideration when making decisions. They can easily identify the flaws of others. They can be seen as insensitive and lacking compassion.

Feelers make decisions based on what they feel is right and just. They like to have harmony, and they value others' opinions and feelings. They are usually very tactful people who like to please others. They are very warm people.

J Versus P (Judging/Perceiving)

This category deals with the way we *live.*

Judgers are very orderly people. They must have a great deal of structure in their lives. They are good at setting goals and sticking to their goals. They are the type of people who would seldom, if ever, play before their work was completed.

Perceivers are just the opposite. They are less structured and more spontaneous. They do not like timelines. Unlike the judger, they will play before their work is done. They will take every chance to delay a decision or judgment. Sometimes, they can become involved in too many things at one time.

After you have identified your own personality type and studied the different types discussed here, you can begin to think more seriously about your career choices. For instance, if you scored very strong in the extroversion section, it may not serve you well to pursue a career where you would be forced to work alone. Likewise, if you scored very low in the sensing category, you may not enjoy a career in the sciences.

SUCCESS NOTES:

_____
_____
_____
_____
_____
_____
_____
_____
_____
_____
_____
_____
_____
_____
_____
_____
_____
_____
_____
_____
_____
_____
_____
_____

SOLUTION 4   KNOW WHAT YOU WANT FROM LIFE AND WORK

Some of the strongest, most dedicated people in the world struggle. Why? They struggle because they have never really thought about what they want out of life or from their careers. They have never done the work required to answer this question—and it is work. What is it that you really want and need to be happy, fulfilled, and successful? You may have never thought about the questions here,

but consider them as you try to formulate an answer to the question, "What do I want from my life and my work?"

- ☑ Is my success tied to the amount of money I make?
- ☑ Are my friends and family more important than career?
- ☑ What would I be willing to do to get ahead?
- ☑ What can I contribute to the world through my career?
- ☑ What really makes me happy? Will my career choice give this to me?
- ☑ Does my career choice suit my genuine interests?
- ☑ Does my current career choice really motivate me?
- ☑ Am I working toward this career for convenience or passion?
- ☑ Would I rather work inside or outside?
- ☑ Am I more of a leader or a follower?
- ☑ Do I want to travel with my work?
- ☑ Am I truly grounded in my ethics?

An old quote says, "If you don't know where you're going, that's probably where you'll end up." Many people have found this to be true in their personal and professional lives. Sometimes it is called a "midlife crisis" and sometimes people think of it as burnout. Regardless of the title, knowing what you want and need from your career and your life will be ultimately important to your happiness and success.

In the space provided, jot down a few things you think you want and need from your career. Remember, the two categories are different.

I need . . .	I want . . .
_____	_____
_____	_____
_____	_____
_____	_____
_____	_____
_____	_____
_____	_____
_____	_____

SOLUTION 5　IDENTIFY AND EMULATE YOUR ROLE MODELS

Who do you admire most in your life right now? Is it a parent or grandparent who struggled to raise you and offer you things he or she never had? Is it your current supervisor who treats people well and with respect? Is it a famous person who overcame adversity to help make life better for others?

We all have role models in our lives for a reason. They help us see what is possible. They help us see a better future. Think about a person you greatly admire. Who is that person?

_____

_____

What personal and professional qualities do they possess that you would like to have someday?

Personal Qualities

_____

_____

_____

_____

_____

Professional Qualities

_____

_____

_____

_____

_____

Choose one of the qualities from the list you just created. How will this quality help you become successful and advance in your chosen career? Be specific in your answer.

_____

_____

_____

_____

_____

_____

SOLUTION 6 DETERMINE WHAT YOU VALUE

Values are strange and unique. What you value and consider to be ultimately important to *your* life and success may be at the bottom of the list for someone else. First, it is important to understand what values are and why our value system is important to us. A value is simply a principle or quality that we think is worthwhile. It is something we highly regard. You may value honesty or love or friendship in your life. Others may put primary importance on money or possessions. In a study by the National Opinion Research Center, "97% of respondents reported that their own families and children were important to them. Career or work was second, with 87% indicating it was important to them" (Arkoff, 1995).

So why are values important to us? They usually drive our decisions, determine how we treat others, guide us in reacting to certain situations, and help direct our moral

Michal Heron/PH College

behavior. When we act in a way that goes against what we value, our conscience begins to gnaw at us. That little voice inside our head begins to let us know that what we have done, or what we are about to do, goes against our moral code, our values. When we make decisions or act in a way that goes against the values established by society or our workplace, we begin to suffer in different ways, such as being incarcerated or terminated. Therefore, knowing what *you* value *and* what society and your workplace values will be exceedingly important to your success and mobility.

A time may come in your personal or professional life when you are asked to go against your value system. The degree to which you hold your values dear will determine the likelihood of your decision. If you are asked to "distort a few numbers" to make the books look better for investors, you, and only you, will know if this is something you can tolerate. A good question to ask is this, "Would my mother be proud of me for making this decision?"

Also, a time may come when your value system is at odds with your employer. If you've never really placed a high value on time management or punctuality and it's a quality your new employer values greatly, you will quickly find that your value system must change—or you will have to change employers and find one who does not value punctuality as much. Again, it will be an interesting journey to discover what others do or do not value.

Our personal value system also serves as a motivational force in our lives. What we value, we protect. What we value, we work to keep. What we value, we work to enrich. What we value, we work to get more of. We are motivated by what brings us joy and peace, and unless we hold a firm picture of our value system in our hearts and minds, we may be working for the wrong things.

Take a moment and circle the words here that best indicate what you value. If *one* or more of your personal values is not on the list, add them to the bottom.

service to others	privacy	interaction
a healthy love relationship	money	honesty
fairness	challenges	respect
the environment	family	friends
friendship	success	education
leisure time	faith	material things
leadership abilities	fun activities	beauty
a nice home	fine car	great clothes
safety	health	comfort
fame/popularity	independence	control
reputation	physical activity	pets
decision making	speaking	writing
_____	_____	_____
_____	_____	_____
_____	_____	_____

Now for the hard part: If you could only have one thing in your life that you valued and it had to sustain you in your personal and professional life, which value from the preceding list would you choose?

_____

_____

Why?

_____

_____

_____

How will this *one* value help you be successful in your career?

_____

_____

_____

_____

SOLUTION 7 RECOGNIZE THE POWER OF YOUR VALUES AND BELIEFS

It has been said, "If you think you can't, you can't. If you think you can, you can." Countless studies have been conducted on the power of personal beliefs. A belief is what we consider to be true or false. It is what we deem to be real or fake, fact or opinion. A belief is a conviction that we hold so dearly that it literally causes us to act in one way or another.

If you believe you are going to fail your math test, you probably will. If you believe you have nothing to offer to the world, you probably do not. Our beliefs are powerful and central to our self-esteem and personal motivation. Consider the following short examples:

Abraham Lincoln lost eight elections, went bankrupt twice, lost a child, had a complete nervous and mental breakdown all *before* he became president of the United States. He believed that he could govern his country, and he did and is today renowned and highly respected for his leadership and courage.

Walt Disney was fired from his first job because his boss thought he did not have any creativity or good ideas and considered him to be a poor sketch artist. Walt Disney believed he was much more talented than his boss gave him credit for.

Tina Turner, raped and beaten by her own husband, Ike, had to file suit in court to keep her identity—her name. Ike believed she would never be successful without him. She believed otherwise. After their divorce and business partnership ended, she recorded many songs, won several Grammy awards, and has sold over 300 million albums. Her beliefs paid off.

THINK ABOUT IT

How will being able to control your emotions help you become a more effective employee and/or leader?

Ray Romano was fired from the TV show *News Radio* while it was still in rehearsal. He believed he had talent as a comedian and went on to develop, produce, and write the Emmy-award-winning series *Everybody Loves Raymond*.

Maya Angelou has won three Grammy awards for the spoken word and has been nominated twice for Broadway's prestigious Tony award. However, as a young girl, she was raped by her mother's boyfriend and did not speak again for four years. By the time she was in her twenties, she had been a cook, streetcar conductor, cocktail waitress, dancer, madam, high school dropout, and unwed mother. However, she believed she had talent as a writer and poet. Her beliefs paid off! She became only the second poet in American history to write and deliver an original poem at a presidential inauguration (for President Bill Clinton).

Here are some examples of beliefs:

- ☑ I believe in God.
- ☑ I believe honesty is always the best policy.
- ☑ I believe it is important to save 10 percent of my paycheck each month.
- ☑ I believe love conquers all.
- ☑ I believe hard work will always pay off in the end.
- ☑ I believe people are basically good, not evil.
- ☑ I believe all people are created equal.

> **QUOTE**
>
> I am somebody. I am me. I like being me. And I need nobody to make me somebody.
>
> Louis L'Amour

Our beliefs can guide us through many troubled times. They can help us when everything seems to be going against our hopes and dreams. They influence our attitudes and behaviors. However, even though our beliefs are very powerful, alone they will not get you an Emmy or the presidency of the United States. Beliefs must be followed by hard work, active goals, and many sacrifices.

Most importantly, however, our belief system may be guiding us to act in one way or another when we don't even know why. Our beliefs are very powerful, and without understanding them, where they came from, and how they direct our actions, we can act or think or feel things we really don't understand. You must have a firm grasp on *what* you truly believe to be true and concrete in your life.

Note also that when we truly believe something and still go against that belief, once again, our conscience begins to gnaw and nag at us. For example, you may believe sensible eating is essential to your overall good health yet continue to eat cream-filled donuts each morning. You may believe honesty is the best policy, but you continue to tell little white lies to your spouse.

In thinking about your career, consider if your choice is consistent with what you believe, what you value, and what you think. If it is not, it is likely that you will not find happiness or fulfillment in that career. For example, you may hold the firm belief that it is important to protect our environment but you know your employer is one of the leading polluters in America. Can you live with this? Can you be happy knowing that your work and your company are counter to one of your central beliefs?

Think about a belief you hold dear. What is that belief?

_____

_____

_____

_____

How can this belief help guide you in your career or job-making decisions?

_____

_____

_____

_____

 SOLUTION 8 UNDERSTAND YOUR EMOTIONAL RESPONSES

Should evolution be taught in the public school system? Should the drinking age be lowered to 18? Should 16-year-olds be allowed to drive a car? Should hate crime laws be abolished? Should same-sex couples be allowed to marry and adopt children? What emotions are you feeling right now? Did you immediately formulate answers to these questions in your mind? Do your emotions drive the way you think or act?

Emotions play a vital role in our lives. They help us feel compassion, offer assistance to others, reach out in times of need, and they help us relate with compassion and empathy. But our emotions can cause problems in our thinking process. They can cloud issues and distort facts. They can make us act in inappropriate ways when normally we would not, which can affect our performance and attitude in the workplace.

Emotions are not bad. As a matter of fact, they are good and help make us human. However, it is of paramount importance that you know how to identify when your emotions are calling the shots and how to control them. You do not have to eliminate emotions from your thought or action process, but it is crucial that you know when your emotions are clouding an issue.

Consider the following controversial questions:

 Should all drugs and prostitution be legalized?

 Is affirmative action reverse discrimination?

 Should illegal aliens be given amnesty and made U.S. citizens?

 Should terminally ill patients have the right to state-assisted and/or privately assisted suicide?

As you read these statements, did you immediately form or call on a previously held opinion? Did old arguments surface? Did you feel your emotions coming into play as you thought about the questions? If you had an immediate answer, you probably allowed some past judgments, opinions, and emotions to enter the decision-making process.

If you were to discuss these issues among friends or peers, how would you feel? Would you get angry? Would you find yourself groping for words? Would you find it hard to explain why you held the opinion you voiced? If so, these are warning signs that you are allowing your emotions to drive your decisions. If we allow our emotions to run rampant and unchecked, serious issues can arise.

If you feel your emotions sometimes cause you to be less than objective, consider the following tips when you are faced with an emotional decision:

- ☑ Listen to all sides of the story before you make a decision or form an opinion.

- ☑ Make a conscious effort to identify which emotions are causing you to lose objectivity.

- ☑ Do not let your emotions turn you off from the situation.

- ☑ Don't let yourself become engaged in "I'm right, you're wrong" situations.

- ☑ Work to understand why others feel their side is valid.

- ☑ Physiological reactions to emotions, such as increased heart rate and blood pressure and an increase in adrenaline flow, should be recognized as an emotional checklist. If you begin to experience these reactions, relax, take a deep breath, and concentrate on being open minded and fair.

- ☑ Control your negative self-talk or inner voice toward the other person(s) or situation.

- ☑ Determine whether your emotions are rational or irrational.

POSITIVE HABITS

WORK

When you hear someone gossiping and spreading rumors, do not participate in the conversation. It can only lead to resentment and trouble.

SOLUTION 9 ARTICULATE YOUR HOPES AND GOALS

"Go tell it on the mountain, over the hills and everywhere." *"Why would I want to do that?"* you might ask. *"If I tell everyone my hopes and dreams and goals, they'll know if I don't make it."* Yes, that is correct, but they will also know when you do—and, they can help you make it.

By letting others know what you want from your life or your career, they can help you bring your goals to fruition. By sharing what type of position you want or where you would like to work, others can be on the lookout for you, and you can do the same for your peers.

Consider this: You have a secret desire to become an animation artist for Pixar Films. Yes, it is a major film company producing such hits as *Finding Nemo, Cars,* and *Toy Story. "How stupid to think that someone from Newell, Iowa* [population 887] *could ever go to work for one of Disney's major studios,"* you might think. Wrong. Wrong. Wrong.

Everyday people get their fabulous dream jobs. Someone became the veterinarian for Gwen Stefani's pets, someone became Oprah's personal trainer, and someone became an animator for an upcoming Disney-Pixar Film. And yes, someone became the head mechanic for Delta Airlines and a chef at MGM Grand in Las Vegas, a nurse at Mercy Hospital, a firefighter for New York City, and a fashion design intern for Federated Department Stores. Why? Because they had talent, they worked hard, they had a belief they could do it, and because they let others know of their hopes and dreams.

By letting others know the "thing" for which you're working, you've put positive energy out there. You have put the world on notice that "I plan to be somebody in a position that I've dreamed of for a long time." How often have you looked at someone doing something great and you said to yourself, "*Jeez, I could have done that*!" Yes, you could have. Perhaps the only difference between you and the new assistant to Wolfgang Puck is that someone knew of his new assistant's dream.

Conversely, you need to ask others about their hopes and dreams. Ask that person sitting next to you this question: "What do you want to do in your career and who has the dream job you really want?" By finding this out, you can help them too. Suppose for a moment that you find out your classmate wants to be a history teacher. The next time you're reading a magazine or newspaper and you see an article on teaching, snip it out and give it to him or her. Tell your friend about the new TV series you saw on the History Channel. Bring them the flyer you picked up from the museum when you visited with your child. Before you know it, others are doing the same for you. Remember, good goes around.

Consider this. You told your classmate you really want to become a physical therapist. Your peer takes his mother to physical therapy one day and overhears a conversation between two staff members about an opening. She mentions this to you. You stop by the therapy center to inquire, and they are very impressed that you knew about the position and took the initiative to stop by. You fill out an application, leave your résumé, and two days later, you're called in for an interview to become an intern. Does this sound far-fetched? Crazy? Impossible? It happens everyday. Speak your dreams.

> QUOTE
>
> You had better live your best and act your best today, for today is sure preparation for tomorrow and all of the other tomorrows that follow.
>
> Harriett Martineau

 SOLUTION 10 CHOOSE OPTIMISM AND SURROUND YOURSELF WITH OPTIMISTIC PEOPLE

Your attitude is yours. It belongs to you. You own it. Good or bad, happy or sad, optimistic or pessimistic, it is yours and you are responsible for it. However, your attitude is greatly influenced by situations in your life and by the people with whom you associate. Developing a winning, optimistic attitude can be hard yet extremely rewarding work. Motivated and successful people have learned that one's attitude is the mirror to one's soul.

Optimism has many benefits beyond helping you develop a winning attitude. Researchers have found that people who are optimistic live longer, are more motivated, survive cancer treatment at a greater rate, have longer, more satisfying relationships, and are mentally healthier than pessimists. Thus developing and maintaining a winning, optimistic attitude can help you have a longer and more satisfying quality of life. It also suggests that by thinking positively, your motivation level increases and you are able to accomplish more.

Listen to yourself for a few days. Are you more of an optimist or a pessimist? Do you hear yourself whining, complaining, griping, and finding fault with everything and everybody around you? Do you blame others for things that are wrong in

Photolibrary.com

IF YOU WERE IN CHARGE

SOLVE THE PUZZLE

Maribeth and Jim do not like each other and constantly clash over various issues. Their personalities are very different, and they disrupt meetings with rude comments about each other. If you were in charge, what would you do?

your life? Do you blame your bad grades on your professors? Is someone else responsible for your unhappiness? If these thoughts or comments are in your head, you are suffering from the *"I CAN'T Syndrome"* (**I**rritated, **C**ontaminated, **A**ngry, **N**egative **T**houghts). This pessimistic condition can influence every aspect of your life negatively, from your self-esteem to your motivation level to your academic performance, to your relationships, and to your career success.

If you want to eliminate **I Can't** from your life, consider the following tips:

☑ Work every day to find the good in people, places, and things.

☑ Discover what is holding you back and what you need to push you forward.

☑ Visualize your success: Visualize yourself actually being who and what you want to be.

☑ Locate and observe positive, optimistic people and things in your life.

☑ Make a list of who helps you, supports you, and helps you feel positive; then make a point to be around them more.

☑ Take responsibility for your own actions and their consequences.

☑ Force yourself to find five positive things a day for which to be thankful.

You've seen the difference between an optimist and a pessimist. They are both everywhere—at work, at school, and probably in your own family. Think of the optimist for a moment. You've probably sat next to him or her in one of your classes or seen the person at work—someone who always seems to be happy, motivated, bubbling with personality, organized, and ready for whatever comes his or her way. Optimists greet people as they enter the room, they respond in class, they volunteer for projects, and they have a presence about them that is positive and lively. You may even look at him or her out of the corner of your eye and ask, "What is he on?"

Positive, upbeat, and motivated people are easy to spot. You can basically see their attitude in the way they walk, the way they carry themselves, the way they approach people, and the way they treat others.

Learn from them as you move through the days and months ahead. Choose your friends carefully. Seek out people who have ambition, good work habits, positive attitudes, and high ethical standards. Look for those who study hard, enjoy learning, are goal oriented, and don't mind taking a stand when they believe strongly about something. Befriend people who have interests and hobbies that are new to you. Step outside your comfort zone and add people to your circle of friends who are from a different culture, are of a different religion, or who have lived in a different geographic region. You'll be happily surprised at how much enrichment they can bring to your life.

Be wary, however, of "the others," the ones you need to avoid. Whiners. Degraders. Attackers. Manipulators. Pessimists. Back stabbers. Abusers. Cowards. Two-faced racists, sexists, ageists, homophobics, ethno- centrists. These people carry around an aura so negative, it can almost be seen as a dark cloud above them. They degrade others because they do not like themselves. They find fault with everything because their own lives are a mess. They do nothing and then attack you for being motivated and trying to improve your life. We call them *contaminated people.*

Examine the following two lists. As you read through the lists, consider the people with whom you associate. Are the majority of your friends, family, peers, and work associates positive or contaminated?

POSITIVE PEOPLE ARE THOSE WHO	CONTAMINATED PEOPLE ARE THOSE WHO
☑ Bring out the best in you	☒ Bring out the worst in you
☑ Find the good in bad situations	☒ Find the bad in every situation
☑ Are gracious and understanding	☒ Are rude and uncaring
☑ Build people up	☒ Sabotage people, even loved ones
☑ Support your dreams	☒ Criticize your hopes and plans
☑ Make you feel comfortable and happy	☒ Make you feel uneasy, nervous, and irritable
☑ Tell you the truth and offer constructive criticism	☒ Are two-faced and always use harsh language to "put you in your place"
☑ Are open minded and fair	☒ Are narrow and ethnocentric
☑ Are patient	☒ Are quick to anger
☑ Are giving	☒ Are jealous and smothering
☑ Love to learn from others	☒ Know everything already

Think about the preceding list and the people in your life, and ask yourself, "Do I surround myself mostly with positive or contaminated people?" As you consider your friends, family, classmates, and work associates, use the space provided to compare and contrast one *positive person* with one *contaminated person* in your life.

Positive Person _____

    His or Her Attributes _____

_____

_____

_____

_____

Contaminated Person _____

    His or Her Attributes _____

_____

_____

_____

(continued)

Compare and Contrast _____

_____

_____

_____

_____

_____

How can an optimist help you in your career? _____

_____

_____

_____

_____

PUTTING IT ALL TOGETHER

By thinking about who you really are, what you want, what you need, and what you have to offer an employer, you can better determine the type of position you will need to be happy, successful, and continue growing. If you focus on matching your vocation together with your passion, you will never face a day of "work" in your life.

Dr. Wayne Dyer is quoted later in this book as saying, "You *must* be what you *can* be." By this statement, he suggests that you already know in your heart and soul what you want and need from life, family, friends, and yes, even your profession, to be happy. Don't settle for less. Don't compromise your dreams. Don't give up on yourself. Strive to become one of the few who truly enjoys getting up in the morning and heading off to their place of employment.

REFERENCES

Arkoff, A. (1995). *The Illuminated Life*. Boston: Allyn & Bacon.

Buscaglia, L. (1982). *Living, Loving and Learning*. New York: Fawcett Columbine.

Gordon, E. (2005). *The 2010 Meltdown: Solving the Impending Job Crisis*. Westport, CT: Praeger.

Solomon, A., Tyler, L., and Taylor, T. (2007). *100% Career Success*. Clifton Park, NY: Thompson Delmar Learning.

The Language of Opportunity: Expanding Employment for Adults with Limited English Skills. (2003). Washington, DC: The Center for Law and Social Policy.

Tieger, P., and Barron-Tieger, B. (2001). *Do What You Are: Discover the Perfect Career for You Through the Secrets of Personality Type* (3rd ed.). Boston: Little, Brown.

Cultivating Your Character and Ethics

Who Are You When No One Else Is Looking?

WHY?

do ethics, character, and name matter? Why do I have to be concerned about what others think of my work ethic? Why is everybody so concerned with trustworthiness? Why is my moral character important at work? Why should I spend time thinking about my work and if I'm proud of it?

What if there were no rules or laws to govern your behavior? What if there were no consequences or ramifications for any of your actions? Let's pretend for a moment that you could never go to jail or face fines or be shunned for your actions, behaviors, or thoughts. If these statements came to pass, what would your life—or the lives of those you love—look like? This is one of the best ways to offer a practical definition of ethics. Basically, ethics is the *accepted* moral code or standard by which we all live. Codes of ethics vary from culture to culture, country to country, and group to group, but each carry with them a certain code that members of that culture, country, or group are expected to follow.

Ethics, however, is about much, much more than following the law, adhering to your society's accepted code, or following your religion's teachings. Each usually contains ethical standards, but as argued in the article *What Is Ethics?* (Velasquez et al., 1987), entire societies can become corrupt, and following that society's so-called 'moral' standard can have dire consequences. Nazi Germany is a perfect example of this situation. Consider America's slavery laws prior to the Civil War. Few people would now suggest those laws were ethical. And think about the Christian Crusades in which hundreds of thousands of people were murdered in the name of religion. Was that ethical?

Think back in history for a moment (and you won't have to think back too far), and consider some national and international leaders, entertainers, sports figures, or even local professionals in your community who, at the height of fame, made paramount ethical mistakes that cost him or her dearly. Richard Nixon. Michael Vick. Barry Bonds. Bill Clinton. Martha Stewart. Prince Harry. Oral Roberts, Jr. O. J. Simpson. Eliot Spitzer. Each of these people, to varying degrees, failed to maintain the *accepted* moral code of his or her community, and the consequences were grave. From jail sentences to public shame, each suffered a demoralizing defeat and a tarnished public image because of their ethical errors.

The word **ethics** is derived from the Latin *mores* (which translates to customs) and from the ancient Greek *ethos* (which loosely translates to "habit" or "custom" or "character"). The study of ethics has also been called "moral philosophy." Many factors influence our ethics, from our family and friends to our teachers and relatives. TV, music, media, religion, and politics also play a tremendous role in how our ethical footprint is developed. We are constantly bombarded with conflicting messages about what is right and wrong or good and bad. Thus more and more people slip into the gray twilight where it is hard to determine what the "right" thing to do really is. To prove this point, consider the following facts:

Ethical errors end careers more quickly and more definitively than any other mistakes in judgment or accounting.

Unknown

- ☑ 25 San Diego State University students failed a Business Ethics class because they were caught cheating.

- ☑ Seventy-five percent of college students admit cheating at some point.

- ☑ According to a Who's Who Among American High School Students poll, 80 percent admitted cheating to get to the top of his or her class.

- ☑ Sixty-one percent of surveyed adults have gone against personal ethics for money.

As you enter the professional world, your moral conduct will become increasingly more important to you, your managers, and your colleagues. The following solutions are included to help you learn more about ethics, morality, and character to better enable you to make informed, logical, and smart decisions.

SOLUTION 11 UNDERSTAND THE DYNAMICS OF ETHICS, INTEGRITY, AND CHARACTER

Ethics, integrity, and character can be hard to pin down because in today's discussions, they are all mixed up together. Basically, they all have to do with how you behave. Your actions are usually guided by a combination of your own personal ethical code, integrity, and character. As discussed earlier, ethics is a habit or a custom for behavior. Integrity, from the Latin *integri* (which means wholeness, as in wholeness of action and wholeness of thoughts) deals with fairness, courage, respect, temperance, and sound judgment. It is about choosing *right* over *easy* and *fairness* over *personal gain.*

Character, from the Greek *charakter* (which means "to stamp", "to scratch or mark," or "to engrave"), refers to the attributes that make up or distinguish you as an individual. In essence, your character is how your soul is "marked" or "engraved," which is directly related to your ethical and moral behavior.

Making ethical choices usually involves three factors or levels: the law, fairness, and your conscience (Anderson & Bolt, 2008). You might also consider adding three other levels: time, pride, and publicity. When you are faced with a challenging professional or personal decision, ask yourself this vitally important question: *"Is it legal, is it fair, can I live with my decision, is this decision in my long-term best interest, could I tell my mother about it, and how would I feel if this showed up on the front page of the newspaper?"*

If you can answer yes to all six levels, most likely this decision would be in your best interest and the best interest of those around you.

FIGURE 2.1 The Six Levels of Ethical Decision Making

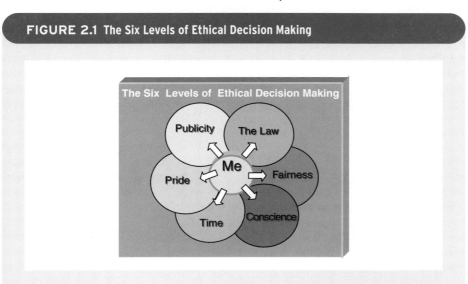

SOLUTION 12 BE PROUD OF YOUR NAME AND REPUTATION

What's in a name? Smith. Johnson. Alexander. Ortiz. Aharonian. Brannon. "Nothing, really," you might say. "It's just a name. It was given to me when I was born." Few statements could be further from the truth. The pride that you have in your name and how protective you are of your name (your reputation) will drive many of your decisions. If you don't care what others think about your name or if your name has no value to you, then your decisions and actions will reflect this. If you are fiercely protective of your name's standing and meaning, your decisions and actions will reflect this. Having pride in your name and your reputation is paramount in considering ethics, integrity, and character.

Consider *The Crucible,* a play by Arthur Miller (1953/2003). It was written in 1953 and set in 1692 Salem, Massachusetts, during the witch trials. However, the play is really Miller's statement on McCarthyism in America (Congressman Joseph McCarthy's Committee on Un-American Activities intended to sniff out any communists living in America).

John Proctor, a main character in the play, is a husband, father, and farmer and one of the people accused of being a witch. Later in the play, he is convicted of witchery and sentenced to hang. During the last act of the play, another character from the play, Reverend Hale, begs the accused to confess to witchcraft so they can be cleansed and not put to death. Hale sends John's wife Elizabeth to try to convince him to confess so he can save his life for the sake of his family. Reluctantly, he agrees to confess to the *false charge* and signs a confession. Later, when he learns that the judges in the matter intend to nail his confession to the church door for all of Salem to see, he recants and refuses to confess.

When the judges hear of this, they are angry and frustrated. They cannot understand why he won't simply sign the paper and *live.* They confront him again. Again, he refuses. In an angry confrontation, one judge, trying again to make him sign the paper, says, *"I must have good and legal proof . . . explain to me, Mr. Proctor, why you will not let . . ."*

To this, Proctor interrupts in a passionate, soul-wrenching scream, *"Because it is my name! Because I cannot have another in my life. . . . How am I to live without my name? I have given you my soul; leave me my name."*

When you care this passionately about your reputation and character, your life is governed by protecting your name. Your actions, beliefs, and decisions are all tied to this one belief: "My name and my reputation matter and I will do nothing to bring shame or embarrassment to my name."

To protect your name and reputation, when in doubt about what to do, reflect on the six levels of ethical decision making (Figure 2.1). You might also consider the following tips:

- ☑ Define what is "right" *before* you are faced with an ethical decision.
- ☑ Have faith in what you know to be right and just.
- ☑ Trust your heart and your conscience.
- ☑ Don't let your desires for bigger, better, faster, prettier, and greener cloud your judgment.
- ☑ Never let competition or the "need to win" overtake your knowledge of what you know is right.

QUOTE

Your character is determined by how you treat people who can do you no good and how you treat people who can't fight back.

Abigail Van Buren

THINK ABOUT IT

How will practicing the six levels of ethical decision making help you become a more trusted employee?

SOLUTION 13   DEVELOP AND MAINTAIN A STRONG MORAL CHARACTER

The word *morality* is associated with many terms such as *ethics, principles, decency, honesty, integrity, honor, virtue,* and *goodness.* So what does it mean to have a strong moral character? If you remember from Solution 11, the word *character* comes from the Greek *charakter,* which means "to stamp or engrave." Therefore, in today's terms, your character is defined by the "markings or stamping" of honesty, virtue, decency, and goodness.

You might be asking yourself, *"Why does character matter in the workplace?"* Character matters because it is important that your employer be able to trust you, that he or she knows you will keep your word and you will honor the company's confidentiality policy. Character also matters because many professions require that records and information be kept private. If your character is suspect and you can't be trusted, most likely you will not remain employed very long.

The CHARACTER COUNTS!_sm Coalition (2007), a project of the Josephson Institute of Ethics, suggests these Six Pillars of Character®:

Stockbyte/Jupiter Images Picturequest-Royalty Free

Trustworthiness   Be honest • Don't deceive, cheat or steal • Be reliable—do what you say you'll do • Have the courage to do the right thing • Build a good reputation • Be loyal—stand by your family, friends and country

Respect   Treat others with respect • Be tolerant of differences • Use good manners, not bad language • Be considerate of the feelings of others • Don't threaten, hit or hurt anyone • Deal peacefully with anger, insults and disagreements

Responsibility   Do what you are supposed to do • Persevere: keep on trying! • Always do your best • Use self-control • Be self-disciplined • Think before you act—consider the consequences • Be accountable for your choices

Fairness   Play by the rules • Take turns and share • Be open-minded; listen to others • Don't take advantage of others • Don't blame others carelessly

Caring   Be kind • Be compassionate and show you care • Express gratitude • Forgive others • Help people in need

Citizenship   Do your share to make your school and community better • Cooperate • Get involved in community affairs • Stay informed; vote • Be a good neighbor • Obey laws and rules • Respect authority • Protect the environment

> **QUOTE**
>
> Every time you make a choice, you choose your character.
>
> Unknown

By employing these Six Pillars of Character®, you can begin to develop a strong moral character that will serve you well in the world of work and in your personal life as well.

SOLUTION 14   DEVELOP A RESILIENT WORK ETHIC

The word **work** is derived from the Greek *ponos,* taken from the Latin word *poena,* which meant "sorrow." Manual labor was not meant for free men. "The cultural norms allowed free men to pursue warfare, large-scale commerce, and the arts, especially architecture or sculpture" (Hill, 1996). Sadly, the word *work* is still equated with sorrow for many people in today's workplace, and work ethic is given little consideration.

Your work ethic is how you perform at work without a job description and without being told to do so. Your work ethic is not tied to what you do for a raise,

what you do to impress others, or what you do to be promoted. Your work ethic is what you do at work because you know it is "the right and just thing" to do. Pride, ownership, and honor all play a role in one's work ethic.

Your work ethic can also be defined by how you approach the day. Do you only do what is required of you and the things that are laid out in your formal job description, or are you willing to go beyond based on your own initiative and values? Do you bring a sense of energy and optimism to the workplace on a daily basis? Do you enjoy your colleagues and do all you can to assist them without thinking of what rewards may come from offering this help? Do you feel like what you do for a vocation is contributing to the good and whole of humanity? All of these questions get at the heart of the matter with regard to work ethic.

A work ethic is a set of values based on the ideals of hard work and discipline. Building a reliable work ethic means training yourself to follow these values. Training yourself so that work becomes automatic instead of a struggle. A work ethic is based on four habits:

- ☑ Persistence
- ☑ Focus
- ☑ Do it now
- ☑ Do it right

These are the key habits in building a dependable work ethic. (Lifehack. org, 2007).

With **persistence**, you are building a habit of working until the job is completed. Some days, you may have to work 12 hours; other days, you may only have to work for 7 hours. Persistence involves putting the effort forward to do what is needed to get the job done.

Focus involves having clarity (and persistence) while working on a task. It is better to have a clear focus for 1 hour than to work in a cloud for 8 hours. Focus means you have taken every precaution to eliminate distractions, interruptions, and needless wandering.

The habit of **Do it now** involves eliminating procrastination in your work and personal life. Yes, we advocate taking time for relaxation and joy, but those can only come once your work is done. If you procrastinate with completing a task *and* try to have time for joy, your spare time will be filled with stress and worry over not getting the work done.

Finally, **Do it right** means you are going to bring your very best to the table every time you do a task. It means you have considered that your *name* is going to be attached to this project and it has to be the very best it can be. Consider this: If your supervisor told you your work would be posted or displayed for everyone to see *and* that your *name* would be displayed with your work, Do it right takes on an entirely new meaning.

Some suggest that the work ethic in America is dead:

Younger generations in the workforce have killed it off. If you're under 30, "work" has a different meaning than it did . . . work is something to do with your hands while chatting on your cell phone . . . unless it's something to do with your mouth while text messaging. And it's nobody's fault but ours, the boomers. We're the ones who were squealing with delight if the kid drew an egg. We were the ones who said, "Johnny *tried,* and that's what counts." They see "work ethic" as "show up and shut up," and no wonder they want no part of it. (Dauten, 2007)

Dale Dauten suggests that what is needed now is a "contribution ethic." He suggests that those who make a valued contribution to their place of work are the "rare people who drive the economy and the world conversation." His contribution ethic includes these suggestions:

- ☑ Just help. Make yourself useful. You aren't just there, waiting. There's no waiting. Just help.
- ☑ Your half is *60 percent.*
- ☑ Innovation is a subversive activity. You can't expect management and/or co-workers to be excited when you say, "I have an idea!" After all, most ideas are suggestions, and most suggestions are complaints. But, if an idea is truly original, then expect resistance; indeed, welcome it as a measure of originality.
- ☑ Giving time without attention is a gift-wrapped empty box.
- ☑ Being right is overrated. If your goal is usefulness, then what matters is progress.
- ☑ Being wrong is underrated. Admitting you were wrong is wisdom gained.
- ☑ Always bring something to read.
- ☑ Think like a hero; work like an artist. When kindly attention meets curiosity, you move gracefully through the world.

POSITIVE HABITS

WORK

Work hard to be a person who always gives more than is expected, works harder than is required, contributes more than you are obliged to do, and complains less than everyone.

SOLUTION 15   UNDERSTAND THE TRUE NATURE OF RESPECT

The world is full of powerful people who have no respect. Conversely, the world is filled with people who have an abundance of respect but no power. Why? Because most people confuse the two or have no idea what either mean. Few people understand that *true* respect can only come to you by earning it. Yes, there are people who think they are respected, but they are only fooling themselves if they believe their respect is real or meaningful—if they did not earn it.

Respect can be earned by many acts; some include:

- ☑ Giving respect, you earn respect
- ☑ Being fair
- ☑ Being honest, even in difficult times
- ☑ Doing the right thing
- ☑ Listening
- ☑ Asking for opinions and suggestions and creating ownership
- ☑ Empowering others
- ☑ Standing up for those you see mistreated
- ☑ Helping others reach their dreams and goals
- ☑ Engaging in open communication

QUOTE

Change occurs, progress is made, and difficulties resolved if people merely do "the right thing." And rarely do people *not* know what is the "right thing" to do.

Father Hessburg,
Notre Dame University

- Being knowledgeable and constantly learning more
- Observing your day-to-day conduct
- Owning your mistakes and admitting when you are wrong
- Maintaining your principles, even when things are turbulent
- Treating people who are in positions lower than yours in a respectful and honorable way

Each of these acts shows that you care not only about other people but you care about yourself as well. If you think about your actions and what they mean to another person and your place of employment, you will begin earning the respect of those around you. Respect is not an immediate gift to you from others. Respect comes with time, proven trust, open communication, and living a life above reproach.

SOLUTION 16 AVOID MORAL BANKRUPTCY

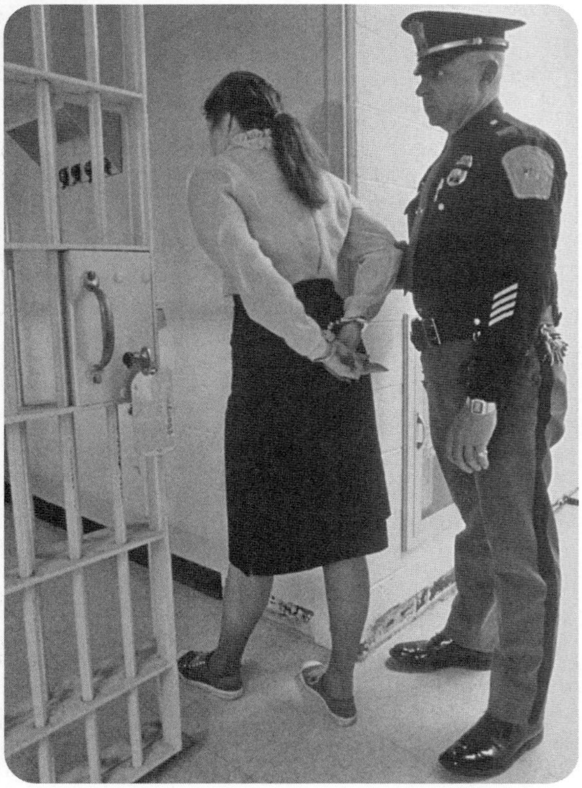

Rhoda Sidney/PH College

You know who they are—the people you've met in your personal and professional life who will do anything, say anything, avoid anything, betray anyone, and change like a chameleon to get what they want. Seldom do we have positive or endearing things to say about these people because we see them as morally bankrupt. They have no scruples, no values, no guiding belief system, and no loyalty.

But worst of all, they have no continuity. You can't depend on them for anything because although you may have witnessed them being loyal or displaying values one day, you also saw them toss their loyalty and values aside for the sake of personal gain. They change from day-to-day trying to carve out a power base, a leadership position, a promotion, or even to maintain their own status quo. Morally bankrupt people are impossible to befriend, depend on, or trust because you never know *who* they are from day to day.

Seldom do morally bankrupt people see themselves as "broken." They say to themselves, "I have done nothing to break the law or disobey the rules of our company." This may be completely true, but morality and integrity involve much more than following the written law or adhering to company policy. Although those two factors are important, you need to understand they are not the only two factors that make you moral and give you integrity.

There are many indicators to identify behaviors and traits of a morally bankrupt person, but the following are the most prominent:

- They have *unhealthy self-esteem.*
  - Morally bankrupt people care little about themselves; therefore, they cannot care about you. They value themselves so little that they can't even see how their actions damage their credibility and reputation.

☑ They lack *courage*.

- Morally bankrupt people only have the courage to stand up for what is right for them. They do not stand up for what is simply right. Courage is a quality of strong people, and morally bankrupt people are weak.

☑ They use *poor judgment*.

- Just as is the case with courage, morally bankrupt people make judgments and decisions that only affect them in a positive way. They base their judgments more on personal gain and loss than on right and wrong.

☑ They are always *looking for more* (especially money).

- Morally bankrupt people never have enough. They cannot be satisfied with abundance; they have to have superabundance. They are driven by the pursuit of money or power, and they will stop at nothing to have more of both.

☑ They are *untruthful*.

- "Truth is an expendable commodity to the morally bankrupt person" (Sherfield, 2004). Winning, money, power, status, and "more" always trump truth.

☑ They are *jealous and arrogant*.

- If morally bankrupt people see you have more than them—more respect, more power, more money, a nicer car, a bigger home, more friends—they will work with diligence to take this from you or, at best, outdo you. They use what little status or power they have to make you look small so your accomplishments pale in comparison to what they have.

☑ They practice *deception and betrayal*.

- Deception and betrayal are not necessarily loud. Morally bankrupt people know how to practice quiet deception and hushed betrayal. They stab anyone in the back to get what they want and to advance as far as they can. They use blame, shame, and lies to quietly turn the tides in their favor.

☑ They are *unfair*.

- Fairness is an unknown word to morally bankrupt people, unless, of course, the unfair act is directed toward them. They have learned how to convince themselves that any means justify a positive end for themselves, and fairness simply does not fit into the equation.

☑ They put *self-interest ahead* of everything.

- Self-interest is not a bad or morally wrong trait. In fact, it can be good and healthy to look out for yourself. However, when your every thought, action, and decision is based on what is good and right for you, this can be dangerous and immoral. When you look out for others and help them along, they will help you along.

We do not mean to suggest that every person with whom you come into contact will be morally bankrupt. In fact, the opposite is probably true. There are countless wonderful, remarkable, talented, truthful, honest people in the world of work, and you will meet many of them. It is important, however, that you know the signs of moral bankruptcy so you can avoid the personal and professional pitfalls of this deadly characteristic.

As you enter the world of work, you are going to be faced with so many demands on your time, effort, energy, and talents. You may be pulled in various directions and called on to do numerous tasks at one time for several managers. All of those things are possible, but to truly succeed, you need to do them both by developing and adhering to a strong moral code you are committed to uphold. If you can do this, and you *can* do it, you will soon be recognized as a team player, a leader, a trusted colleague, and someone whom your superiors can depend on to "do the right thing."

SOLUTION 17   BE TRUSTWORTHY

 **QUICK FACT**

Whether choosing a mate or someone to work closely with, trust really matters. University of Florida research finds that of all the major character traits, people value trustworthiness the most in others.

Source: http://news.ufl.edu/2007/10/03/trustworthiness/

There are two types of people in the world: Those who distrust everyone until it is proven they can be trusted, and those who trust everyone until it is proven that they cannot be trusted. Neither is right nor wrong, but rather a fact of life. Gaining trust and giving trust are both about time. It either happens immediately or is built over time.

Trustworthiness is a quality that most people admire and want in friends, employees, and co-workers. People want to know that you can be trusted to keep your word, adhere to moral standards, do what is right, remain ethical under dire pressure, and tell the truth even in times of struggle. If you are perceived as trustworthy, you will most likely be treated with respect and adoration. Further, people will count you among those they are proud to know.

Trustworthiness can be earned by acts as simple as delivering packages when you said you would to as complex as being loyal to your co-workers even when they are in trouble. Consider the following factors that promote trustworthiness.

 QUOTE

Watch your thoughts; they become words. Watch your words; they become actions. Watch your actions; they become habits. Watch your habits; they become character. Watch your character; it becomes your destiny.

Frank Outlaw

Trustworthy people:

- ☑ Are truthful even in times of personal turmoil.
- ☑ Do the right thing even if it's not popular.
- ☑ Are courageous and do what they say they will do.
- ☑ Listen to their conscience.
- ☑ Support and protect family, friends, and community.
- ☑ Work hard to build and maintain their reputation.
- ☑ Seek advice from others when in doubt about the "right" thing.
- ☑ Are honorable in all actions.
- ☑ Do not go against his or her personal beliefs for gain.
- ☑ Constantly try to improve.

SOLUTION 18 HONOR YOUR COMMITMENTS

You're waiting for a ride and it doesn't show. You were promised a report by noon yesterday and it never arrived. The check was supposed to arrive this morning but it never came. Your date was supposed to arrive at 7 P.M. It is now 11:30 P.M. He or she was a no show and a no call. How would any of these situations make you feel? Would you be angry? Sad? Confused? Hurt? Perhaps you would feel a bit of all these emotions because someone you trusted broke their commitment. They did not keep their word.

Commitments are a vital and real part of trust and character. Learning to honor your commitments is perhaps one of the most mature, rational, and loving things you can do in this world. Always think deeply and consider all angles before you make a commitment to another person, whether that commitment is picking up your friend from work or marrying a loved one. There are no degrees of commitment. It is black and white. Either you keep your word or you do not. You can't be a little pregnant. You can't be a little dead, and you can't be somewhat committed.

Making a commitment, whether in writing or by word, means you pledge to do something mutually agreed on. You can (and should) also have commitments with yourself. A commitment is an obligation. Some people consider the word *obligation* as negative and restrictive. Yes, it can be, but you can view both commitment and obligation as an anchor. They are the characteristics that ground us, the qualities that make life worth living. When we are committed to others *and* ourselves, our lives begin to have purpose and meaning. Without commitment, we are kites in the wind with no string attached. We are not connected to anyone or anything.

Strangely, however, being "anchored down" through a commitment or obligation is one of the most liberating feelings on earth. With commitment, we are still kites, free to fly and float and wander, but we are tethered to the earth and the people we love.

People who honor their commitments enjoy a variety of benefits that both enrich and improve the quality of life. For example, people who make a full and lasting commitment to their personal goals are among some of the most successful and notable in history (Arkoff, 1995). Commitment awakens action, and action triggers results.

Vincent van Gogh, considered one of the world's greatest painters, only sold one of his works during his lifetime. He did not let this deter him from painting. Recently, a van Gogh painting sold for over $75 million. He was committed to his profession and his talents.

Lucille Ball was dismissed from drama school because her teacher thought she was too shy to ever do any effective stage work. She went on to earn thirteen Emmy awards, was a Kennedy Center honoree, and was awarded the Presidential Medal of Freedom. She was committed to her profession and her talents.

Decca Recording Studio turned down a chance to sign **The Beatles** because the company's executives did not like their sound and felt the guitar was a thing of the past. The Beatles went on to have over forty number-one hits, sold more than a billion songs worldwide, and are listed as the most successful recording act of all time. They were committed to their profession and their talents.

BIGGEST INTERVIEW BLUNDERS

Meyer was asked by the interview committee, "Suppose that we offered you a position here at Ace Medical Supplies tomorrow with a twelve-month contract. Then, in three months, another company offered you more money to move to their company." Meyer responded, "Well, I hope you would understand that I have my family to consider and I'd have to really consider taking the other position. I know I'm under contract and all, but seriously, my future is important too." The committee appreciated his honesty but not his level of commitment.

QUOTE

I *am* my choices.
Jean-Paul Sartre

Michael Jordan was cut from his high school basketball team and went home in tears. He later went on to join the Chicago Bulls, was named as the NBA's Most Valuable Player, holds the NBA record for highest career regular season scoring average, and is considered by most basketball aficionados as the greatest basketball player of all time. He was committed to his profession and his talents.

Commitment, then, is a powerful and dynamic quality that can sustain you in times of doubt, lift you in times of defeat, inspire you in times of creative stillness, and guide you in times of turbulence. If you work to honor your commitments, the rewards will be powerful.

SOLUTION 19   DEVELOP A STRONG GUIDING STATEMENT AND INTEGRITY PLAN

IF YOU WERE IN CHARGE

SOLVE THE PUZZLE

If you noticed that several employees seemed to lack direction and did not seem to have any focus, what could you do to help those employees change for the better?

You're wearing a T-shirt to class. It is not your normal run-of-the-mill T-shirt, however. You designed this T-shirt for everyone to see and read. It is white with bright red letters. On the front of the T-shirt is written your personal guiding statement, the words by which you live. The words that govern your life. What will your T-shirt read? Perhaps you will use the golden rule, "Do unto others . . ." It might be an adaptation of the Nike slogan, "Just Do It," or it might be something more profound such as, "I live my life to serve others and to try to make others' lives better."

Whatever your guiding statement, it must be yours. It can't be your parents' or your professor's or your best friend's statement. It must be based on something you value, and it must be strong enough to motivate and carry you in hard, tough times. Your guiding statement must be so powerful that it will literally *guide you* when you are ethically challenged, broke, alone, angry, hurt, sad, or feeing vindictive. It is a statement that will guide you in relationships with family, friends, spouses, partners, or would-be love interests. It is a statement that will earn you respect and rewards in the world of work.

As you've been reading, have you thought of your statement? If you already have a statement, be proud. However, if you do not, you are not alone. This is a very difficult question, and most likely, you've never been asked to develop a guiding statement before. It may take you some time to write your statement, and this section is included to help you.

One of the best places to start working on your guiding statement is to look back at those qualities you circled as valuable to you in Solution #6 of Chapter 1. If you value something, it may appear in your guiding statement. Also, you should look back at Solution #2 in Chapter 1 and include your strengths in your Guiding Statement. Giving attention to the information just provided on moral bankruptcy in this section will also help you develop a statement that will work well for you.

For example, if you circled the words *respect, giving,* and *optimistic* among those you value the most in Solution 6, this is a basis for your statement. A guiding statement based in these words may read something like this: "I will live my life as a positive, upbeat, motivated person who respects others and enjoys giving to others on a daily basis."

If your circled words included *integrity, truth,* and *fairness,* your statement may read something like this: "My integrity is the most important thing in my life and I will never act in any way that compromises my integrity. I will be truthful, fair, and honest in all my endeavors."

As you can see, if one of these statements was your guiding statement, and you truly lived your life by that statement, your actions would be in alignment with your values. This is the purpose of a guiding statement: to give you direction and support in hard, troubling times.

In the space provided, transfer the most important words from your Strength List in Solution 2 and your Value List in Solution 6, and then work to develop your guiding statement from those words.

My dominant strengths include

_____

_____

_____

_____

The most important values were:

_____

_____

_____

_____

Draft of my **Guiding Statement** (Take your time and be sincere. You will need this statement to complete the following four questions.)

_____

_____

_____

_____

_____

_____

_____

_____

How will your guiding statement help . . .

With your overall job search plan?_____

_____

_____

_____

_____

_____

_____

If you have a disagreement with your supervisor at work? _____

_____

_____

_____

_____

_____

If you are asked to do something at work with which you fundamentally disagree? _____

_____

_____

(continued)

_____

_____

_____

_____

If you are having a disagreement with someone you care deeply about (friend, spouse, partner, parent, work associate, etc.)? _____

_____

_____

_____

_____

_____

_____

PUTTING IT ALL TOGETHER

Reflect on the words of John Proctor from Salem: *"Because it is my name! Because I cannot have another in my life."* If you allow these words to be your guiding mantra, you will begin to see a vast difference in how you approach work, relationships, commitment, fairness, and ethics. Being proud of yourself and your work is a powerfully important aspect of being fulfilled and happy. When you know your moral compass is pointing in the direction of your dreams, you will have no trouble sleeping at night—or getting up in the morning.

REFERENCES

Anderson, L., & Bolt, S. (2008). *Professionalism: Real Skills for Workplace Success.* Upper Saddle River, NJ: Pearson Prentice Hall.

Arkoff, A. (1995). *The Illuminated Life.* Boston: Allyn & Bacon.

Character Counts! Coalition. (2007). *The Six Pillars of Character.* Los Angeles: The Josephson Institute of Ethics. Available from www.charactercounts.org.

Dauten, D. (2007, March 25). "Today's Work Ethic Just No Longer Works." *Boston Globe:* B13.

Hill, R. (1996). "Historical Context of the Work Ethic." Available from www.coe.uga.edu/~rhill/workethic/hist.htm.

Lifehack. org. (2007). "How to Build a Reliable Work Habit." Available from www.lifehack.org/articles/management/how-to-build-a-reliable-work-ethic.html.

Miller, A. (2003). *The Crucible.* New York: Penguin Press. (Original work published 1953)

Sherfield, R. (2004) *The Everything Self Esteem Book.* Avon, MA: Adams Media.

Velasquez, M., Andre, C., Shanks, T., & Meyer, M. (1987, Fall). "What Is Ethics?" *Issues in Ethics* IIE V1 N1.

Designing Your Job Search, Writing Your Cover Letter, and Selling Yourself through Your Résumé

Selling Yourself

 WHY?

read and work through a list of "dos" and "don'ts" about résumé writing? Why do I have to create a "job search plan"? Why can't I just apply for the job I want? Why do I have to write a cover letter? Why is it important to know what type of résumé to write?

Remember the old saying, "You are what you eat"? When searching for a professional position, you could change that to read, "You are what you write." Most likely, the people conducting the job search have never met you and know nothing about you except what you provide to them. A carefully crafted résumé communicates your past history (skills and experience) that makes you the ideal candidate for their position. Your résumé is the first marketing piece and in many cases must stand alone when a recruiter is determining whether or not to interview you. Just as a well-designed and written résumé can be a wonderful first step, a poorly designed and written one can doom you before you ever leave your house. Remember this: A résumé gets you the interview; the interview gets you the job. Although there is no single way to develop your career résumé and formats may vary from discipline to discipline, this chapter outlines the key components of résumés and discusses how to develop one that will represent your best efforts.

Your second "advertising tool" is your cover letter. A cover letter is basically an expansion of your résumé. A cover letter gives you the chance to link your résumé, skills, and experience together with your interest in *a specific company's* position. You will need to write many cover letters to make this link work properly; in other words, you most likely need to write a cover letter designed for each job for which you apply. Your cover letter will often be the stepping-stone to get an employer to even look at your résumé. Consider it a teaser, if you will, to all of your talents and experience. Just as you would never send someone a greeting card and not sign it, you would never send a résumé and not tell the person or committee *why* you sent it. Your cover letter tells why.

Once you have designed a dynamic résumé and written a compelling cover letter, ideally you will be called for an interview. You will need to present yourself in a professional manner in person just as you did on paper. You will need to know how to answer *and* ask important questions. You will also need to know how to answer questions that you may consider trivial, illegal, or unethical. Further, you will need to know how to evaluate the benefits package that may come with your position. This chapter will help you prepare yourself to stand out among the hundreds of people who want the same job for which you are applying.

SOLUTION 20 FOCUS ON YOUR JOB SEARCH PLAN

When searching for your dream job, it is quite possible it will not be listed in this Sunday's want ads. It may be there, but in today's job market, it is more likely you will hear about the position from a friend, peer, or instructor. It may be posted on the Internet, or you may even find it posted on one of the many job search sites such as **monster.com, employment911.com,** or **career.com.** The traditional want ads describing the position for which you may have been trained are quickly fading away. To find the job you want and deserve, you must leave no stone unturned.

The first thing you need to know about searching for a job is this: Getting a job—the right job—is hard work! Most people in the career development field will tell you that finding the right job is a "full-time job." It may even be that your job search leads you to a shocking surprise: more training. Some majors are challenging and interesting but, unfortunately, do not prepare graduates for careers that afford the lifestyle they want. Thus in some cases, you may find that the best solution is to continue your education with another focus or possibly enroll in graduate school.

Your job search is just that—*yours*. It is an individual matter, and it must be given serious thought. Again, getting the right job is hard work, and the time to start is now. To assist you in developing your job search plan and eventually finding the career that suits you, consider the following *four focus tips:*

Focus on Your Interests

What do you want to do? Where do you want to live? What kind of organization appeals to you? Because getting a job usually takes a great deal of time and energy, you want to get the right one the first time if possible. Chapter 1 helped you identify your interests and strengths, which can be an invaluable tool for you.

Do you like to work with people or do you prefer numbers and data? Are salary and benefits the prime factors driving your choice? Do you mind relocating and continuing to relocate? Do you want to travel or are you a homebody? Do you need the company of colleagues or do you work best with a computer at home? Before you start the search and draft your résumé, hone in on your interests and try to match your job with what you love.

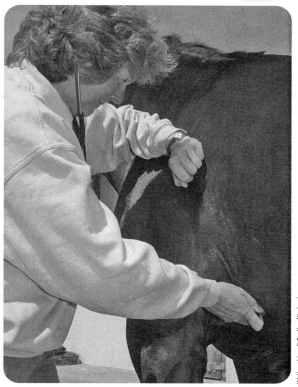

Kit Houghton © Dorling Kindersley

Focus on Your Qualifications

Employers want to know what you have to offer them. What are your assets, your strengths and weaknesses, your work experience? Have you managed other people? What have you learned from extracurricular activities and part-time jobs? Do you write well? Are you excellent with computers? Do you speak a second language fluently? Once you have evaluated your interests and your qualifications, you can begin compiling the information needed to write your résumé.

QUOTE

There can be no happiness if the things we believe in are different from the things we do.

Freya Stark

Focus on Your Needs

When you have defined what you want to do and have evaluated your qualifications realistically, you need to narrow your search to those companies that are at the top of your list. Consider the following: Do you want to be in the South? Or the Southwest? Are you unwilling to work anywhere but Atlanta or New York or San Francisco? Are you unwilling to relocate even when it means a promotion? Is change very difficult for you? Be realistic about geographic location before you take the job. If you accept a job in Denver because you have always lived there and the company wants to transfer you to Connecticut after a year, can you deal with this? Does the position pay enough for you to have an acceptable standard of living? Does it pay enough for you to repay your student loans if this is a factor?

If you take a position knowing it is not going to offer the salary and benefits you want in the long run, you are simply prolonging the job search.

Focus on Your Overall Objective

If your current career objective states, "I want to work with computers," can you narrow your career objective to something more focused, such as "I wish to work at a computer animation company in Birmingham, Alabama, as a digital artist," or "I wish to work for a major publishing company in New York City as an editorial assistant," or "I wish to work as an assistant buyer for a major retailer in the Northwest, preferably Seattle"? The narrower you can define your focus, the easier it is to plan your search.

SOLUTION 21 LEAVE NO STONE UNTURNED

GRADUATE QUOTE

The most important thing that I learned about interviewing is to begin preparing for your professional interview years before it occurs. It is very important to take advantage of internships, volunteer, join clubs, and participate in professional organizations. I learned that it was important to do more than the minimum. Stacking your resume with activities that were not "required" will be looked upon favorably by any employer.

BRAYTON WILLIAMS, Graduate!
The University of Nevada, Las Vegas, NV
The William F. Harrah College of Hotel Administration

CAREER: Assistant Front Office Manager The Fairmont, Newport Beach, CA

Now that you have spent some time focusing, consider the following avenues to begin your job search.

Campus Career Center

One of the best places to begin your job search is usually through the career center on your campus. Not only does this center help you with résumé writing and interviewing skills, staff members typically schedule career fairs to connect you with potential employers. It is much easier to get an interview with recruiters who are looking to hire students rather than responding to a newspaper ad. You might also check the bulletin board or online postings in the career center.

Internships or Cooperative Work Experiences

If your college offers an internship or a cooperative work experience, you may want to explore this as a career opportunity. If you work for a company as an intern and perform well on the job, you will most likely be offered a permanent position. If you take an internship, be sure to do your very best work even if you decide after being on the job for a while that this is not for you. You need references, and the best ones are supervisors where you have worked and performed well.

Employment Agencies (or Headhunters)

Often companies work with employment agencies because they screen applicants for them and send them only the top candidates. Only leave your résumé with reputable companies. Ask them for references of people they have placed in successful positions. Never sign anything with an employment company without reading it carefully. You may be agreeing to give them several months of your salary for locating you a job. Be sure and ask the agent if the employment fee is paid by the company that has placed the job with the agency. If the company does not pay the fee, do not sign anything and look for another agency to assist you.

Newspapers and Classified Ads

Newspapers can be a good source for one part of your job search, but do not limit your search to classified ads. First, as stated earlier, the competition today is usually much tougher, and many of the very best jobs are never placed in the newspaper. Do include this source as one of your targets, however.

Professional Journals, Associations, and Organizations

If you have the opportunity to join the student chapter of a professional organization such as the American Institute of Architects or subscribe to a professional journal such as the *New England Journal of Medicine,* do it! You can usually find professional journals in your library or maybe your instructor can make suggestions. Many professional organizations offer student memberships for a greatly reduced price. This membership not only gives you a professional organization to put on your résumé, it provides contacts and may offer mentors and job opportunities.

Networking

Develop a network among the people you know who may work for a company in which you have an interest. People on the inside have an advantage in helping you get your foot in the door. What about your dad's golf partner? Someone who is your mom's friend? What about a graduate who is your friend and knows your work style and may be working for a company in which you have an interest? Use every method you have to get the interview.

Professors

Your professors are excellent people to include in your network. If you have excelled in a professor's class, he or she may be very willing to help you. But if you have constantly cut class or showed up late, you probably cannot count on a professor to recommend you. Professors feel their credibility is on the line when they recommend someone to their colleagues in their profession. If you plan to use your professor (or anyone from your institution) as a reference, always ask permission first.

Direct Contacts

Even if there is no advertised position, you can write an unsolicited letter, include your résumé, and follow up with a phone call. Many times this results in very little, but sometimes your résumé hits their office at just the right time. Don't be too discouraged if you get a lot of form letters or never hear from them at all. Some companies get many more letters of application than they can review.

Guest Speakers

If guest speakers present in your class, pay attention, take notes, and stay afterward to ask questions. On the days you have speakers, be sure to look your best, from your clothing to your hair to your fingernails. You may not want to wear a suit, but don't wear sweat pants either. Give the speaker a card and express an interest in the company. These people usually want to help students or they would not have showed up to speak. After the speaker has finished, approach the person and ask for a business card. Follow up with a note telling him or her how much you enjoyed the presentation. At this time, you can also express an interest in any career options at his or her company. Many of them have good contacts and may be helpful to you even if you are not interested in their particular company.

The Internet

The Internet has changed the rules of almost everything, and job searches are not an exception. You can now sit at your computer and research companies of interest. You can find out if they have open positions, read about their history, their mission, their values, and sometimes even read testimonials from current employees.

As you explore the Internet, you will find thousands of jobs listed all over the world. In this space, we cannot list all the possibilities, but some of the major sources are listed here.

www.monster.com
www.career.com
www.jobsonline.net
www.ejobsearch.org
www.employment911.com
www.job-hunt.org
www.indeed.com
www.jobfactory.com

SOLUTION 22 KNOW YOUR EMPLOYER'S EXPECTATIONS

Keith Brofsky/Getty Images, Inc.–Photo Disc

Next we discuss some of the talents and qualities that are becoming increasingly rare, yet constantly sought after, in today's workplace. By understanding more about these qualities and striving to learn as much about them as possible, you can put yourself miles ahead of the competition.

Writing, Speaking, and Listening Skills

As you read through this book, you may think we are beating a dead horse. Over and over again, in almost every chapter, we offer some type of advice, suggestion, or tip for becoming a more effective communicator in written, verbal, and nonverbal forms. We do so because these are constantly listed as

top skills needed for success—in *any* profession and because so few people actually possess these qualities. If you want to put yourself ahead of the competition, then attend every class, every seminar, every meeting, and every function where you can learn more about effective writing, speaking, and listening skills.

A Strong Work Ethic

Contrary to popular belief, most employers don't want you to work yourself to death. In today's environment, however, they do want to make sure they are getting their money's worth. Our suggestion is to develop a strong work ethic that is healthy for you and your employer. Here are some suggestions for developing a strong work ethic:

- Come to work on the days you are assigned.
- Come to work on time.
- Try to give more than is expected.
- Give your very best to every project.
- Strive to get along with others.
- Think of the company's best interest.

You will be rewarded for these attributes.

Loyalty and Trustworthiness

Today competition is extremely strong among companies vying for the same customers. In some instances, you may have to sign a legal document that forbids you from discussing or sharing your work with anyone. Some industries also ask for a noncompete clause. If you leave Company X or Hospital Y, this clause prohibits you from working with Company Z or Hospital C—and sometimes in the same industry—for six months to one year, and maybe even longer.

> ### QUICK FACT
>
> In a recent survey, employers ranked Honesty, Integrity, and a Strong Work Ethic in the top five most desired personal skills and qualities they seek in an employee.
>
> National Association of Colleges and Employers, *Job Outlook 2005*

David Young-Wolff/PhotoEdit Inc.

In this light, loyalty to your employer is a highly regarded trait. However, loyalty cannot be measured by a résumé or determined by a simple interview. Proving you have loyalty and are trustworthy comes over time. It may take years to establish these characteristics with your company and within your industry, but be warned, it only takes seconds to destroy what took years to create. Remember, it *really* is a small world after all.

Teamwork

Employers are looking for people who not only understand the details of teamwork but who excel as team members. There is a humorous cartoon figure who says, "Teamwork is a bunch of people doing what I say!" Unfortunately, many people think this *is* teamwork. A true team has shared responsibilities, shared purposes, shared goals, shared visions, and, most important, shared accountability.

Team players understand that successful and efficient teamwork involves listening, respecting, and supporting each other; lifting one another up in times of trouble; working together to resolve conflicts quickly; making each other look good; and ultimately, bringing your personal best to the table every time you meet. Strive to be a team player; you will quickly reap the benefits.

Professionalism

The term *professionalism* varies from workplace to workplace. What is professional for one office or setting may be totally inappropriate for another. This includes everything from language usage to dress to personal grooming to conduct to your overall demeanor. Unlike loyalty and trustworthiness, professionalism *can be* judged before a potential employer ever meets you. Most interviewers can establish the level of your professionalism by your résumé and cover letter. Some even judge the quality of paper on which your résumé is printed. We have never actually met a person who lost a job over a watermark being turned the wrong way on your cover letter, but it certainly says something about your professionalism to many who will interview you.

Confidence and Decision-Making Abilities

QUOTE

Courage is a quietness, born of facing up to life, even when afraid.

Emily Councilman

There is a difference between confidence and the ability to make decisions, and being cocky. Confidence comes from experiences and calculated risk taking. Employers are looking for people who are not afraid to make hard decisions and for individuals who have confidence in their abilities. When you meet with the person interviewing you, move away from saying (and believing), "I'm a nurse," or "I'm an accountant," or "I'm a computer networking engineer." Instead, move toward discussing your overall qualities. Steer the conversation to your general and specific abilities and characteristics.

Priority Management Skills

Today, maybe more than any other time in history, we are faced with more and more to do and what seems like less and less time in which to do it. Your success depends on how well you manage your priorities both personally and professionally. Priority management not only involves getting today's work accomplished, it also involves the ability to plan for the future.

Contribute all you can to your career and employer, but also take time to enjoy your life, your family, your friends, and your relationships. If you are sacrificing your personal life, your personal time, and taking people in your life for granted, you will soon begin experiencing burnout, and then you're of no use to anyone. Guard your time wisely.

The Ability to Change and Grow

A decade ago, few people could have predicted there would be full-time, well-paid positions called webmasters or computer animation engineers. This is a perfect example of how changes in technology drive changes in business, health professions, and industry. If you are unable or unwilling to change and grow, thousands of your peers can *and will.* Our advice is to keep abreast of trends and technology pertaining to your field. Attend conferences, read professional literature, take classes, and have open discussions with colleagues and mentors regarding the issues surrounding your company and industry.

Critical Thinking Skills

Not only do employers want associates who can make decisions and proceed with confidence, they also demand that you be able to think your way through problems and challenges. Employers are looking for people who can distinguish fact from opinion; identify fallacies; analyze, synthesize, and determine the value of a piece of information; think beyond the obvious, see things from varying angles, and arrive at sound solutions.

Multitasking

A recent newspaper cartoon suggested you are too busy if you are multitasking in the shower. This may be true, but in keeping pace with today's workforce, this is another essential task: the ability to do more than one thing at a time—and the ability to do them all very well. If you have not had much experience in multitasking, we suggest you begin slowly. Don't take on too many things at one time. As you understand more about working on and completing several tasks at a time, you can expand your abilities in this arena.

BIGGEST INTERVIEW BLUNDER

When Maxine was asked about the most important decision she had made on her current job, she replied, "I don't think I've ever made a decision at work. I just do what they tell me to do."

Human Relation Skills

Human relation skills are listed last, certainly not because it is least important, but because this quality is an overriding characteristic of everything listed previously. Employers are looking for individuals who have people skills. This concept goes so much further than being a team player; it goes to the heart of many workplaces. It touches on your most basic nature, and it draws from your most inner self.

The ability to get along with grouchy, cranky, mean, disagreeable, burned-out colleagues is, indeed, a rare quality. But don't be mistaken: There are those who do this, and do it well. Peak performers, or those at the top of their game, have learned this world is made up of many types of people, and those cranky, grumpy people will always be in our midst. Human relation skills will be one of the most important traits you can develop.

 SOLUTION 23 USE EFFECTIVE KEYWORDS TO SHOWCASE YOUR TALENTS AND EXPERIENCES

All writers know that when writing a paper, speech, lecture, novel, or poem, they must know their audience. This is also true of the résumé writer. For effective résumé writing, one size does not fit all. The résumé and cover letter you send to one company for position X will not be the same one you send to another company for position Y. Your target audience (the employer) has changed, and so should your résumé and cover letter.

Accomplishment Keywords

When constructing your résumé, especially your accomplishments, think about these keywords used to gain attention:

organized	trained	maintained	increased	performed
developed	reduced	created	administered	designed
modified	constructed	delivered	trained	wrote
achieved	approved	arranged	doubled	facilitated
coordinated	upgraded	solved	revised	replaced
headed	launched	modernized	raised	tested
installed	mastered	managed	saved	solved
conserved	analyzed	assisted	corrected	won
wrote	repaired	introduced	started	negotiated
drafted	expanded	streamlined	monitored	finalized
implemented	directed	participated	processed	sold

Consider the following "before" and "after" statements and how effective keywords can change the tone and professionalism of an accomplishment statement.

EXAMPLE

Before

I helped my supervisor put together a new log-in system for incoming animals. Then, we put this information into the computer. I was responsible for checking the system daily. I reported any miscommunication.

After

- Assisted management in the creation and implementation of a computerized log-in system for lost animals using Microsoft Excel.
- Responsible for the daily animal log monitoring and spreadsheet reporting from Excel.
- Analyzed lost animal data and communicated findings to management.

As you can read, the bulleted "after" statements are more polished, give more information, and present your skills in a more professional, action-oriented manner.

Now, you try it. Read the following statement and make it more appealing using some of the keywords listed earlier.

"Worked in customer relations. Trained supervisors to work with employees. Trained supervisors to work better with customers. I helped the company write a new employee application. I helped them put the application online. This helped us manage our personnel information better."

Your turn:

_____

_____

_____

_____

Personal Trait Keywords

When you begin to describe yourself, you will need to think about another list of keywords to help the potential employer recognize your individual skills. Here are some of these keywords:

self-disciplined	successful	organized	motivated	energetic
mature	responsible	creative	dependable	efficient
team player	trustworthy	loyal	friendly	active
pleasant	reliable	resourceful	honest	outgoing
experienced	talented	open minded	tactful	caring
hardworking	enthusiastic	humorous		fair
genuine	sincere			

Consider the following "before" and "after" statements and how these keywords can change the tone and professionalism of your self-description.

EXAMPLE

Before

I am good at helping others and working with other people. I work hard and think that I am fair and honest.

After

I am an enthusiastic, open-minded individual who enjoys helping others, being a team player, and creatively solving problems. Honesty, tactfulness, and genuine concern are my strongest attributes.

Although some people may be uncomfortable touting their strong points, consider this statement: *If you don't sell yourself through your language and keywords, you'll never get the opportunity to sell yourself through an interview.* In more common words, "If you don't toot your own horn, it won't get tooted."

SOLUTION 24　SELL YOURSELF WITH CONFIDENCE

THINK ABOUT IT

How will using positive keywords enhance your own personal résumé and make your skills, experience, and education stand out? In looking over the keywords, which traits make you most proud?

As you write your cover letter and design your résumé, consider what skills, qualities, abilities, and attributes you have to offer. It is up to *you* to make sure future employers know all about you and what you will be able to bring to their workplace. Don't be afraid to ask your references to write about certain qualities you have.

Think of this as an ad for the newspaper. What if you had to literally sell yourself in the want ads to even get an interview? What would your ad say? What adjectives would you use to describe your abilities? In the space provided, write an ad to sell your abilities to an employer. It may be helpful to refer to the list of strengths you created for Solution #2 in Chapter 1 on page 9. You may also find the list of personal trait keywords in Solution #22 helpful. Be brave and take risks. If you can't speak positively about your abilities, few others will do so.

OUTSTANDING, QUALIFIED PROFESSIONAL ON THE MARKET

An Exercise in Self-Discovery

ATTENTION

_____ **FOR SALE**

(your name)

_____
_____
_____
_____

_____

_____

_____

_____

_____

SOLUTION 25 WRITE A POWERFUL AND CONCISE COVER LETTER

The most important part of the job search process is the preparation that must be done *before* the interview process. Two key elements of this preparation are your cover letter and résumé. Both are vital components in your career search. A carefully crafted letter and résumé communicate your past history (education, skills, and experience) that makes you the ideal candidate for their position. They are the first marketing pieces, and in many cases must stand alone when a recruiter is determining whether or not to interview you.

Whenever you send your résumé to a company, whether it is in response to a posted advertisement or requested, you must send a cover letter with it. Cover letters are extremely important; in fact, most recruiters say they read four times as many cover letters as they do résumés because if the cover letter does not "strike a chord," they never look past it to the résumé.

Carolyn Robbins (2006), career development expert, author, and speaker, states, "During my 25 plus years that I've been involved in career development, I have found that of all the paperwork associated with job searching, cover letter give job searchers the most difficulty." The information presented here will help you overcome any anxiety associated with writing your cover letter or résumé.

As you begin your cover letter and résumé process, consider the following: *"Gotta do it, can't skip it, No excuse for missing it."*

GENERAL TIPS

☑ Both your résumé and cover letter *Must* be typed. There are no exceptions to this rule, ever!

☑ Your cover letter and résumé must be printed on the same type and color of fine-quality paper. Cheap paper sends the message that you don't care. This is not the place or time to pinch pennies; buy excellent quality, 100% cotton stock paper.

☑ Check your printer and be sure the print quality is impeccable. Never send a cover letter or résumé with smudges, ink smears, or poor print quality.

☑ When you print your cover letter and résumé, be certain the watermark on the paper is turned in the correct direction. Hold it up to the light

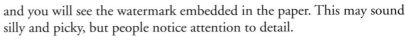

and you will see the watermark embedded in the paper. This may sound silly and picky, but people notice attention to detail.

☑ Do not fold your cover letter or résumé. Purchase a packet of 9 × 13 envelopes in which to send your materials.

☑ Do not handwrite the address on the envelope. Use a label or type the address directly on the envelope. Remember, first impressions are important.

☑ Never send a generic photocopy of a cover letter or résumé, even on the finest paper.

☑ Layout, design, font, spacing, and color must be considered in the building of your cover letter and résumé.

☑ Unless you are specifically asked to do so, *never* discuss money or salary history in either your cover letter or résumé. This could work against you. When asked for a salary history, use ranges.

☑ Your résumé and cover letter *must* be error free. That's right, not one single error is acceptable including grammar, spelling, punctuation, layout/spacing, dates, or content.

Simply put, the cover letter's purpose is to get the interviewer to read your résumé. It sets the tone for who you are, what you have to offer, and what you want. *"It screams—ever so politely—that you have the intelligence, experience, and soft skills to be the answer to an employer's staffing problem"* (Britton-Whitcomb, 2003). The cover letter should say to the reader, "You have an opening, you have a detailed description of what you need done, and I can fill your opening and be the person who gets the job done—and done well."

Consider the following **four steps to success** when writing your cover letter:

1   STEP ONE: **An effective cover letter is *personally addressed and job specific.***   If at all possible (and yes, it is possible with just a little research), address your letter to a specific person. Avoid at all cost the dreaded "Dear Sir or Madam" or "To Whom It May Concern." In most cases, a phone call to the company will provide the name of the person, their title, and their address. Always verify spelling, even with common names. This single step can set you apart from lazy job seekers. Also, make sure you spell the company's name correctly.

2   STEP TWO: **Once your letter is correctly addressed, your first paragraph should be an attention grabber and answer the question "Why am I writing?"**   Susan Britton-Whitcomb, author of *Resume Magic* (2003), calls this "the carrot." This simply means your first paragraph has an interesting fact, an appeal, or maybe even a quote—something that makes the reader (ideally, your future employer) read further. Your first paragraph should also have a transition statement that makes the reader want to read on. For example, your last statement might read, "With a degree in medical assisting and four years experience at Desert Medical Center, I know I can make a valued contribution to Grace Care Center."

3   STEP THREE: **Your second (and maybe third) paragraph(s) should clearly state why you are qualified for the position you are seeking.**   Use your cover letter to highlight those areas of your experience that specifically qualify you for the job. Your cover letter is not the time to list all of your qualifications but to indicate the two or three components that most qualify you for the position and closely match the position announcement. You may also include specific attributes that may not be on your résumé. The keyword to consider here is your value. Relate your education, experience, and talents to their need. Mention facts and statistics of how you've been successful in the past. Remember, "Employers are not interested in you for your sake, but rather because of what you can bring to the organization. This might sound harsh, but businesspeople have an obligation to improve the success of their organization. If you consistently show how you can help them do this . . . they will be much more motivated to talk to you." (Farr & Kursmark, 2005).

4 STEP FOUR: **Your final paragraph should address the question of** *Where do we go from here?* Do not be ambiguous here by saying something trite like "I hope to hear from you in the near future," or "If you have any questions, please do not hesitate to call me." Remember, *your* job search is none of their business, nor is it their responsibility. Be proactive by stating that *you will be following up* with a phone call to discuss your résumé and experience(s) in more detail. Make sure that once you have told them you are going to call, you actually do call.

Your final paragraph should also continue to express what you can do for the company. End your letter with a statement about your qualities and their needs such as, "Mr. Thompson, I will call you on Monday, January 24 at 11:30 am to discuss how my past experiences can help streamline operations and continue superior patient care at Grace Care Center."

Don't forget to *sign your letter.* Figures 3.1 and 3.2 provide Sample Cover Letters. Figure 3.1 indicates the correct format and spacing in red.

SOLUTION 26 UNDERSTAND THE DOs AND DON'Ts OF MEMORABLE RÉSUMÉS

Eight seconds. That is all you have to gain the attention of your potential employer, according to Susan Ireland (2003), author and consultant. "In eight seconds, an employer scans your resume and decides whether she will invest more time to consider you as a job candidate. The secret to passing the eight-second test is to make your resume look inviting and quick to read" (p.14).

A resume is the blueprint that details what you have accomplished with regard to education, experience, skills acquisition, workplace successes, and progressive responsibility and/or leadership. It is a painting (that *you* are able to paint) of how your professional life looks. It is the ultimate advertisement of you! Your résumé must create interest and ideally a *desire* to find more about you.

When choosing your personal résumé format, take into careful consideration the field in which you wish to be employed as well as the company where you hope to interview. The one-size-fits-all ideology does not work with résumés. Personalizing your résumé can set you apart from all of the other job seekers wanting your position.

As you begin to develop your résumé, make sure to allow plenty of time to develop it. Plan to enlist several qualified proofreaders to check your work. We cannot stress strongly enough the need for your résumé to be perfect. A simple typo or misuse of grammar can disqualify you from the job of your dreams. Don't allow a lack of attention to detail to stand between you and your future career.

Further, your résumé must be 100 percent completely accurate and truthful. Do not fabricate information or fudge dates to make yourself look better. It will only

FIGURE 3.1 Sample Cover Letter with Formatting Information

Your name and address on high-quality paper. Your name should be larger and/or in a different font to call attention.

BENJAMIN SHAW

1234 Lake Shadow Drive, Maple City, PA 12345   (123) 555-1234   ben@online.com

The date (then double space) → January 3, 2008

The specific person, title, and address to whom you are writing (then double space) →

Mr. James Pixler, RN, CAN
Director of Placement and Advancement
Grace Care Center
123 Sizemore Street, Suite 444
Philadelphia, PA 12345

The formal salutation followed by a colon: (then double space) →

Dear Mr. Pixler:

Paragraph 1 (then double space) →

Seven years ago, my mother was under the treatment of two incredible nurses at Grace Care Center in Philadelphia. My family and I agree that the care she was given was extraordinary. When I saw your ad in today's *Philadelphia Carrier*, I was extremely pleased to know that I now have the qualifications to be a part of the Grace Care Team as a medical assistant.

Paragraph 2 (then double space) →

Next month, I will graduate with an occupational associate's degree from Victory College of Health and Technology as a certified medical assistant. My résumé indicated that I was fortunate to do my internship at Mercy Family Care Practice in Harrisburg. During this time, I was directly involved in patient care, records documentation, and family outreach.

Paragraph 3 (then double space) →

As a part of my degree from Victory, I received a 4.0 in the following classes:

✓ Management Communications
✓ Microsoft Office (Word, Excel, Outlook, PowerPoint)
✓ Business Communications I, II, III
✓ Anatomy and Physiology, I, II, III
✓ Medical Assisting
✓ Medical Coding, I, II
✓ Medical Office Procedures
✓ Principles of Pharmacology
✓ Immunology, I, II, III, IV
✓ Urinalysis and Body Fluids
✓ Therapeutic Interventions
✓ Clinical Practicum, I, II, III

This, along with my past certificate in medical transcription and my immense respect for Grace Care Center makes me the perfect candidate for your position.

Final paragraph or closing (then double space) →

I have detailed all of my experience on the enclosed résumé. I will call you on Monday, January 24, at 11:30 am to discuss how my past education and experiences can help streamline operations and continue superior patient care at Grace. In the meantime, please feel free to contact me at the number above.

The Complementary Close (then four spaces) →

Sincerely yours,

Your handwritten signature in black or blue ink →

Benjamin Shaw

Your typed name → Benjamin Shaw

Enclosure contents → Enclosure: Résumé

FIGURE 3.2 Sample Cover Letter

Rosetta M. Alverez

August 18, 2008

Ms. Marilyn McAllen, President
TinyTot Day Care Center
125-A Adobe Falls Road
Crystal City, NJ 45678

Dear President McAllen:

After reading your ad in *Education Today,* reviewing your website, and giving serious consideration to your specific needs, I have determined that my past experience in directing day care activities and my degree in early childhood education make me the perfect candidate for your open position as director of infant care.

My earliest recollection of a career field was that of a preschool teacher. I have loved children all of my life, and this led me to seek early employment and a college degree in caring for infants and preschoolers. As my résumé indicates, I have spent the past 14 years directly involved in almost every aspect of child care, preschool education, and infant development. In my current position as assistant director of education for ChildPlay, my responsibilities involve:

- ✓ direct supervision of 12 child-care specialists,
- ✓ development of weekly nutritious meal and snack plans,
- ✓ development of educational curriculum, activities, and lessons,
- ✓ toddler and infant artistic development, and
- ✓ oversight of office management, personnel, and budget matters.

I am certain that once you review my résumé and we have an opportunity to speak in person, you will agree that my attitude, values, and work ethic are in complete alignment with those you promote at TinyTot. I will call you on Monday of next week to establish an appropriate time to stop by.

Thank you for your consideration,

Rosie Alverez

Rosetta M. Alverez, CCCS

Enclosures: Résumé, Specialist Certificate

---

come back to haunt you in the long run. Dennis Reina, organizational psychologist and author of *Trust and Betrayal in the Workplace,* states, "I think that what you put in a resume absolutely has to be rock-solid, concrete, and verifiable. If there are any questions, it will immediately throw both your application and your credibility into question" (Dresang, 2007). People have been fired from positions after they were hired because they misrepresented themselves on their résumé, cover letter, or application.

As you begin to build your résumé, remember to "call in the **DOCTOR**."

D = Give attention to **D**esign and format

O = Write an effective, clear, and specific **O**bjective

C = Check for **C**larity and concreteness

T = Tell the **T**ruth

O = Use an **O**rganized format to sell yourself (chronological, functional, accomplishment)

R = **R**eview for mistakes in content, grammar, and spelling

D Visual **design** and format are imperative to a successful résumé. Think about the font that you plan to use, whether color is appropriate, the use of bullets, lines, or shading, and where you are going to put information. Also pay attention to the text balance on the page (centered left/right, top/bottom). The visual aspect of your résumé will be the first impression. "Make it pretty" (Britton-Whitcomb, 2003).

O Writing a clear and specific **objective** can help get your foot in the door. The reader, usually your potential employer, needs to be able to scan your résumé and gather as much detail as possible as quickly as possible. A job-specific objective can help. Consider the following two objectives:

EXAMPLE

Before:

Objective: *To get a job as an elementary teacher in the Dallas Area School District.*

After:

Objective: *Seeking an elementary school teaching position that will utilize my 14 years of creative teaching experience, curriculum development abilities, supervisory skills, and commitment to superior instruction.*

C **Clarity** is of paramount importance, especially when including your past responsibilities, education, and job growth. Be certain you let the reader know exactly what you have done, what specific education you have gained, and what progress you have made. Being vague and unclear can cost you an interview.

T When writing your résumé, you may be tempted to fudge a little bit here and there to make your résumé look better. Perhaps you were out of work for a few months and you think it looks bad to have this gap in your chronological history. Avoid the urge to fudge. Telling the absolute **truth** on a résumé is essential. A lie, even a small one, can (and usually will) come back to haunt you.

O Before you begin your résumé, think about the **organizational** pattern you will need to use. For some jobs, chronological might be best. For others, you may want to use an accomplishment format. It might serve you well to construct one of each so you will have them if you need them. Plus, this gives you experience in writing each type of résumé.

R **Reviewing** your résumé and cover letter is important, but having someone else review them for clarity, accuracy, spelling, grammar, placement, and overall content can be one of the best things you can do for your job search.

The following basic tips will help you as you begin building a dynamic résumé.

● Here are general topics you *must* include, *should* include, should *consider* including, or *should not* include on your résumé:

Contact information (name, complete mailing address, phone and cell numbers, fax number, e-mail address, web page URL)	MUST include
Education, degrees, certificates, advanced training (to include dates and names of degrees)	MUST include
Current and past work history, experience and responsibilities	MUST include
Past accomplishments (this is *not* the same as work history or responsibilities)	MUST include
Specific licensures	MUST include
Specific career objective	SHOULD include
Summary or list of qualifications, strengths, specializations	SHOULD include
Special skills (including special technical skills or multiple language skills)	SHOULD include
Volunteer work, public service, and/or community involvement	SHOULD include
Internships, externships, and/or extracurricular activities	SHOULD include
Awards, honors, certificates of achievement, special recognitions (at work or in the community)	SHOULD include
Military experience	CONSIDER including
Professional / Preprofessional memberships, affiliations, and/or associations	CONSIDER including
Publications and presentations	CONSIDER including
Current *business* phone number and/or address (where you are working at the moment)	DO NOT include
"Availability" date/time to begin work	DO NOT include
Geographical limitations	DO NOT include
Personal hobbies or interests	DO NOT include
Personal information such as age, sex, health status, marital status, parental status, ethnicity, or religious affiliations	DO NOT include
Photos	DO NOT include
Salary requirements or money issues	DO NOT include (unless specifically asked to provide a salary history)
References	DO NOT include, but have the information ready on a separate sheet of paper that matches your résumé

- Do not date-stamp or record the preparation date of your résumé in any place.

- Limit your résumé (and cover letter) to one page each (a two-page résumé is appropriate if you have more than ten years of experience).

- Use standard résumé paper colors such as white, cream, gray, or beige.

- Use bullets (such as these) to help profile lists.

- Avoid fancy or hard to read fonts such as curlz or borg s.

- Use a standard font size between 10 and 14 points.

- Do not staple anything to your résumé (or cover letter)

- Avoid the use of "I," "Me," or "My" in your résumé.

- Avoid contractions such as "don't," and do not use abbreviations.

- Keep your résumé formal and professional.

- Use action verbs such as "designed," "managed," "created," "recruited," "simplified," and/or "built."

- Avoid the use of full sentences; fragments are fine on a résumé.

- Use the correct verb tense. You will use past tense (such as "recruited") except for your current job.

- Remember when phrasing your information, less is more.

- Do not include irrelevant information that does not pertain to this particular job search.

- Choose a format that puts your best foot, or greatest assets, forward.

SOLUTION 27   BUILD A TIMELY CHRONOLOGICAL RÉSUMÉ

There are different types of résumés, but primarily they can be classified as chronological, functional, accomplishment, or a combination of each.

- ☑ A *chronological résumé* organizes education and work experience in a reverse chronological order (your last or present job is listed first).

- ☑ A *functional résumé* organizes your work and experience around specific skills and duties.

- ☑ An *accomplishment résumé* allows you to place your past accomplishments into categories that are not necessarily associated with an employer but shows your track record of "getting the job done."

- ☑ A *combination résumé* generally combines elements of one or more of the above.

A *chronological résumé* is the most common type. It can easily highlight your career and education progression. It is relatively easy to construct because it's straightforward. However, it *may not* be the most effective type if you have had gaps in your employment or if you wish to show off your skills and talents more than your past positions or educational degrees.

You must determine which type of résumé best profiles your education, skills, and experience. Your choice may be based on the wording of the job advertisement. Figure 3.3 shows an example of a chronological résumé.

FIGURE 3.3 Chronological Résumé

BENJAMIN SHAW

1234 Lake Shadow Drive, Maple City, PA 12345   **(123) 555-1234**   **ben@online.com**

OBJECTIVE: To work as a medical assistant in an atmosphere that uses my organizational skills, compassion for people, desire to make a difference, and impeccable work ethic.

PROFESSIONAL EXPERIENCE:

January 2006-Present   **Medical Assistant Intern**

Mercy Family Care Practice, Harrisburg, PA
- Responsible for completing patient charts
- Took patients' vitals
- Assisted with medical coding

February 2003-December 2006   **Medical Transcriptionist**

The Office of Brenda Wilson, MD, Lancaster, PA
- Interpreted and typed medical reports
- Worked with insurance documentation
- Assisted with medical coding
- Served as office manager (1/05-12/06)

March 1998-February 2003   **Ward Orderly**

Wallace Hospital, Lancaster, PA
- Assisted nurses with patient care
- Cleaned patient rooms
- Served patient meals

August 1995-March 1998   **Administrative Assistant**

Ellen Abbot Nursing Care Facility
- Typed office reports
- Organized patient files

EDUCATION:

Occupational Associate's Degree – Medical Assistant
Victory Health Institute, Harrisburg, PA
May 2008 (With Honors)

Certificate of Completion – Medical Transcription
Philadelphia Technical Institute
December 2002

Vocational High School Diploma – Health Sciences
Philadelphia Vocational High School
August 1995

SOLUTION 28   CONSTRUCT A SKILLFULLY WRITTEN FUNCTIONAL RÉSUMÉ

A **functional résumé** emphasizes (highlights) the skills and talents you have gained. This is a fine résumé format if you want to show what you know rather than emphasize where you've worked or from where you gained your training. This type can be effective when you are trying to get a potential employer to look at what you have to offer the company in terms of usable, transferable skills. The functional résumé allows the reader to identify emphasized skills quickly and downplays past employers or education.

FIGURE 3.4 The Functional Résumé

BENJAMIN SHAW

1234 Lake Shadow Drive, Maple City, PA 12345   (123) 555-1234   ben@online.com

OBJECTIVE: To work as a medical assistant in an atmosphere that uses my organization abilities, people skills, compassion for patients, desire to make a difference, and impeccable work ethic.

SKILLS:

Bilingual (English/Spanish)	Data Protection
Claims Reimbursement	Client Relations
Highly Organized	Problem-Solving Skills
Motivated, Self-starter	Team Player
Priority Management Skills	Delegating Ability
Strategic Planning	Budget Management

PROFESSIONAL PREPARATION:

Occupational Associate's Degree – Medical Assistant
Victory Health Institute, Harrisburg, PA
May 2008 (With Honors)

Certificate of Completion – Medical Transcription
Philadelphia Technical Institute
December 2002

Vocational High School Diploma – Health Sciences
Philadelphia Vocational High School
August 1995

PROFESSIONAL EXPERIENCE:

January 2006–Present	**Medical Assistant Intern** Mercy Family Care Practice, Harrisburg, PA
February 2003–December 2006	**Medical Transcriptionist** Office of Brenda Wilson, MD, Lancaster, PA
March 1998–February, 2003	**Ward Orderly** Wallace Hospital, Lancaster, PA
August 1995–March, 1998	**Administrative Assistant** Ellen Abbot Nursing Care Facility

REFERENCES: Provided upon Request

One problem with the functional résumé is that it does not show where you gained or learned the skills mentioned, whether past work experiences and/or educational training. Some employers do not like functional résumés because they assume you are trying to hide something. However, a well-constructed functional résumé can highlight your skills, talents, work experience, and training. Figure 3.4 (see page 60) offers an example of a functional résumé.

SOLUTION 29 CONSTRUCT A TELLING ACCOMPLISHMENT RÉSUMÉ

An accomplishment résumé gives the same basic information as the chronological or functional résumé; however, it showcases what you were able to accomplish in your past positions rather than your skills, your work history, or your training. Susan Britton Whitcomb, author of *Resume Magic* (2003) refers to this type of résumé as showing your "trophies." An accomplishment résumé often downplays or omits previous job descriptions, dates, and experiences. A powerful accomplishment résumé, however, shows your accomplishments *and* job descriptions, dates, and experiences. Figure 3.5 shows an example of an accomplishment résumé.

YOUR RÉSUMÉ WORKSHEET

Now it is your turn. After reviewing the information for résumé writing and the examples of several résumés, begin compiling information to build your own chronological résumé using this template.

Personal Information

Name _____

Address _____

_____

Phone Number(s) _____

E-mail address _____

Website _____

Work Experience (Employment History)

1. (most recent)

Company name _____

Your position _____

Your duties _____

_____

_____

(continued)

FIGURE 3.5 Accomplishment Résumé

BENJAMIN SHAW

**1234 Lake Shadow Drive
Maple City, PA 12345
(702) 555-1234**

**ben@online.com
www.bjs@netconnect.com**

Career Target:

MEDICAL ASSISTANT

A highly qualified medical professional with eight years of experience in patient care, client relations, and medical coding seeking a challenging career that utilizes my strong problem-solving skills, deep compassion for the people, and medical training.

PROFESSIONAL ACCOMPLISHMENTS

Mercy Family Care Practice
- ✓ Revised and updated medical coding procedures
- ✓ Increased insurance payments by 11%
- ✓ Revised and streamlined new patient intake process
- ✓ Assisted lead MA with ethics plan revision and implementation
- ✓ Revamped treatment procedure guidelines

Office of Brenda Wilson, MD
- ✓ Developed new medication administration checklist
- ✓ Implemented new guidelines for lab specimen collection
- ✓ Assisted with compliance of OSHA regulations

SKILLS / STRENGTHS
- ✓ Highly organized
- ✓ Team player
- ✓ Impeccable work ethic
- ✓ Bilingual (English and Spanish)
- ✓ Budget Minded
- ✓ Motivated, self-starter
- ✓ Excellent client relations
- ✓ Superior time management skills

PROFESSIONAL PREPARATION

Occupational Associate's Degree – Medical Assistant
Victory Health Institute, Harrisburg, PA
May 2008 (With High Honors)

Certificate of Completion – Medical Transcription
Philadelphia Technical Institute
December 2002 (With Honors)

Vocational High School Diploma – Health Sciences
Philadelphia Vocational High School
August 1995

PROFESSIOINAL EXPERIENCE

January 2006-Present   **Medical Assistant Intern**
                                Mercy Family Care Practice

February 2003-December, 2006   **Medical Transcriptionist**
                                Office of Brenda Wilson, MD

March 1998-February, 2003   **Ward Orderly**
                                Wallace Hospital

August 1995-March 1998   **Administrative Assistant**
                                Ellen Abbot Nursing Care Facility

2. (next most recent)

Company name _____

Your position _____

Your duties _____

_____

_____

3. (next most recent)

Company name _____

Your position _____

Your duties _____

_____

_____

Education and Training

1. (latest degree)

Name of institution _____

Name and date of degree _____

Honors / Recognition _____

_____

2. (degree)

Name of institution _____

Name and date of degree _____

Honors/Recognition _____

_____

Additional Training

Name of institution _____

Name and date of certificate or training program _____

_____

_____

Name of institution _____

Name and date of certificate or training program _____

_____

_____

Special Skills and Qualifications

List any skills and qualifications that you possess that may be of interest to an employer.

_____

_____

(continued)

_____

_____

_____

College or Community Service (optional)

List any relevant service you have performed that the potential employer might need to know.

_____

_____

_____

_____

_____

References

List the names, addresses, and phone numbers of at least three people you could call on to serve as a reference for you if needed.

1. _____

_____

_____

_____

2. _____

_____

_____

_____

3. _____

_____

_____

_____

SOLUTION 30   CHOOSE APPROPRIATE REFERENCES

If an employer is interested in you, he or she will most likely ask that you provide three to five references, people who can attest to your professional skills, work ethic, and workplace knowledge. There are five steps to soliciting letters of reference successfully.

1   STEP ONE: **Select three to five people with whom you have had professional contact.**   As you determine the best ones to select, choose people who are very familiar with your work ability. Current and former employers with whom you have experienced a good working relationship are excellent sources of references. Your instructors are also an excellent source. If you do not have anyone who falls into these two categories, consider asking friends of your family who are respected members of the community. As you consider possible reference sources, be sure to choose individuals who are responsible and timely in their reply to your request. Typically, do not use your minister, rabbi, or other religious leaders as references.

References are a reflection of you, and if the reference sources do not respond in the appropriate manner, they will cast a shadow on your credibility. Your references should have excellent written communication skills. A poorly written recommendation letter reflects badly on you.

2 STEP TWO: **Request permission from your reference sources.** Always ask someone before you list them as a reference on an application or résumé. During your conversation with them, discuss your career goals and aspirations. Give them a copy of your résumé and cover letter. Ask them to critique them for you and make any necessary changes. Also ask the person to put your letter on the company letterhead and send your potential employer an original copy, not a photocopy.

3 STEP THREE: **Obtain all necessary contact information from them.** Know your references' professional name, job title, business address, e-mail address, phone number, and fax number so your potential employer can contact them with ease.

4 STEP FOUR: **Send thank-you letters to those who agree to serve as references for you.** Stay in contact with your references throughout your job search. Give them updates and a periodic thank you in the form of a card, an e-mail, or a phone call. At the end of your job search, a small token of your appreciation may be appropriate, but a thank-you note is essential.

5 STEP FIVE: **Develop a typed list of all references—including contact information—and take it with you to all interviews.** It is now customary *not* to include the names of references on your résumé. You simply state, "References available on request" or do not mention references at all. Employers will ask if they need them.

In the space provided, list three people you could ask to serve as references for you (or write you a reference letter). Once you have identified these three people, list the skills that each person could speak about on your behalf. Think about this carefully because it is important to choose references who can speak to your many qualifications, not just one or two. Choose people who know you in different areas of success.

IF YOU WERE IN CHARGE

SOLVE THE PUZZLE

Understanding that people only solicit references from those whom they hope will give them a positive recommendation, what weight would you place on a reference letter or reference phone conversation when hiring a new employee? Why?

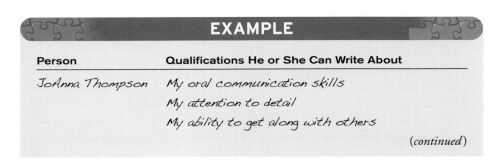

Person	Qualifications He or She Can Write About
JoAnna Thompson	My oral communication skills
	My attention to detail
	My ability to get along with others

(continued)

EXAMPLE

Person	Qualifications He or She Can Write About
Beau DeTiberious	My ability to form a team
	My ability to motivate team members
	My ability to meet deadlines
Person #1	Qualifications He or She Can Write About
Person #2	Qualifications He or She Can Write About
Person #3	Qualifications He or She Can Write About

SOLUTION 31 DESIGN AND DISTRIBUTE ATTRACTIVE PERSONAL BUSINESS CARDS

POSITIVE HABITS

WORK

Never use your company's supplies for your own personal projects or monetary gain, not even your company business cards. Always keep your personal life and projects separate from your company's projects. This way, you can always have a clear conscience regarding any conflict of interest.

Setting yourself apart from other job seekers is important, and designing/distributing attractive personal business cards can help. Business cards give you a professional edge, provide your potential employer another contact source, and help contacts stay in touch with you.

Business cards should be the standard size and, if possible, be professionally designed and printed. If this is not possible, many computer programs and graphic packages can assist you. You can also purchase sheets of blank business cards for your home printer. You simply design, print, and break them apart.

Although including a simple graphic is fine (and can be very helpful), avoid flashy, unprofessional colors or overly cute graphics. Be certain to include your vital information:

Full name
Full address with zip code
Phone numbers (residence, business, cellular, and fax)
E-mail address
Website

Nearby you will find examples of appropriate and inappropriate personal business cards.

BENJAMIN SHAW

BIKER • SKIER • ALL AROUND COOL DUDE

Babes, call me at
(702) 555-1212

or email me at
realDude@online.com

Inappropriate personal card for business use.

Benjamin Shaw

1234 Lake Shadow Drive, Maple City, PA 12345

702-555-1212   ben.shaw@online.com

  student
Victory Health Institute
Medical Assistant Program

More appropriate personal card for business use.

 SOLUTION 32 GIVE SERIOUS ATTENTION TO JOB APPLICATION GUIDELINES AND DETAILS

Some employers will ask you to fill out a job application in addition to or as a substitute for your résumé. Don't take this task lightly. This application can be as important as your résumé and cover letter and should be given serious consideration. Neatness, accuracy, and effective verbiage still apply. Consider the following guidelines when completing a job application:

- Don't take the directions for granted. Read them carefully before beginning.

- Type the application if possible. If this is not possible, be very neat with your penmanship. Make sure your write legibly and neatly. Use a pen, not a pencil.

- Ask if the application is available online. If so, complete it this way so you can use the computer's spell and grammar check and make corrections.

- Ask if you can take the job application home so you can take your time with it and/or type it. (Consider making a copy of it to use for practice.)

- Be certain you answer each and every question. If the question does not apply to you, simply put N/A (not applicable).

- Check all of your information for accuracy. Take your address book and a small dictionary to the interview with you. If you submit an application and a résumé, be certain the information matches exactly.

- Just as you would never lie on your résumé, do not lie or fudge information on your application.

- If you application states, "Résumés are not substitutes for this answer," do not write, "See résumé."

- Never turn in an application that has been mutilated, folded, soiled, or damaged. This makes just as big an impression as turning in a handwritten dirty résumé.

- Be certain to sign and date your application if space is provided to do so.

PUTTING IT ALL TOGETHER

As you begin the construction of your résumé, cover letters, and business cards, consider that these pieces of paper must represent you when you are not present. They speak volumes in your absence and can mean the difference between an interview and a rejection letter. Take your time, proofread your work, call potential references, tell the truth, and think about your needs and what you have to offer. Moreover, always sell yourself with confidence, grace, and pride.

REFERENCES

Britton-Whitcomb, S. (2003). *Resume Magic: Trade Secrets of a Professional Resume Writer.* Indianapolis: JIST Works Publishing.

Dresang, J. (2007, April 23). *Liar! Liar! Won't Get Hired. In Age of Easy Information, Resume Fibs Can Sabotage Hunts for Work.* The *Las Vegas Review Journal;* reprinted from the *Milwaukee Journal Sentinel.*

Farr, M., & Kursmark, L. (2005). *15 Minute Cover Letter: Write an Effective Cover Letter Right Now.* Indianapolis: JIST Works Publishing.

Ireland, S. (2003). *The Complete Idiot's Guide to the Perfect Resume.* Indianapolis: Alpha Publishing Company.

Robbins, C. (2006). *The Job Searcher's Handbook* (3rd ed.). Upper Saddle River, NJ: Prentice Hall.

Communicating and Interviewing with Confidence and Class

The Impression of a Lifetime

WHY?

read and work through an entire chapter on communicating and interviewing? Why do I have to have to be concerned about my confidence level? Why is my body language important at an interview? "Hey, I'm not the interviewer, so why do I have to ask questions at the interview?"

In Chapter 3, we stated that your résumé gets *eight seconds* to make an impression. Consider this: During the interview process, you have even less. A judgment is made immediately about you: your dress, your grooming, your stance, your handshake, and your overall visual impression. Right or wrong, the interviewer will form an immediate first opinion of you—just as you will form an immediate first impression of your interviewer.

Think of your interview in terms of establishing a meaningful and positive relationship, just like with friends or family. You may have positive interpersonal relationships with your family, your current co-workers, and certainly your close friends. You've nurtured and fostered those relationships for years, but in the interview, you only have a short while to form the same type of "positive relationship" and "comfortable feeling" with this new acquaintance.

The interviewer will not know what type of brother or sister you have been. They will not have seen you helping your friends or volunteering with a service agency. They will not know how powerful you are in mediating conflicts with family members. They do not know about your parenting skills or caring nature. Those qualities are personal and only the people closest to you know them. But your interviewer needs to sense the same friendliness, confidence, trust, class, professionalism, and intelligence about you that those closest to you know to be true.

As you begin to prepare for your interview, consider the following mnemonic. If you confidently *carry* **REWARDS** with you to an interview, you will most likely *get* rewards after the interview, such as a job offer, benefits, and a career in which you can grow and prosper.

> **R = Rapport**   Rapport is basically your "relationship" (intended or unintended) with another person, the emotional alliance you establish with someone. Consider how you come across to others. Rapport involves your verbal and nonverbal communication efforts. Strive to establish a positive relationship with potential employers and future colleagues.

> **E = Education and Training**   Be confident about what you know and promote your abilities, skills, and talents eloquently to the interviewer. Remember, if you don't promote yourself, it is unlikely anyone else will.

> **W = Willingness**   Project a sense of willingness to learn new things, to become a team member, to assist the company with growth and new projects, and a willingness to keep up with advancements and changes in the modern world of work. A recent survey by the consulting firm Towers-Perrin found that only 21 percent of current employees are engaged and willing to exert any extra effort at work (*Las Vegas Review Journal,* November 5, 2007). Potential employers enjoy seeing an attitude of willingness and engagement.

> **A = Appearance**   Dress for success. Pay close attention to your grooming, your hygiene, your hair, your clothing, and yes, even your shoes and socks (or hosiery). It all matters—and it is all noticed. Never make the mistake in thinking that appearance is not important.

> **R = Response**   Project positivity and optimism in your responses to the questions asked in the interview. Even if you have to talk about your weaknesses or past experiences of conflict and turmoil, put a positive spin on them. Let the interviewer know you have learned from adversity.

> **D = Demeanor**   Cast a quality of confidence (not cockiness), intelligence, professionalism, and positivity. Carrying yourself with confidence during the

interview will not go unnoticed. Pay attention to your handshake, eye contact, posture, mannerisms, and facial expressions.

S = Sincerity   No one likes phony people, especially a potential employer. Be yourself and strive to be sincere in your answers, your emotions, and your passion.

This is a great deal of information to consider, but this chapter will help you make a powerful first impression, assist you in honing your interpersonal and oral communication skills, and prepare you to interview with confidence and class.

 SOLUTION 33   UNDERSTAND THE IMPORTANCE OF HUMAN COMMUNICATION

You do *not* have a choice. If you are in the presence of another human being, you are communicating. Silence is communication. Smiling is communication. Reading a newspaper is communication. Turning your back to the wall and hiding your face from everyone is communication. It is just the law of nature: If you are around one or more people, you are communicating with them. With that said, understanding the impact of effective communication can help you in the interview, on the job, and with every type of personal and professional relationship.

Consider this: Nothing in your life is more important than effective communication. Your family is not. Your friends are not. Your career is not. Your religion is not. Your money is not. Why, you may ask? That is a harsh statement. We make this assertion because without effective communication, you would not have a relationship with your family and friends. You would not have a career or money or even religious beliefs. Communication is that important. In fact, it is so important that communication gives us our identity. Without it, we would not even know we were human beings.

Take into account the true story of the Wild Boy of Aveyron. In January 1800, a gardener in Aveyron, France, went out one morning to collect vegetables for the day. To his surprise, he heard an unusual moaning. Upon further inspection, he found a "wild boy" squatting in the garden eating vegetables as an animal might do. This boy showed no signs or behaviors associated with human beings. He appeared to be about twelve years old, but stood just a little more than 4 feet tall. He had scars and burns on his body and his face showed traces of smallpox. His teeth were brown and yellow and his gums were receding. It can only be assumed that when he was an infant, he was abandoned in the woods and left to die. It has also been suggested that someone may have tried to kill him as an infant because of the long scar across his trachea (Lane, 1976).

When he was found in 1800, he could not speak and barely stood erect. "He had no sense of being a human in the world. He had no sense of himself as a person related to other persons" (Shattuck, 1980). Because of his lack of communication and contact with other humans, he had no identity, no language, no self-concept, and no idea that he was even a human being in a world of human beings. That is how *powerful* communication is in our world today: It gives us our identity.

Communication is also important for many other reasons:

   Survival

   Establishing relationships

> **QUOTE**
>
> I see communication as a huge umbrella that covers and affects all that goes on between human beings.
>
> Joseph Adler

- ☑ Gaining knowledge
- ☑ Finding enjoyment
- ☑ Entertainment
- ☑ Expressing opinions and explaining details
- ☑ Delegating responsibilities
- ☑ Articulating our desires and wishes
- ☑ Changing emotions
- ☑ Promoting health and stress reduction
- ☑ Motivating and influencing others
- ☑ Managing conflict and overcoming adversity

The more you learn about all types of human communication, the stronger you become in each of the areas just listed and the more effective and powerful your interview will be. Further, the more you understand about your own communication habits, the more powerful first and lasting impression you will make.

SOLUTION 34   MAKE A POWERFUL, POSITIVE, AND LASTING FIRST IMPRESSION

Rick Friedman/CORBIS-NY

You never get a second chance to make a good first impression. So what do you need to do to impress people? Remember that the impression starts with the résumé and cover letter you send to a company. Your impression continues when you talk to someone from a company on the telephone or send an e-mail. These actions need to be perfect because they are speaking for you even though you are not physically present.

According to Susan Bixler and Nancy Nix-Rice (1997), "Books are judged by their covers, houses are appraised by their curb appeal, and people are initially evaluated on how they choose to dress and behave. In a perfect world, this is not fair, moral or just. What's inside should count a great deal more. And eventually, it does, but not right away. In the meantime, a lot of opportunities can be lost."

If you are fortunate enough to get an interview, that first impression begins as soon as you arrive at the company. When interviewing, this is an extraordinarily important point to remember. If you make a poor impression on the job interview, you will never get a chance to prove how smart you are, what a hard worker you are, or how likeable you are. A poor first impression is usually the kiss of death on a job interview.

Remember that personal impressions begin as soon as you walk in the door of a company. You are being evaluated by potential colleagues, administrative assistants, and the people who interview you. They are determining if you are likeable, friendly, assertive, educated, and confident. They are drawing conclusions about your ability, communication style, manners, etiquette, and attitude. In short, they are deciding if they want you for a colleague by the image and impression you are portraying.

You might say, "Well, I don't want an image." Unfortunately, that is not something over which you have control. Everyone has an image, and it is usually determined by what you allow people to see—your dress, grooming, manners, attitude, etiquette, confidence, appearance, and communication skills.

If you ask yourself these questions and answer them honestly, it will help you understand the importance of image and impressions. How many people really know who you are? How many people know your hopes and dreams? Your fears and desires? Truthfully, not many. Most people will say, "one or two people." All anyone knows about you is what you allow them to see, so image and impressions become the measuring sticks by which others judge you, whether you like it or not.

You may not like the fact that these factors are expressly important to the interviewer, but, let's face it, they are!

- ☑ Your résumé and cover letter and yes, *even* the quality of paper and the envelope in which you send your materials

- ☑ Your telephone conversations with *everyone* at the company with whom you are interviewing

- ☑ Your e-mails

- ☑ Your appearance—what you wear to the interview

- ☑ Your grooming—how you smell (perfumes, colognes, etc.), your clothing, your shoes, etc.

- ☑ Your personal confidence, including your handshake, your eye contact, and your facial expressions when you meet someone

- ☑ Your verbal tone and whether you appear congenial and friendly

- ☑ Your "presence" or "got-it-together" confident demeanor

Not only are overall impressions, dress, and grooming significant factors when getting a job, they are also very important when it comes to being considered for a promotion. You can do few things more crucial for your career than to have impeccable dress and grooming, respectful manners, a friendly and caring demeanor, and impeccable etiquette skills.

Do yourself a favor. Take a few minutes and look in the mirror and judge yourself as though you are looking at someone else. What do you really see? What can you improve? Is there something about your appearance holding you back? What do your posture and facial expression say about you? What can you do to improve your ability to make a good first impression? As you begin to consider first impressions, consider the following advice:

Be nice to everyone. This should be a natural behavior you practice daily, but nowhere is it more important than while interviewing. As soon as the interviewer sees you, he or she begins to make a decision. You are immediately sending out verbal and nonverbal signals that help form that crucial first impression. Few interviewees realize this, but you can be ahead of the pack by simply mentally acknowledging how important the first few seconds are to your success. In an instant, the interviewer performs a quick eye sweep and takes in your attire, your grooming, your posture, and your smile. They also begin forming impressions such as these:

- Are you confident?
- Do you appear to be comfortable in this environment?
- Are you glad to be there?
- Are you sincere?
- Are you impeccably groomed and dressed?
- Are you warm and friendly?

Basically, a successful interview begins with you being respectful, looking your best, coming prepared, and displaying a positive, can-do attitude.

 SOLUTION 35   HONE YOUR INTERPERSONAL COMMUNICATION SKILLS

Masterfile Royalty Free Division

Communication is not something we do *to people;* rather it is something done *between people.* Communication can take on a variety of forms, such as oral speech, the written word, body movements, and even yawns. All of these actions communicate something to another person. When thinking about your interpersonal communication encounters, remember: Communication is continuous, irreversible, and unrepeatable.

Communication is continuous, so if you are in the presence of another human being, you are communicating; it can't be helped. If you walk into the back of a crowded room, sit by yourself and never open your mouth, you are still communicating. The message might be unclear, but you are communicating. The message to some may be that you want to be alone; to others, it may be that you are shy, and still to others, the message may be that you do not mix well with people. In reality, you may have sat at the back of the room because you had to leave early and did not want to disturb others. The simple fact remains: You were communicating.

Communication is irreversible   Once you have said something, it can never be taken back. You can apologize for it, explain it, and try to make it go away, but the fact it was said can never be erased. The most important lesson here is that we should know what we are saying before we say it. Relationships have been lost, feelings hurt beyond repair, and friendships derailed because of words uttered before thinking. This lesson is of ultimate importance as you begin your new career.

Communication is unrepeatable This is the most abstract aspect to be discussed but one of immense importance. Communication is unrepeatable because you have only *one* time to make the impact you want to make. Once the words have been said, they will never mean the same thing again. For example, think of the first time you ever heard a person tell you, "I love you." You may have heard it a hundred times since, or you may have never heard it again. The fact of the matter is this: It may mean more now or less now, but it will never mean to you what it meant to you the first time you heard it. You will never feel the same emotion again you felt the first time you heard those words from that person.

If you remember these three aspects of interpersonal communication, you are already miles ahead of many others seeking employment. You might also consider the following excerpt:

STANDARDS OF INTERPERSONAL COMMUNICATION

General Tips for Interpersonal Communication

- You never know what type of day, month, year, or life a person has had . . . act accordingly.
- Ask people about themselves. This puts people at ease.
- Interpersonal communication involves a great deal of trust on your part.
- The healthier your self-esteem is, the better you treat and respect others, so work to enhance your self-esteem. Never try to diminish another's self-worth.
- Try to greet and treat everyone as if he or she was your close, personal friend.
- Show empathy for others and most of the time, you will be treated the same.
- ALWAYS select and use your words carefully. Words are immensely powerful tools.
- Pay very close attention to your nonverbal communication such as: gestures, facial expressions, clothing, proximity, posture, touch, and eye contact.
- Understand that first impressions are NOT always correct. Get to know the person and the situation.
- NEVER use your "power" or position to control a person just because you can.

Listening to Others

- Remember this fact: ***Listening is HELPING***.
- The number-one rule to effective listening is this: "STOP talking."
- Look at the other person's facial expressions.
- Concentrate on what the other person is saying. Give him/her your full attention.
- Eliminate distractions such as phones, other conversations, and outside noise.

(*continued*)

- DO NOT judge the situation before you hear what is being said. Judging current situations on past experiences hampers listening. Put past prejudices aside.
- Leave your emotions out of the situation. They can cloud your listening ability.
- Ask questions for clarification.
- Repeat what you have heard so that you are assured you heard it correctly.
- Listen for what is NOT being said. Listen "between the lines."
- Avoid jumping to conclusions. Keep your cool and don't make immediate assumptions.

Dealing with Difficult People

- Don't become the same type of difficult person as the ones with whom you are dealing. Fighting fire with fire will only make the flame hotter. In most situations, you will need to be the "cool" one.
- Don't take the other person's attitude or words personally. Most of the time, they don't know you or your life. You are their sounding board.
- AVOID physical contact with others.
- If you must give criticism, try to do so with a positive tone and attitude. If possible, provide some positive comments to the person before you offer your criticism.
- Don't save up a list of the person's faults and problems and "sandbag" him or her all at once.
- NEVER verbally attack the other person.
- Allow the other person to save face. In other words, don't beat the dead horse.
- If you have a problem with someone or someone's actions, be specific and let them know before it gets out of hand. They can't read your mind.
- Ask yourself, "If this were my last action on earth, would I be proud of how I acted?"
- If someone shows signs or becoming physically aggressive toward you, get help early, stay calm, talk slowly and calmly to the other person, and if necessary, walk away to safety.

Resolving Conflict

- Remember that conflict will more than likely happen throughout your entire life. It is a natural occurrence. It is a natural force in life.
- Allow the other person to vent fully before you begin any negotiation or resolution.
- Try to see the world through the other person's eyes.
- Try to create "win-win" situations where everyone can walk away having gained something. It is always best not to have a loser.
- Determine if the conflict is a "person" conflict or a "situation" conflict.
- Ask the other person or people what he/she needs. Try to understand the situation.

- Realize that you (or your company or office) may very well be "in the wrong."
- Try to face the conflict head-on and quickly. To avoid conflict only makes it worse.
- OWN your words. If you're making a statement, let it come from YOU, not "them."
- Show your concern for the other person.
- Try with all your might to end on a positive note.

SOURCE: © Robert M. Sherfield, Ph.D., 2007.

> **QUOTE**
>
> The #1 rule for effective interpersonal communication: Be nice. Be nice. Be nice.
>
> R. Sherfield

 SOLUTION 36 OBSERVE AND IMPROVE YOUR BODY LANGUAGE (NONVERBAL COMMUNICATION)

Often your body language reflects how you really feel about yourself on the inside. You might be saying all the right things verbally, but if words and vocal tones are not in sync with your body and facial expressions, observers, especially prospective employers, will not believe you. You cannot be convincing in your speech if you slump over, drag around, or fail to make eye contact. Your body language speaks volumes about you.

According to Steven McCornack (2007), Michigan State University professor and author, nonverbal communication is more flexible and ambiguous than verbal communication, governed by fewer rules, and has more meanings than verbal communication. It is controlled by gender and culture on a level greater than verbal communication.

First, consider some of these "actions" that constitute nonverbal communication (body language):

Race/gender	Smiles or frowns
Age	Handshakes
Touching or any physical contact	Appearance and grooming
Facial expressions	Walk and posture
Proximity	Silence
Color	Breathing

As a brief exercise in decoding nonverbal communication, examine the photo on page 74. Jot down what you think is being communicated. Do not share your ideas with anyone until asked to do so by your instructor. Pay close attention to how your observations compare with those of your classmates. This can be a powerful lesson in how others perceive us and what we do with our bodies.

My observation: _____

_____

_____

_____

_____

QUOTE

What you're doing speaks so loudly I can't hear what you're saying.

Anonymous

Observe your body language in a mirror. Are you surprised at some of the messages you are sending out? Consider why you have your current mannerisms (positive and negative). Did anyone call you names when you were growing up or were you taught that what you believe about yourself is more important than what others believe? Were you bullied by someone who chipped away at your confidence or were you raised to feel confident and proud? Were you praised by your parents and made to feel strong or did you have critical parents who constantly berated you? Did a teacher embarrass you and make you self-conscious or were you complimented on your efforts and talents? Are you critical of yourself or have you worked to strengthen your self-esteem? Do you make negative comments about yourself or do you forgo harmful self-talk?

You may be asking why someone ask these types of questions. The simple answer is this: The first step toward building positive nonverbal body language is to learn to love yourself, respect yourself, and to believe you really are okay. If you are still struggling with inner confidence, review Chapters 1 and 9 of this text. You might also consider reading more about self-esteem and inner strength to help you build more confidence. By "feeling good" on the inside, you begin to "look good" on the outside.

To enhance your body language, consider the following tips:

- ☑ Pay close attention to your facial expressions

- ☑ Make eye contact with the person you are communicating with

- ☑ Work to establish respectable boundaries of personal space and proximity. When communicating, respect the other person's personal space, or bubble

- ☑ Develop a confident handshake; harder is not always better

- ☑ If you are a "touchy-feely" person, understand that others may not enjoy, and may misinterpret, your touch

- ☑ Know that your clothing and hygiene are strong nonverbal indicators, and never ignore your appearance

- ☑ Work to understand the meanings of different colors and learn what different colors mean to different cultures

- ☑ Pay close attention to your gestures and body movement such as posture, needless movement, and nervous energy

SOLUTION 37   SPEAK WITH AUTHORITY AND CLARITY

Although nonverbal communication is massively important, you cannot ignore that what you *say* and *how you say it* matters, too. The power of words is staggering. They can make a person's day or break a person's spirit. They change nations, free masses, and even start wars. The most interesting thing about words (verbal communication) is that they must have a medium; they must be written or spoken, and here is where you come into the picture. In truth, the phrase "the power of words" is a misnomer. Words have little power until they are used by humans. *You* determine how words and phrases are to be used, and, in turn, *you* determine their power.

For example, if you began a conversation with an employee or co-worker by saying, "The job you did on the AT&T account last week was some of the worst work I have ever seen," you are setting the entire conversation up for failure. Because communication is *irreversible* and *unrepeatable,* you have now inflicted damage from which neither party will soon recover.

However, if you had begun the conversation on a more positive note, using language that was constructive and empowering instead of destructive and degrading, the outcome may be entirely different. Consider the different atmosphere that could have been created if you had said, "James, you are one of the most capable and talented accountants this company has ever had. You're attentive to detail, you care about your work, and you make us all look good. However, we do need to talk about what happened with the AT&T account last week." The power of words is, indeed, staggering.

Your ability to speak with confidence, clarity, and sincerity will be paramount to your success. To improve the *quality* of your verbal communication skills during your interview and when working with others, use these simple strategies:

- ☑ Be sincere and honest.
- ☑ Be clear, accurate, and detailed.
- ☑ Mean what you say and work hard to say what you mean.
- ☑ Choose your words carefully.
- ☑ Use examples and stories to clarify your point.
- ☑ Ask for feedback during the discussion.
- ☑ Get to the point as quickly as possible.
- ☑ Make sure you emphasize your main points.
- ☑ Pay attention to others' feelings and emotions.
- ☑ Respect others and their opinions.
- ☑ Don't use language that is threatening or demeaning to you or others.
- ☑ Work to put other people at ease.
- ☑ Remember the power of silence; force yourself to listen.

🔍 QUICK FACT

Effective communication skills are constantly rated among the top five attributes that employers seek in today's workforce. According to the National Association of Colleges and Employers (2005), communication skills are ranked at number one and interpersonal skills are ranked at number three among the most desired personal skills employers seek.

Think about your own communication efforts at this point in your life. Make a list of the positive communication strategies you now possess. An example might be, "I am very good at making my point clear."

1. _____

2. _____

(continued)

3. _____

4. _____

5. _____

Now consider the areas where you may need improvement. List that area and at least one strategy for improvement. Example: "I am not a very good listener." Strategy for improvement: "I plan to make it a point to stop talking when others are talking."

1. _____

Strategy for Improvement: _____

_____

_____

2. _____

Strategy for Improvement: _____

_____

_____

3. _____

Strategy for Improvement: _____

_____

_____

4. _____

Strategy for Improvement: _____

_____

_____

5. _____

Strategy for Improvement: _____

_____

_____

SOLUTION 38　BE PREPARED FOR THE INTERVIEW

You may have several interviews before you find the job you want, and you will probably spend many hours preparing for these interviews. In the beginning it is advisable for you to go to all interviews even if you're not sure you want the job. The more you interview, the more confident and comfortable you should become. The interview is the determining factor in getting a job and must be taken seriously. An outstanding résumé is important, but it will not secure the job for you. The résumé gets the interview; the interview gets the job!

Just as you prepared for exams, you will need to prepare for the interview. Do not make the common mistake of thinking that your degree or past work experience will get you the job. It may, but more often than you would believe, it is the interview and the relationship you establish that day that gets you the offer. Your experience and credentials are important, but nothing is more important than you and how well you are prepared for this day. As you prepare for your interview, consider the following sound advice.

DAYS BEFORE THE INTERVIEW

☑ Prepare extra copies of your résumé to take to the interview. Although one person typically conducts interviews, some employers designate several people to sit in on the interview process.

☑ Place your extra résumés, references, and other job search information in a professional portfolio (leather binder) or attractive folder. Avoid carrying loose papers, and never carry a backpack to an interview.

☑ Prepare a typed reference sheet and take several copies to the interview.

☑ If achievement portfolios are required, update your portfolio with any last-minute applicable information.

☑ Using the research you have done on the company, make a list of questions you want to ask the interviewer. Never attend an interview without asking questions yourself. You are interviewing them just as they are interviewing you. Interviewers are much more impressed if they think you have researched the company and if you have questions to ask.

☑ Have a friend or colleague sit with you and ask you questions that you might anticipate. A list of potential questions is provided in Solution #39. Have them throw a few "surprise questions" your way too.

☑ Ask someone whose opinion you trust to look at your interview outfit and give you advice and suggestions for improvement.

☑ Make sure you know how to get to the interview site. Make a dry run if necessary. Being late for your interview will be the kiss of death for that job.

☑ Check the night before to make certain you have transportation and that all of your personal needs are met such as child care.

THE DAY OF—AND ON THE WAY TO THE INTERVIEW

☑ Get up early and spend some time alone reviewing the job announcement, your résumé, your portfolio, the company's profile, and other important information.

☑ Bring a pen, paper, and calendar with you to the interview. These can be kept in your portfolio too.

☑ *Know* where your items are located so you do not have to search for them during an interview. Fumbling around makes you look unorganized and unprepared.

☑ Prepare for the unknown: For example, take an umbrella, even if it is sunny; leave early, even though the interview site is only a few miles away.

☑ Be certain your clothes are clean and pressed.

☑ Be certain your shoes are spotless and shined.

☑ Be certain you are groomed and your breath is fresh. Breath mints or sprays go a long way.

☑ Arrive at the interview at least 15 minutes early.

☑ If you are a smoker, *do not* smoke in the car on the way to the interview, and try to avoid smoking in your interview clothes. Often the smell of cigarette smoke lingers for hours and clings to your clothing. For many, this is an immediate turnoff.

☑ Do not take any type of food or drink into the interview with you.

☑ Do not chew gum during the interview.

☑ Before you enter the building, turn off your cell phone, pager, Blackberry, I-Pod or any other electronic device except your hearing aid, pacemaker, or other life-assisting device. TURN THEM OFF. Period! There is *no* excuse for your cell phone to ring during an interview. No one, including you, is that important.

Nothing splendid has ever been achieved except by those who dared believe that something inside them was superior to circumstance.

Bruce Barton

DURING THE INTERVIEW

☑ Establish eye contact.

☑ Work to develop an immediate rapport.

☑ Shake the hand of everyone in the room.

☑ Pay close attention to your posture (straight shoulders, positive stride, etc.).

☑ Speak with clarity and enunciate your words.

☑ Ask where to sit if you are not told upon entering the room.

☑ Enter with a positive and upbeat attitude.

☑ Jot down the names of everyone in the room as they are introduced to you. You may even draw an impromptu seating chart to remind you of who's who in the room.

☑ Refer to people by their names if you address them during the interview.

☑ Take notes during the interview.

☑ Answer every question asked as long as the question is legal.

☑ You don't have to be deadly serious or stodgy, but it is advisable to avoid jokes or off-color humor during the interview process.

☑ Consider your grammar and strive to use correct speech.

☑ If you need clarification on a question, ask for it before you begin your answer.

☑ *Never* downgrade or talk badly about a past job or employer. This will only come back to haunt you.

☑ If at all possible, do not discuss any aspect of your personal life, such as children, marriage, family, and so on.

☑ During the interview, jot down any questions that may arise you did not already consider.

Esbin-Anderson/The Image Works

☑ If you are offered anything to eat or drink, accept only water just in case your mouth becomes dry during the interview.

☑ *Never* ask about money or company benefits during the first interview, unless the interviewer approaches the topic. Let him or her lead this discussion.

☑ Strive to never appear desperate or begging for the job. There is a difference between excitement and desperation.

AFTER THE INTERVIEW

☑ Shake hands with everyone in the room and thank them for the opportunity to meet with them. Let them know you were honored to have the opportunity. Humility goes a long way.

☑ Politely let them know that you enjoyed the interview and you are very interested in the position.

☑ Ask each person in the room for a business card. This gains you their correct name spelling, address, and e-mail address.

☑ Don't linger around the site unless you are told to wait. This makes you look desperate.

☑ Always follow up with a personalized thank-you note. Solution #44 will help you write an effective follow-up thank-you note.

GENERAL TIPS

☑ Remember the cardinal rule of interviewing: Interviewers are not interested in what the company can do for you; they are interested in what you can do for the company. Therefore, you must present your case on why you want to work for the company and the contributions you are prepared to make.

☑ Be truthful in every aspect of the job search: the application, your résumé, your cover letter, your portfolio, your references, your question responses, your salary history, and yes, your interest in the position.

☑ If you take someone with you to the interview, he or she should wait outside the building. Under no circumstances should you take anyone inside with you.

☑ Be nice and gracious to everyone you meet. That may be the person with whom you interview in a few moments.

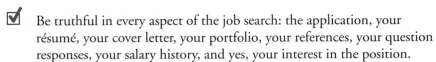

SOLUTION 39 ANTICIPATE THE INTERVIEWER'S QUESTIONS

Richard Nelso Bolles, author of *What Color Is Your Parachute?* (2007) the most widely published job-hunting book in history (with over 9 million copies in print), makes an astounding assertion. He states, "You don't have to spend hours memorizing a lot of 'good answers' to potential questions from the employer; there are only five questions that matter." Wow. Five questions!

With this statement, *do not* think you will only be asked five questions, but rather Bolles is suggesting that with every question asked of you, the interviewer is trying to get to the heart of the matter. Here are the five basic questions, if you will:

1. Why are you here?

2. What can you do for us?

3. What kind of person are you?

4. What distinguishes you from the nineteen other people who can do the same tasks that you can?

5. Can I afford you?

These are the five principal questions that most employers are dying to know the answers to. *This is the case, even if the interview begins and ends with these five questions never once being mentioned overtly by the employer* (Bolles, 2007).

So how do interviewers get to the heart of the matter? How do they pull the answers to these five questions from you? Ironically, they do it by asking many, many other questions. This section will offer you insight into some common and not so common questions asked by today's employers.

It is usually customary for the interviewer to make small talk for a few minutes to give you time to relax and get comfortable. Avoid answering questions with a simple "yes" or "no." Briefly elaborate on your answers without talking too much. For example, if the interviewer says, "I hope you had no trouble finding our building," don't just answer "no." You might say something like, "Not at all. I live near here so I was familiar with the location. Actually, I had a part-time job when I was a sophomore and I brought materials to one of your managers from my department chair."

Interviewers will often say to you, "Tell me about yourself." They are not looking for your life history as much as they are gathering background information on you and observing how well you can present information. Be yourself and enjoy the process. This will show.

The interviewer might then ask you, "What do you know about our company?" This is a good opportunity for you to show how prepared you are. You could open your portfolio and tell the interviewer, "When I was researching the company, I found some interesting facts on your website. I know that you are an international company based in New York and that you have over four thousand employees. I learned that you have several divisions, including food processing and distribution, restaurants, and contract food sales. In fact, this information is the reason I applied for a job with you through our Career Center. My minor in college is restaurant management, and I think this company will be a great place to put my knowledge and the skills to great use."

You will, of course, have to adapt your answer to your own situation. There is no way to be completely prepared for questions an interviewer may ask. The key is to have anticipated the interviewer's questions and to be so comfortable with the message you want to convey about yourself that you sound confident and decisive. As you talk, remember to look at the interviewer and to lean forward slightly, which indicates you are listening intently.

After a brief, "Let's-get-to-know-each-other" session, you can anticipate more direct and important questions. Here are some of the more common questions you might expect:

- ☑ Why should we hire you?
- ☑ Why are you interested in this company and in the position?
- ☑ When did you decide on a career in _____?
- ☑ Tell me about your extracurricular activities.
- ☑ What are your strengths?
- ☑ What are your weaknesses?
- ☑ Why did you leave your last job?
- ☑ Do you have a geographical preference? Why?
- ☑ Are you willing to relocate?
- ☑ Are you willing to travel?
- ☑ Do you have job experience in _____?
- ☑ What can you do for the company?
- ☑ What other companies are you interviewing with?
- ☑ Tell me about a difficult problem you have had and how you solved it.
- ☑ Tell me about a time when you worked under stress.
- ☑ What kind of accomplishment gives you the greatest satisfaction?
- ☑ What are your long- and short-range goals?
- ☑ Where do you see yourself in five years?
- ☑ What one word best describes you?
- ☑ How do you deal with difficult people?
- ☑ Describe one goal you have set over the past six months and how you went about accomplishing it.

- ☑ What is the biggest mistake you ever made? What did you learn from it?
- ☑ What subject in school gave you the most challenges? Why?
- ☑ What past experiences or courses have prepared you for this position?
- ☑ Would you prefer to work alone or with a group of people? Why?

Some more in depth and less common questions might be:

- ☑ What type of manager would bring out the best in you? Why?
- ☑ What is the most important thing to you in a job? Why?
- ☑ Who has been the most influential person in your life? Why?
- ☑ If I called your past supervisor, how would he or she describe you?
- ☑ In what area do you lack the most confidence?
- ☑ In what area of this position do you lack the most experience? How do you plan to accommodate for this?
- ☑ If you could design your own job evaluation form with only five qualities to be evaluated, what five qualities would you list? Why?
- ☑ Tell us about a time when you put your best foot forward and the end result was still unfavorable. Why do you think this happened? What did you do about it? What did you learn from the situation?
- ☑ What is the biggest change to which you have ever had to adapt? What strategies did you employ to adjust to this change?
- ☑ How do you deal effectively with interpersonal conflicts?
- ☑ How do you deal effectively with miscommunication?
- ☑ How do you deal effectively with gossip?
- ☑ Of what are you most proud in your professional life? Why?
- ☑ If you could not be involved in this job or profession any longer, what would you do for a vocation? Why? Why are you not doing that now?

Regardless of the question asked, your primary responsibility in the interview is to be straightforward, honest, and answer the question to the very best of your ability.

> Look over the position advertisement, the company's website, and your own application materials and think about questions that may be asked of you. Write down five questions that you might anticipate that are *not* listed above.
>
> 1. _____
> 2. _____
> 3. _____
> 4. _____
> 5. _____

SOLUTION 40 ASK INFORMED QUESTIONS

Feel free to ask the interviewer questions during the interview, but the interviewer should lead the majority of the first part of the interview. At the close of the interview, you may be asked if you have any questions. If this opportunity is not offered, you can say, "I have a few questions, if you don't mind." Asking questions of the interviewer is impressive and indicates to them that you are interviewing them as well. Some typical questions follow:

- ☑ How would you describe a typical day in this position?
- ☑ What kind of training can I anticipate?
- ☑ What is the probationary period of employment?
- ☑ What are the opportunities for personal growth and professional development?
- ☑ To whom would I report?
- ☑ Will I have an opportunity to meet some of my co-workers?
- ☑ Would you describe the training program?
- ☑ When will my first job performance evaluation take place?
- ☑ Why do you enjoy working for this company?
- ☑ How would you describe the most successful person working at this company? Why?
- ☑ What objectives do you expect to be met by your new employee in the first six months?
- ☑ Can you tell me about an assignment I might be asked to do?
- ☑ What happened to the last person who held this job?
- ☑ What do you see as the major challenges facing this organization? Why?
- ☑ How would you describe the culture of the workplace in this organization?
- ☑ What does this company value?

A good rule of thumb is never to ask questions just to be asking them. Only ask questions to which you truly want or need a response.

SOLUTION 41 MANAGE INAPPROPRIATE OR ILLEGAL QUESTIONS EFFECTIVELY

Sadly, you may encounter questions that are either inappropriate or even illegal. Remember, federal and state laws may prohibit many questions that deal with your personal life, but, no one agency has "a list" of all questions that cannot be asked. Federal laws such as the Civil Rights Act of 1964 and the American's with Disabilities Act of 1990 do regulate certain questions that can be asked during an interview.

If illegal or inappropriate questions are asked in person or on an application, it can be challenging to manage them and still retain your composure and decorum. It is up to you how much you want to tell a potential employer about your personal life or lifestyle and they cannot demand an answer "unless the question relates to a bona fide occupational qualification" (Lamarre, 2001).

First, review the list of questions that many experts consider illegal, or at best inappropriate and/or taboo, and later in this section, we discuss how to respond if you are asked an illegal or unethical question.

With some exceptions, employers should not ask you about the following:

- ☑ **Your age**   You should not be asked this question; however, some professions are age restricted (such as airline pilots and bartending) and this question is perfectly legal.

- ☑ **Your marital status, your parental status, or your living situation (who lives with you or why)**   If you are asked this question, they are really trying to find out if you will be at work on a regular basis or maybe if you can travel. It is legal to ask, "Does your personal schedule permit extensive travel?" but it is not legal to ask, "Would you get into trouble with your wife or children if you were asked to travel a lot?"

    It is illegal to ever ask if you are planning a family, if you are pregnant, or if you have ever had an abortion.

- ☑ **Your race or national origin**   You should not be asked about either of these categories, nor should you ever be asked to provide a photo of yourself. However, every employer can, upon your employ, ask you to provide legal documentation that you are eligible and clear to work in the United States. Upon employ, they can also ask for a photograph for security and identification purposes.

- ☑ **Your sexual orientation**   This is tricky, but generally, yes, an employer may ask about your sexual orientation. However, many states and cities ban discrimination based on sexual orientation, especially for federal employment (Smith, 2007).

- ☑ **Your religious affiliation**   This question is illegal and should never be asked. However, if you are asked this question, the interviewer is probably trying to determine if your religion might prevent you from working on weekends, Sundays, or certain holidays. It is legal to ask, "Would you be willing to work on Sunday?" or "Would you be willing to work on Christmas?"

- ☑ **Your political affiliation**   It is legal and allowable to ask this question; however, "Some states ban discrimination on this basis and political affiliation may not be used for discriminatory purposes in federal-government employment" (Smith, 2007).

- ☑ **Your physical limitations or your mental/emotional limitations**   You cannot be asked a question such as, "Have you ever been treated for depression or any mental illness?" but you can be asked a question such as, "This position requires that you deal with many stressful situations and many situations in which you will encounter conflict. Do you feel you have any limitations that might prevent you from managing these situations effectively?"

It is never legal to ask about your HIV status, your disabilities, or any prescription drugs you may take.

☑ **Your physical attributes**   You cannot be asked questions about your height or weight unless this is directly tied to job performance due to specific, predetermined limitations.

☑ **Your financial status**   An employer cannot ask if you have a checking or savings account, how much money you save each month, or any question about your credit rating. However, many states do allow potential employers to run credit checks on applicants.

☑ **Your personal habits**   Generally, employers can ask if you smoke at home, but this question has led to some lawsuits. "Currently, 31 states ban policies prohibiting off-duty smoking" (Smith, 2007).

☑ **Your *arrest* status**   Your arrest status is completely different from your conviction status. It is legal to ask if you have ever been *convicted* of a crime. A few states do allow an employer to ask if you have been arrested *if* it is job related.

☑ **Your affiliations**   It is not legal to ask you to which organizations you belong. It is legal to ask if you belong to certain professional organizations such as the National Association of Architects *if* you are applying for a position in the architectural field. An employer cannot, however, ask if you belong to the Shriners, Free Masons, or any union.

☑ **Military status**   You may not be asked what type of discharge you had from the military. You should not be asked if you ever were in the military unless it is job related.

☑ **Your school and/or college records**   School and college records may be sought *only* with your consent. Usually, you have to order the official transcript and have it sent directly to your employer.

Basically it comes down to money. It is very expensive to hire, train, and retain an employee in today's workforce. An employer wants to know as much about you as possible, and they want to know if you are qualified, if you will get along with others, and if you will be at work when you say you will be there.

So, how do you handle questions that may be illegal or inappropriate? This can be tricky at best and the kiss of death at worst. Consider this: Can an employer ask you if you are married? No, they cannot. However, if this type of question arises, you have to decide if you will answer, but you can always view these types of questions as a positive moment too. You might respond: "Yes, I am married, and my spouse and I fully support each other's careers and advancement possibilities."

Can an employer ask, "Are you gay?" Generally, yes, but again, you have to decide how you would answer this question (whether the answer is yes *or* no). If you are uncomfortable with this question, you may respond, "Before I answer that question, can you discuss how this is related to this particular position?" or "I choose not to answer that question based on my personal beliefs."

Sometimes, *you* will have to do an evaluation of the employer. You may want or need to ask yourself, "Do I really want to work for a company that would ask an illegal or inappropriate question?" Ultimately, the choice is yours.

THINK ABOUT IT

Just what personal traits should really matter to an employer when considering someone for a position? Why? How do those traits play a role in employee rapport, performance, and overall effectiveness?

As an exercise, choose one of the areas just discussed, and pretend you were asked a question that was illegal, inappropriate, or taboo. State the question here and then give your response to this question.

Question:

_____

_____

My response:

_____

_____

_____

_____

_____

_____

_____

SOLUTION 42   CONSIDER THE INTERVIEWER'S EVALUATION

Begin with the end in mind. That is a solid piece of advice for many situations, but it is certainly valid advice for entering an interview. Think about the end of the interview and what you would like to have accomplished when you leave. What do you want the employer to know? What skills do you want them to know you possess? What overall impression do you want them to hold of you and your possibilities? These are important questions to ask yourself *before* you enter the interview.

Employers use a variety of methods to evaluate your performance during the interview: your résumé, your portfolio, and your overall decorum and appearance. They will, of course, evaluate such traits as your attitude, skills, appearance, experiences, self-confidence, verbal and nonverbal communication skills, and level of enthusiasm.

As you think about the interview and what you would like to accomplish during the process, consider this. In a recent study at UCLA, the impact of one's interview performance was based on three items: your words, your vocal quality, and nonverbal communication (Robbins, 2006).

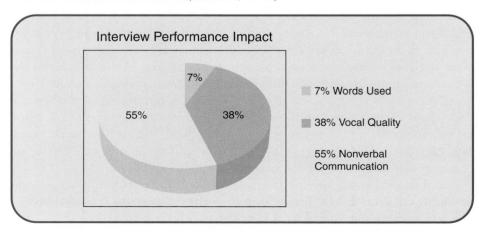

Interview Performance Impact

- 7% Words Used
- 38% Vocal Quality
- 55% Nonverbal Communication

A company may have a standard interview evaluation form, but there are no standardized forms used by all companies nationwide. With that in mind, it is imperative that you consider the many areas of your performance on which an employer might evaluate you:

- ☑ Résumé, cover letter, quality of paper used
- ☑ Timeliness
- ☑ Appearance and grooming
- ☑ Decorum
- ☑ Attitude
- ☑ Nonverbal communication
- ☑ Verbal communication
- ☑ Written communication
- ☑ Treatment of staff
- ☑ Skills, talents, training, preparation
- ☑ Self-confidence
- ☑ Enthusiasm
- ☑ Apparent interest in the position
- ☑ Alertness
- ☑ Listening ability
- ☑ Ability to answer questions
- ☑ Ability to question the interview team
- ☑ Knowledge about the company
- ☑ Sense of positivity and optimism
- ☑ Grammar
- ☑ Comments about others, especially past employers
- ☑ Likability
- ☑ Honesty
- ☑ Straightforwardness
- ☑ Leadership abilities
- ☑ Personal goals
- ☑ Humor
- ☑ Pre-employment tests and assessments

Depending on the profession of your choice, there will be other qualities on this list.

SOLUTION 43   ACCEPT REJECTION WITH CLASS AND GRACE

It has often been stated that few people like a sore loser and fewer people like a bragging winner. Regardless of the outcome of your job search, think only in positive terms. If you happen to be rejected for a position, consider it a learning experience and count yourself lucky to have had the opportunity to go on the interview. View it as a trial run for the next interview. Evaluate your performance and strive to improve on what may have gone wrong, and work to improve challenging areas. Always remember that a certain amount of rejection is always expected in a job search. Yes, you may feel disappointed, angry, depressed, and even revengeful, but don't act on these emotions and do not let them overcome you. They are natural and they will pass.

Above all, never burn bridges. If you were not offered employment after your interview, don't get angry and fire off e-mails, nasty letters, or rude phone calls to the interviewer or committee. After all, they will be hiring again and you may want a position with them in the future. Remember that if you did not get the job, it may have had *very little* to do with you, your experiences, or your training. The company may have decided to promote someone from within. This is often the case, and no amount of interview preparation will ever change that. However, this does mean that another position within the company just opened up, and now you know that they do promote from within.

> **QUOTE**
>
> I am not bound to win, but I am bound to be true. I am not bound to succeed, but I am bound to live up to the light I have.
>
> Abraham Lincoln

Some of the most popular and impressive people in today's mainstream have been turned down for (or even fired from) employment. Walt Disney was fired from his first job because his boss considered him to have no creativity and no ability to draw. J.K. Rowling, author of the highly popular *Harry Potter* series, was rejected by many agents and publishers before she found a company ready to take a chance on her work. Katie Couric was fired from CNN for poor job performance but later went on to host *The NBC Today Show* and was paid over $15 million per year. Tim McGraw was dropped by his first producer because his first few singles failed. His manager told him to go home and try another profession. Failure, adversity, and setbacks are a natural part of the job search process.

If you get the job, be gracious and practice humility. Don't brag or downgrade others who may not have been as fortunate as you. This does nothing to build your own positive personal qualities and will not paint you in a favorable light with management or co-workers. Grace and class are qualities that will carry you a long way and transcend age, employment, race, gender, and money.

SOLUTION 44   WIN, LOSE, OR DRAW, *ALWAYS* SAY "THANK YOU" IN WRITING

Indeed, it is safe to say that failing to send a thank-you note is *"the most overlooked step in the entire job search process"* (Bolles, 2007). Yes, this is a mandatory step for every interview and for every person who interviewed you. In today's world of high-tech and run, run, run, this one act will set you apart from the thousands who interview daily. And yes, you must send a thank-you letter even if you *do not* get the job. "When do I send the thank-you note," you might ask? Immediately after the interview.

It is advisable, as mentioned before, to ask for a business card from the people who interview you so you have the correct spelling of their names and their address.

It is advisable that when you leave the interview, you go somewhere quiet, write your thank-you notes, and mail them before you even go home. Thank-you notes should be received in one to two days after the interview.

Sending a simple thank-you note lets the employer know that you have good manners, you respect other people's time and efforts, you are considerate, you really do care about the position, and you have positive people and communication skills. Yes, all of that from a card and stamp that can cost less than $2.

In a recent *USA Today* Snapshot Poll (September 13, 2007), a survey of 150 senior executives throughout America showed that 88 percent of them felt that receiving a follow-up thank-you note boosted the job seeker's chances of getting the job. With that said, however, be certain your thank-you note is neat, error free, and well written. "A poorly constructed and error-ridden thank-you note will hurt—not help—your chances" (Finnigan & Karasu, 2006).

In Figures 4.1 and 4.2 are examples of two thank-you notes. Review them and consider using them as a template to build your own notes. A well-written, personalized, speedy thank-you note contains these elements:

 The date

 The interviewer's names

FIGURE 4.1 Thank-You Note: After the Interview

Benjamin Shaw
1234 Lake Shadow Drive
Maple City, PA 12345
ben@bl.com

January 20, 2008

Mr. James Pixler, RN
Director of Placement
Grace Care Center
123 Sizemore Street
Philadelphia, PA 12345

Dear Mr. Pixler,

Thank you for the wonderful opportunity to meet with you and the team at Grace Care Center on Monday. Your facilities are amazing and the new wing is going to be a remarkable addition to your center.

I enjoyed learning more about the new position in medical assisting and I think that my qualifications and past experiences have prepared me for this challenging opportunity. I would consider it an honor to answer any further questions that you might have or to meet with you again if you consider it necessary.

I look forward to hearing from you at your convenience. If you need any additional information, you can reach me at 123-555-3454.

Thank you,

Benjamin Shaw
Benjamin Shaw

FIGURE 4.2 Thank-You Note: After a Position Rejection

Benjamin Shaw
1234 Lake Shadow Drive
Maple City, PA 12345
ben@bl.com

January 20, 2008

Mr. James Pixler, RN
Director of Placement
Grace Care Center
123 Sizemore Street
Philadelphia, PA 12345

Dear Mr. Pixler,

Thank you for the opportunity to meet with you and the team at Grace Care Center on Monday. I enjoyed learning more about your center and the planned addition.

Although I was not offered the position, I did want to thank you for your time, and I would like for you to contact me if you have any future openings where you feel my qualifications and experiences would match your needs. Grace is an incredible facility, and I would consider it an honor to hold a position there.

If you need to contact me in the future, you can reach me at 123-555-3454.

Thank you for your time and assistance, and good luck to you and your colleagues.

Sincerely,

Benjamin Shaw
Benjamin Shaw

☑ A sincere statement of thanks

☑ Acknowledgment of those in attendance for the interview

☑ A statement of interest in the position

☑ Restatement of something about the interview

☑ Closing and an invitation to contact you

☑ Your signature

PUTTING IT ALL TOGETHER

Consider developing a Pre-Interview Readiness Checklist such as the one in Figure 4.3. This can be a helpful tool as you make any final preparations for your interview. You may need to add a few position-specific items to the list based on the job announcement.

FIGURE 4.3 My Pre-Interview Readiness Checklist

ITEMS	Yes / No/ NA	Comments
Pre-Interview Résumé is job specific	Y N NA	_____
Objective statement is job specific	Y N NA	_____
Résumé is typed, neat, and free of errors	Y N NA	_____
Cover letter is job specific	Y N NA	_____
Qualifications are clearly spelled out in résumé	Y N NA	_____
Used the DOCTOR method to prepare and review résumé	Y N NA	_____
Reference sheet prepared	Y N NA	_____
Have checked with references to verify use of their names	Y N NA	_____
Have portfolio or binder for interview materials	Y N NA	_____
Have printed personal business cards	Y N NA	_____
Have arranged transportation	Y N NA	_____
Have written out possible interview questions	Y N NA	_____
Have practiced answering mock interview questions	Y N NA	_____
Have considered responses to illegal or inappropriate questions	Y N NA	_____
Have considered the items on which I will be evaluated	Y N NA	_____
Have a list of questions to ask interviewer	Y N NA	_____
Have researched the company	Y N NA	_____
Day of Interview Positive attitude	Y N NA	_____
Well groomed	Y N NA	_____
Leave early to be on time	Y N NA	_____

(continued)

Have portfolio, pen, calendar, extra résumé, and reference sheet	Y	N	NA	_____
Look professional and confident	Y	N	NA	_____
Have breath mints	Y	N	NA	_____
Have materials for the unknown (umbrella, etc.)	Y	N	NA	_____
Cell phone is off or left in car	Y	N	NA	_____

REFERENCES

Bixler, S., and Nix-Rice, N. (1997). *The New Professional Image: From Corporate Casual to the Ultimate Power Look.* Avon, MA: Adams Media Corporation.

Bolles, R. N. (2007). *What Color Is Your Parachute? A Practical Manual for Job-Hunters and Career-Changers, 2008 Edition.* Berkeley, CA: Ten Speed Press.

Finnigan, D., & Karasu, M. (2006). *From Learning to Earning: Success Strategies for New Grads.* New York: Sterling.

Lamarre, H. (2001). *Career Focus: A Personal Job Search Guide* (3rd ed.). Upper Saddle River, NJ: Pearson Prentice Hall.

Lane, H. (1976). *The Wild Boy of Aveyron.* Cambridge, MA: Harvard University Press.

Las Vegas Review Journal, November 5, 2007, Sec. D, p. 1.

McCormick, S. (2007). *Reflect & Relate: An Introduction to Interpersonal Communication.* New York: Bedford/St. Martin's Press.

National Association of Colleges and Employers. (2005). *Job Outlook.*

Robbins, C. (2006). *The Job Searcher's Handbook* (3rd ed.). Upper Saddle River, NJ: Pearson Prentice Hall.

Shattuck, R. (1980). *The Forbidden Experiment: The Story of the Wild Boy of Aveyron.* New York: Farrar, Straus & Giroux.

Smith, R. (2007, August 14). *Don't Ask—Maybe.* Retrieved from www.forbes.com.

USA Today Snapshot ® (2007, September 13). *Post-Interview Thank-You Notes Influential.* Source: Accountemps, Money Section B, p. 1.

Perfecting Your Professional Image and Distinguishing Yourself on the Job

The Importance of a Polished You

 WHY?

is it important that I polish my image? Why do I need to know how to dress for an interview and in the workplace? Why do I need to learn to order from a menu? Why do table manners and personal etiquette play a role in my ability to get and keep a job?

Should I use the shortest fork for my appetizer or the salad? Should I wear French cuffs on an interview? Should I extend my hand to be shaken or wait until a hand is offered? Many people have the mistaken idea that everyone knows how to dress, how to dine properly, and how to demonstrate good manners. Some even believe these qualities are not important. The truth is that these things are not as common as much as they once were, and many people grow up not knowing the basic points. However, do not be mistaken: First impressions, manners, etiquette, and basic grooming remain very important.

Several years ago, John Malloy, a so-called image guru, made this statement: "As much as one-third of your success depends on what you wear." In Malloy's opinion, your appearance, image, and presence contribute greatly to your overall success in your career. When you combine a powerful first impression, professional dress, good basic manners, excellent dining etiquette, proper language skills, and add a winning smile, you have all the makings of an outstanding professional package. More and more colleges and schools are providing educational experiences in all these areas for their students because the professional package is that extra quality that helps students secure the job they want and then move up rapidly in the ranks.

So why do educators have all their students study etiquette and dress? Why do career college faculty care if their students know how to meet and greet people and project themselves in a positive light? What can learning to develop an outstanding professional package do for you in the workplace?

This chapter presents five major tips on how to build an exemplary professional package designed to showcase all the skills you have learned. Ideally, the outcome of this chapter will be that you begin to pay much more attention to how you meet others, how you dress, what kind of manners you demonstrate, your dining etiquette, and your professional demeanor.

 SOLUTION 45   DRESS TO IMPRESS

Many people like to demonstrate their own style and pay little attention to what constitutes appropriate dress at work. Frequently companies today don't spell out exactly what they are looking for in dress for their employees, so you need to pay attention to what the successful people are wearing. Even if you are required to wear a uniform, notice how others present themselves. Is the uniform clean and pressed? Does it fit well?

A company supervisor might tell you not to wear clothes that are too tight or too short or too revealing, but they won't tell you exactly what you should wear to work. You have to be able to determine for yourself what looks good on you, what is over-the-top dressing for your particular environment, and what is considered dress that will impress your superiors, colleagues, and customers.

Look carefully at the people who have already made it and those who appear to be on a fast track. What do they wear to work? Are they overly casual? Do they wear jeans to work on casual day? Do you see any of them with earrings, tongue studs, or bright red streaks in their hair? Do you find any who have tattoos on their necks, heads, and other conspicuous places? Companies are hiring you to represent them, and, appropriate or not, they want a positive appearance from all their employees. The appearance that was appropriate at school and in a casual environment may not be OK in the work environment.

Women's Dress

Women have so many more choices than men and so many more ways to get it right or wrong. Getting it right can be a great asset to someone thinking about promotions or making positive impressions. You have many choices that can complement your individual style and body type and still present you in a positive light.

Whatever your profession, you want to look the part. You don't necessarily want to wear clothes that make you stand out; rather, you want to look good so people will respond to you appropriately. The mark of a well-dressed woman is that she always looks professional and well dressed, but you don't necessarily remember exactly what she had on. If you stand out, you have to be sure it is for the right reasons—perhaps a flair for color, style, jewelry, or the ability to mix styles.

If you need to (or are required to) wear business suits, they should be dark colors. Shoes should be stylish but comfortable, and jewelry should be well made, preferably gold or silver. Shoes should not have open heels or toes. Clothes should be cleaned, pressed, and immaculate—no spots, safety pins, or hems or cuffs in bad repair. Purses and belts should be leather and in good repair. Your blouses should be tailored; avoid busy prints, frilly lace, and sexy garments. Likewise, avoid pastel colors, especially pink (that screams "baby girl") and bright, garish colors. Appearance is a cultivated practice and you can learn to look successful, which will go a long way toward making you successful. To get an idea of how people dress in your profession, purchase magazines or journals that have pictures of people who work in your profession. You might also consider visiting an office where you would like to work and observing the dress of the women who work there.

Although wearing pants is acceptable in most businesses, women should typically stick to pantsuits that have a matching jacket and pants. The pants should be hemmed at the proper length. Sleeves should be hemmed so they do not extend below the wrist. Since most clothes require some alterations, you should avoid buying clothes off the rack that do not fit you properly unless you have them altered to fit.

Here are some universal "Dress for Success" solutions:

> **QUOTE**
>
> You can't depend on your eyes when your imagination is out of focus.
>
> Mark Twain

- ☑ Pantsuits should have a matching jacket and pants.
- ☑ Pants should be hemmed to the right length and never be too short.
- ☑ Sleeves should be hemmed so they do not extend below the wrist.
- ☑ If you wear a skirt, it should come to the top of your knees for work. Fashions my dictate changes in skirt lengths, but they should never be too short at work.
- ☑ Business dresses and pantsuits are fine for most days, but if you have an important meeting, wear a business suit with a skirt.
- ☑ The best colors for business suits are navy, black, gray, burgundy, olive, tan, and khaki.
- ☑ Avoid overpowering perfume.
- ☑ Your hair should be clean and well groomed.
- ☑ Avoid clothes that are too tight or revealing.
- ☑ Have your clothes altered to fit well.

☑ Avoid all extremes, such as trendy clothes, bleached hair, unnatural colors of hair such as green or blue.

☑ Have no tattoos that show.

☑ Avoid any kind of body piercings that are obvious, especially facial piercings.

☑ Jewelry should be simple; gold or silver is best.

☑ Wear no more than one ring on each hand except for wedding and engagement rings.

☑ A modest gold watch and one bracelet are attractive touches at work.

☑ Hose should coordinate with your outfit, but usually a barely black or suntan color works for most business occasions.

☑ Avoid colored hose, fishnet, and other patterns at work.

It is a nice touch to wear a perfume that is light and inoffensive, but never wear a heavy, overpowering perfume or cologne. Some co-workers are allergic to certain fragrances.

Sometimes people get presence mixed up with posture. Posture is what your mother told you about all the time: "Stand up straight." "Don't let your shoulders slump." Presence is that certain something that sets you apart from most other people. Presence is how you enter a room, how you walk, how you shake hands, how you dress, how you speak, how much confidence and energy you demonstrate, how outgoing you are. You probably have seen some people who make others' heads turn, and it's not necessarily because they are extraordinarily handsome or beautiful. Many times it is simple confidence, coupled with extraordinary grooming or clothing and a sparkling personality.

Some of you reading this book will say, "But I can't do these things. I'm very shy. I don't like to bring attention to myself." The answer is to "fake it until you make it." Most people consider themselves shy yet manage to cover it up. You are going to get attention. It's just a matter of whether the attention is positive or negative.

Your image should match your ambitions. If you were going to work today, would your wardrobe reflect your ambitions? Would you look chic and stylish or would you appear frumpy and nondescript? Would you look like a student or like a professional? What would people say about your grooming? What does your body language say about you? Image is a complete package, and anyone can improve personal image. Some people are naturally more attractive than others, and some are more graceful and charming, but anyone can learn to develop presence and build a better image.

BIGGEST INTERVIEW BLUNDER

Mary refused to remove the bright red streak in her hair and insisted on keeping the ring in her lower lip when she interviewed with a conservative company. The interview was very brief.

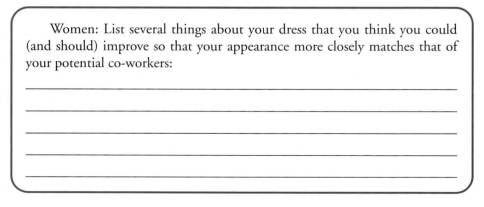

Women: List several things about your dress that you think you could (and should) improve so that your appearance more closely matches that of your potential co-workers:

_____

_____

_____

_____

_____

Men's Dress

One of the best ways for men to stand out is by dressing distinctively. The typical man does not give a great deal of attention to his appearance, so when he does it right, he gets a lot of positive attention. As stated earlier, women have many more choices than men—and many more ways of making bad decisions. Any man can become a very good dresser if he is willing to work at it.

Although you may not work in a job that requires a suit, you need at least one nice suit, especially for the interview. You want interviewers to think they are getting a bargain with you. The best times for men to buy suits are after Christmas and after the Fourth of July when most nice men's stores put their suits on sale. You might also look for warehouse sales, which often provide excellent bargains if you know how to shop for them.

Many suits can be worn year round except perhaps on the coldest or hottest days. If you live in the South, you don't need heavy wool clothes because you will get very little wear from them. Regardless of where you live, however, the fabric in your suits should contain wool because it helps suits keep their shape better after cleaning. If you are taking a traveling position, you need clothes that won't wrinkle badly.

Some tips for becoming a well-dressed man follow:

Michael Jang/Getty Images Inc.–Stone Allstock

- ☑ If you are going to work in a company where you need to wear suits, start building a good wardrobe now.

- ☑ Most men need to own at least two suits; navy and charcoal gray work well for most men.

- ☑ New graduates can interview in a blue blazer and charcoal gray slacks if they don't have a suit. A nice sport coat is a good wardrobe addition.

- ☑ You should own at least six to ten dress shirts including several white shirts and at least two light blue shirts if you are required to wear dress shirts to work. French blue is also a versatile color that can be worn with most of the colors just mentioned. Of course, you can gradually accumulate this collection.

- ☑ The only color shirt to wear to an interview is white, and it should be starched and immaculate.

- ☑ Shirts should be starched; do not rely on permanent pressed because they always look unkempt if not pressed.

- ☑ Dress shirts should always be long sleeved even in the summer; never wear short-sleeved dress shirts.

- ☑ A small monogram on your left cuff is a nice touch.

- ☑ You might want to consider one shirt with French cuffs and cuff links.

- ☑ Suit jackets should either be a two- or three-button style. Stay away from trendy suits that will go out of style soon.

☑ Purchase black and brown belts and shoes because they look good with almost everything.

☑ The dressiest shoe a man can wear is a lace-up wingtip, but young men can wear tasseled loafers or cap-toe lace-up shoes just as well.

☑ Heels of shoes should not look worn, and shoes should always be polished and shined.

☑ Socks should be black if worn with gray, navy, or black and they should not show your bare leg if you cross your legs, so buy long socks.

☑ Never wear white socks with a business suit or sport coat. Patterned socks are one mark of a well-dressed man if they are coordinated well.

☑ Ties should be stylish and bought with careful consideration. If you don't know how to choose a tie, get help from a salesperson at a fine clothing store.

☑ Ties should be made of silk in a stylish width and should have no spots on them.

☑ Men should learn to tie a knot that is in style.

☑ Men should wear a mild, nonoffensive cologne.

☑ Remove fat wallets, large key rings, and excessive change from your pockets.

Before you go to an interview, investigate what men wear at work. A standard rule for interviewing is to dress one step up from the typical daily wear of employees. You might want to visit the building casually if it is a large company and observe what men wear to work.

Dress for interviews should be based on the kind of job for which you are interviewing. If you are dressing to be a machine technician, you would dress differently from someone interviewing for a position in allied health. Regardless of what other people are wearing in the company, managers expect the interviewee to dress professionally and stylishly (Larson, 2000).

> Men: Briefly discuss the type of clothing you are going to need for your profession. Next, list several things about your dress that you will need to improve:
>
> _____
>
> _____
>
> _____
>
> _____
>
> _____
>
> _____

Business Casual: Men and Women

Many businesses are beginning to dress down, especially on Friday. Dressing down does not mean anything goes. Although you don't want to overdress when others are casual, you don't want to go to great extremes with your casual dress either. Actually,

GRADUATE QUOTE

The most important lesson I learned was this: Perfect your capacity to articulate your abilities and skills because you never know what employers are really looking for. *Never* be discouraged. Your dream position is out there.

Jonathan T. Ellis, Graduate!
The University of South Carolina, Columbia, SC Technology Support and Training Management

Career: Network Administrator
The University of
South Carolina

it is just as expensive to dress well for casual occasions as it is to dress for business—and more difficult for some people. A general rule of thumb for success is this: Observe what others, including your supervisors, are wearing.

Here are some basic tips for business casual dress:

- ☑ On casual days, men should wear a good pair of dress slacks and a golf shirt or a knit shirt with a blazer.

- ☑ Men can also wear a button-down-collar shirt with slacks and a blazer.

- ☑ Under no circumstances should you wear T-shirts and wrinkled khakis or tennis shoes. Some people really show poor judgment with casual dress, and they stand out for all the wrong reasons because they don't take it seriously enough.

**IF YOU WERE
IN CHARGE**

SOLVE THE PUZZLE

Mary frequently dresses in very sexy and revealing clothing that is inappropriate for work. If you were her supervisor, what would you do about it?

SOLUTION 46   MIND YOUR MANNERS

You have probably heard this all your life from your mother or some authority figure. "Now, mind your manners." They were giving you good advice! Today, manners seem to be a thing of the past for many people. You can be the exception and should stand out because of it. Businesses expect their employees to demonstrate good manners to their colleagues and their customers. Here are some of the basics of good manners:

- ☑ Follow the golden rule at work. Christians refer to this axiom: "All things whatsoever ye would that men should do to you, do ye even unto them." It is interesting, however, that this same rule is found, although stated differently, in Buddhism, Islam, Taoism, Confucianism, and many other religions.

- ☑ Say "please" and "thank you."

- ☑ Practice outstanding ethics. Be known as a person who has impeccable character. If the situation feels wrong to you or if it is illegal, don't do it. Ask yourself this question, "Will someone else be hurt if I do this?" Another good question is this one: "How would I feel if this made the headlines in the newspaper with my name?"

- ☑ Apologize immediately when you are wrong, as soon as you realize you have made a mistake.

- ☑ When in business settings, refrain from being loud and obnoxious.

- ☑ Never tell off-color jokes or jokes that disparage any race, sex, or religion. You may not even be aware that you have offended someone.

- ☑ Send cards to colleagues for birthdays, weddings, deaths, and promotions. Write a thoughtful note. A card is better than an e-mail. It says you cared enough to purchase a card. Keep a stock of appropriate cards and send them immediately when the occasion warrants.

- ☑ Men should hold doors for women and allow them to enter first; this courtesy includes elevators.

QUOTE

Good manners sometimes means simply putting up with other people's bad manners.

Jackson Brown Jr.

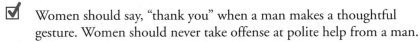

- Women should say, "thank you" when a man makes a thoughtful gesture. Women should never take offense at polite help from a man.

- Men should help women with heavy bags, boxes, and so on, without making a big deal about it. Just do it!

- If you are traveling by plane, by all means, men should help women around you lift heavy bags and place them in the overhead bins.

- If you are walking on the sidewalk, men should walk on the outside.

- If you are entering a cab, women should enter first while the man opens and holds the door. Men should exit first and offer a hand to the woman as she exits the cab.

- Never answer your cell phone during a meal! Actually, turn your phone off during a meal, and, of course, during an interview or business meeting.

- Treat everyone with respect and dignity—from the person who cleans the rest room to the top client in the corporation. Be nice, be nice, be nice!

- Avoid gossip! Stay out of the rumor mill because there are no secrets at work.

- Avoid office romances. No one can help falling in love, but keep your personal life at home and away from work.

- If you are having personal difficulties, keep these problems at home. Never go to work and tell your troubles or share your personal business with anyone who will listen.

- If you are sick, stay at home; if you feel bad, go to work and don't complain. No one wants to be around a whiner!

- Compliment others—and be sincere!

- Present a positive, upbeat presence at work.

POSITIVE HABITS

WORK

Send cards and notes to colleagues on their birthdays, when they accomplish something outstanding, or when they are ill. People never forget a thoughtful note.

SOLUTION 47 DINE WITH CLASS

The mark of a very polished person is the ability to use outstanding dining etiquette and to order food and beverage with confidence. Study and use the finer points of dining etiquette as you enter your career and consider moving up. No one is exempt from needing to know how to sit and eat a meal with dignity and grace. No one! Read a good etiquette book and take it seriously. Research shows that only about 12 percent of new hires are skilled in the social graces, which may mean the difference in great success or failure. Excellent manners will set you apart early in your career. Manners will also make a positive impression on almost everyone!

We assume you know the basics, such as to chew with your mouth closed, keep your elbows off the table, pass food to the right, cut your meat only one piece at a time, and butter only one small piece of bread at a time, but many

Yang Liu/Corbis/Bettman

people don't know these rules! You also need to know the following basic rules of good etiquette and dining:

- ☑ A utensil that has been used should never be placed on a tablecloth.

- ☑ If you use a sweetener or other items that have been wrapped in paper, slip the paper under your bread plate, and don't leave it strewn across the table.

- ☑ Remember LR: liquids to the right. This means you should only drink from or use the glasses on your right. Solids, such as bread plates, are always on your left.

- ☑ As part of your interview, you may be taken to a fine restaurant.

- ☑ Order something that is easy to eat and not the most expensive thing on the menu. A good rule is to follow the price range of the host who is taking you to dinner.

- ☑ Avoid difficult foods (e.g., spaghetti that is difficult to manage, soup that might drip on your clothes, or ribs that can't be eaten easily).

- ☑ If you eat soup, dip your spoon away from you, rather than toward you.

- ☑ Do not push food onto your fork with your knife or a piece of bread.

- ☑ If the host orders dessert, you can do so, but do not if he or she does not.

- ☑ Under no circumstances should you drink or smoke, even if others at the table do. If your host orders wine, you may have one glass of wine if you would like, but don't have any more.

- ☑ If you share foods—and this is not advised on an interview—do not pass your plate back and forth. Using a clean, unused utensil, place a portion on your bread plate, and pass it to the person for whom it is intended or ask your server for a small plate.

Figure 5.1 is a diagram of a formal table setting. Study it carefully so you will know what to do if you are dining at a formal restaurant. Starting at the outer edge, use the appropriate fork with each course. Again, here's the rule to remember: Solids

QUOTE

Etiquette means behaving yourself a little better than is absolutely essential.

Will Cuppy

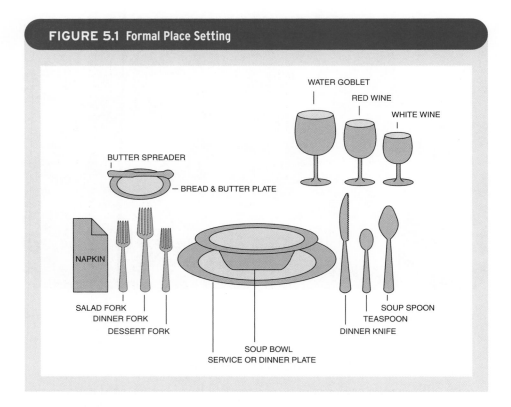

FIGURE 5.1 Formal Place Setting

on the left, liquids on the right; in other words, your personal bread plate is on the upper left-hand side of your plate, and your drink will be on the right. If you can't remember this, wait and watch others at the table and do what they do.

If you leave the table, place your napkin on your chair; do not put it on the table until the meal has been completed and you are leaving the restaurant. When you finish your meal and are leaving the table, fold your napkin loosely and place it back on the table.

When women approach or leave the table, men should stand. If it is a business occasion, women should stand at the beginning of the meal and shake hands as the men are doing. Women do not need to stand when someone leaves the table or returns. A man should help the woman to his right with her chair and then help the woman on his left if no one else is doing so. Take your seat from the right side of the chair.

You may be saying to yourself, "Who cares?" or "What difference does it make which fork I use?" The answer is simple and complex—no one and everyone. However, consider this: It is always better to have knowledge and skills and *not* need them than to need them and *not* have them.

There is much to learn enroute to developing a professional presence, and you might make some mistakes. Learn from them and keep working until you are comfortable in any setting.

 SOLUTION 48 WATCH WHAT YOU SAY

Many people go to work and gossip unrestrainedly. They tell everything they know about themselves, their personal business, their colleagues, and the company's business. Others say things that are very offensive to their co-workers. Remember that the workplace today is very diverse and made up of people from all ages, races, cultures, sexual orientations, and religions. Although you may be protected by freedom of speech laws, that doesn't make it OK to irritate your colleagues. Offensive and inappropriate behavior can cause you to be fired. You may be able to avoid certain behaviors in your personal life, but at work, people are in a captive audience situation, and we all must be respectful of each other (McKay, 2007).

Consider the following:

- ☑ Do not "put your personal business on the streets." Most people don't want to know your business, and those who do will most likely use it against you. Don't talk about your marital problems, your children's problems at school, your husband's firing, your wife's brother-in-law—nothing that is *your personal business.* These are subjects that you discuss only with your closest friends who want to know about you and care about your reputation.

- ☑ Don't use profanity under any circumstances or other inappropriate terminology. Today's movies and television programs have carried over into our personal lives, and many people now use inappropriate language, as a result. For example, "He just pissed me off" is not appropriate for any workplace, and many people use this phrase frequently. Some co-workers would consider this language very offensive.

- ☑ Don't tell religious, political, or off-color jokes or stories that might be offensive to a co-worker. You need to be very much aware that all people don't share your beliefs even if they don't say anything.

- ☑ It is offensive to make broad, sweeping derogatory remarks about any group of people. Comments of this nature can inhibit your ability to be promoted and to become a respected colleague. If you become a supervisor and hear comments that are defamatory, call the person aside and discuss it with the offending person.

- ☑ Avoid political opinions at work. You may not know the political persuasion of your boss or your colleagues, and some people hold strong grudges about politics. Do not promote either your religious or political beliefs at work.

- ☑ Be aware of anything that implies sexual harassment. Even innocent remarks can get you in serious trouble at work if it is construed as sexual harassment.

- ☑ Avoid remarks that might be offensive to a person's sexual orientation.

- ☑ Avoid loud, obnoxious language at work—or anywhere, for that matter. You want to be viewed as a respectable person, and respectable people do not conduct themselves in this manner.

SOLUTION 49   APPRECIATE AND RESPECT DIFFERENCES

More than likely, you have already encountered many people at school and perhaps at work who are different from you in a variety of ways. The United States is made up of a highly diverse population, and becoming more so every day. You simply must learn to accept, appreciate, and work with people who are different from you.

Myrleen Ferguson/Photo Edit Inc.

First, simply have an open mind about people. Give them a chance before you form a quick opinion based on how they dress, their accent, skin color, or other ways that they might be different from you. If you have a derogatory mind-set toward a race, an ethnic group, a sexual orientation, or a religion, for example, you have internal barriers that can keep you from getting to know who a person really is. If you are guided by prejudices, you will miss out on knowing many great people who can enrich your life and teach you many valuable lessons.

Learning to interact with people from other cultures is an act of growing and maturing. If you only know people who are just like you or who are very similar to the people with whom you grew up, you will likely miss some great opportunities and experiences. You need to learn to look at each person with whom you come in contact as an individual, not as a race, a class, or a religion. We cannot help but be influenced by what we have been taught and what we have experienced, but we can overcome prejudices and biases if we view people as individuals. If you intend to grow as an educated person and as a human being, you will need to expand your capacity to accept and understand people from different cultures and backgrounds.

Culture is learned. We are born into a culture, and we develop many of our beliefs from our family, neighbors, and friends. Culture appears to seep through our skins like osmosis. Many of our beliefs are passed from one generation to another, and, in many cases, prejudices are passed along to the next generation.

Education should enlighten you—open up your mind to all kinds of new people and new ways of thinking. As a college student, you may have many of your beliefs challenged, questioned, and perhaps ridiculed. Expect to experience changes in your beliefs as you grow and mature. This does not mean you must abandon everything you have always believed. Just because you have grown doesn't mean you have to give up your family, place of worship, values, and friends. It may mean, however, that you have to rethink and reevaluate some of your beliefs. You may have been taught that people belonging to one group or another are not acceptable. As you become more educated and mature, you may find that these people aren't so bad after all—just different. You are encouraged to explore and celebrate differences!

 **QUICK FACT**

Approximately 80 percent of job openings are in the "hidden job market" and are never advertised and are filled through networking.

Carleton University
Career Services

Think about a person you have met at school who is very different from you. The difference could be religion, race, sexual orientation, or nationality. Try to have a conversation with this person and see what you can learn about him or her. In the space provided, write at least three good qualities you learned about this person:

_____

_____

_____

_____

SOLUTION 50 MAKE THE SUPERVISOR LOOK GOOD

Learning to make your boss look good is very important! Some people might find this offensive, but we think it is vital to your professional success.

Supervisors are usually very busy people who lead stressful lives at work because of a variety of responsibilities. Bosses quickly learn to rely on certain people because they can count on them to come through when they need someone to help them get something done quickly. This person is willing to come in early and stay late if necessary. Clock watchers are not the kind of people who endear themselves to their bosses.

To support your boss and make him or her look good, you need to know what the boss is trying to accomplish. See if there is a written set of goals and objectives that should be accomplished by the group your boss is supervising. Your work should support those goals and objectives as much as possible.

Here are some other helpful hints:

- Remember that establishing a good relationship with mutual trust takes time. Observe your superior's work habits. What can you do to help your boss? Ask your boss exactly what is expected of you.

- Keep your boss informed; bosses don't like unpleasant surprises. You certainly don't want your boss to hear something negative from her boss that she should have known.

- If you hold a meeting, provide your boss with a set of written notes of what took place.

- *Never* discuss your superiors with colleagues at work or in social settings; it always gets back to the boss. If you have an opportunity to say something complimentary about your boss, and you sincerely mean it, do so.

- Earn your boss's trust by keeping confidential information to yourself. As you move up the ladder, you will be privy to more confidential information. This information should not be treated as juicy tidbits that are shared up and down the halls.

- Follow up on assignments given to you by your boss as soon as possible (ASAP). Remember, bosses do not know everything you are doing but know if you are doing what they assign to you.

- If you see that your boss is extremely busy, and you have some time you could devote to helping, say something like this: "You seem to have so much on your plate today. Is there any way I can help?"

THINK ABOUT IT

Consider the three major ways you can improve your overall professional package right now. Appearance? Grooming? Hairstyle? Clothing?

SOLUTION 51 LEARN AS MUCH AS YOU CAN

This is a very important tip! Many people go to work everyday and learn nothing new. They merely do what their narrow job demands or what someone tells them to do. If you want to be promoted, learn everything you can possibly learn about your company.

Some helpful suggestions follow:

- Make a list of 25 things you need to know to do your job better and learn the answers.

- Ask questions of the people who seem to be outstanding at their jobs.

- Seek opportunities to work on certain projects so you can learn.

- Sign up for training and workshops offered internally by your company.

- If a special program is coming to your area, ask permission to attend and see if the company will pay for this training.

- After you have been with the company for a while and have proved you are a hard worker, you might ask to attend training in a location other than your city if you can justify it to your boss.

- If there is a job above you that you would like to have, find out what the qualifications are and be sure you have them, even if it means going back to school.

- If your company has a tuition reimbursement program, by all means take advantage of it and earn an advanced degree.

- Observe the leaders in your company and see what you can learn from them. How do they dress? How do they treat people? How do they handle crisis situations?

- When you feel comfortable, schedule some time with a person above your position and see if he or she has time to mentor you. Many times people are flattered that someone wants to be like them.

- If you are nervous about speaking in front of a group or about speaking up in a committee meeting, join Toastmasters or some other group that will help you improve.

Make up your mind that you will learn something new everyday and you will push yourself out of your comfort zone as you work hard to become better in all ways.

> Trust people with opportunities they never have had; identify ability and potential; and match the right skills to the right job.
>
> Truett Cathy, Founder, Chic-fil-A

SOLUTION 52 SPEAK UP WITH GOOD IDEAS

Many people have great ideas, but they are socially shy and refrain from speaking up. When you have to speak in front of a group or at a meeting, do your knees fold up like Gumby? Are you afraid of saying something so dumb that you will be embarrassed forever? To be successful at work and in social settings, you have to work hard to learn how to express your good ideas.

According to a book of lists, the fear of speaking in public is the number-one fear of all fears. The fear of dying is number seven ! More than 41 percent of people have some fear of anxiety dealing with speaking in front of groups. People who have this fear can experience all kinds of symptoms: sweaty palms, accelerated heart rate, memory loss, and even difficulty breathing (Laskowski, 1996). There are few people—even accomplished public speakers—who have not had to overcome their fear of speaking up.

Making a formal presentation to an audience is covered in Chapter 4. It is equally important to be able to present your ideas well at a committee or department meeting. Here are some pointers that will make you more at ease:

- ☑ Be comfortable with the place where the meeting will take place.
- ☑ Learn as much as you can about the people who will be attending the meeting.
- ☑ Prepare, prepare, prepare!
- ☑ Study the agenda and get comfortable with your thoughts about each item.
- ☑ If you are new, don't comment on everything. Speak when you have something worthwhile. Your job is to be sure you have something important to say.
- ☑ Make at least one solid suggestion or ask one thought-provoking question at each meeting.
- ☑ Sit close to the Chair of the meeting, but don't get in a superior's preferred seat. The closer you sit to the Chair, the more power you are perceived as having.
- ☑ Before you go to the meeting, visualize yourself speaking and actually practice in front of a mirror.
- ☑ Don't make excuses, apologies, or put yourself down *ever* in front of a group.
- ☑ Remember that the more you speak up, the easier it becomes.

 SOLUTION 53 PLAY WELL WITH OTHERS

We all have mannerisms that annoy others, but some people seem to have a special talent for getting on their co-workers' nerves. Some co-workers simply fall into the classification of "difficult people," who come in all sizes, ages, shapes, and nationalities. Every workplace has them. Some of these people can be ignored, but some have to be dealt with if they are attacking your professional integrity and reputation.

Every workplace has at least three generations of workers with a great variety of needs and wants all trying to inhabit space with many people who might be very different from each other. Add in a diversity of cultures, religions, ethnic backgrounds, regional differences, and political opinions, and navigating the hallways at work can become tricky.

One of the most frequently asked questions when references are called about a potential employee is, "Does he get along well with others?" Being able to work well with all kinds of colleagues and not become embroiled in arguments, disagreements, and pettiness is a big plus in your employment background.

Exactly how do you play well with others? Heathfield (2007) stated seven ways you can play well with others, which we have adapted here:

1. Bring suggestions and solutions with the problems to the table. Many people can identify problems, but few have good solutions. Thoughtful solutions will earn you respect and admiration. Become a problem solver and not a problem creator.

2. Don't ever play the blame game. Avoid pointing your finger publicly at other people and blaming them for failures because this habit will quickly earn enemies.

3. Your verbal and nonverbal communication matters. If you talk down to people, use sarcasm, or use a nasty tone of voice, the other person will hear this in your voice.

4. Never deliberately blindside a co-worker, your boss, or reporting staff person. If a co-worker hears information you provided for the first time in a staff meeting, and it has direct bearing on that person, then you have blindsided him or her. Discuss problems with the person involved before ambushing a colleague in a meeting.

5. Keep your commitments. Work is interconnected. If you fail to meet deadlines or commitments, you affect the productivity of other colleagues.

6. Share credit for accomplishments, ideas, and contributions. Always share the glory! Compliment others and recognize them for their accomplishments. Notice what others do, and say something positive about their work.

7. Help other employees find their greatness. Everyone has special talents. If you can help other people be productive, you will benefit the entire organization.

> **QUOTE**
>
> Nothing we do, however virtuous, can be accomplished alone.
>
> Reinhold Niebuhr

SOLUTION 54   EXPRESS YOURSELF TACTFULLY

Anyone can blurt out insensitive remarks about others! It takes intelligence and common sense to express yourself in a tactful manner that is not offensive to your colleagues. Tactful communications will endear you to your colleagues. Acting assertively with others' feelings will quickly create workplace problems for you.

To express yourself tactfully, consider the following tips:

- ☑ Know exactly what you are trying to express and be able to verbalize it clearly.

- ☑ Use precise language that clearly identifies what you are trying to accomplish.

- ☑ Think about other peoples' perspectives. Everyone has an agenda. Are you trampling on what someone else wants with your words?

- ☑ Realize that you don't have to fill up every second with words. Pause and use the effectiveness of silence sometimes.

- ☑ Conflict is going to happen. You can count on it! When it does, go out of your way to communicate professionally with the person with whom you have a problem. As stated earlier, we have diverse workplaces, and conflict is the result of a broad range of backgrounds.

- ☑ Being able to express yourself tactfully requires that you listen very keenly to the other people involved. Watch their body language and listen to the tone of their voices so you get the real message.

- ☑ If you feel that you have not been heard correctly, try to rephrase your thoughts so people understand better.

- ☑ Everyone has a perspective from which they hear and listen. Think about others' perspectives as they relate to what you are trying to accomplish.

SOLUTION 55 GROW FROM POSITIVE AND NEGATIVE FEEDBACK

Everyone loves positive feedback, but most people try to avoid negative comments. We don't want to hear negative things about ourselves because we are all sensitive. Negative feedback is comments made about past behavior where we did not perform well. Positive feedback, in contrast, is affirming and includes compliments about our past behavior. Some managers only provide negative feedback. One person made this comment: "The only time I know that I am doing OK is that I haven't been chewed out lately." This is a sad commentary on that person's manager because this is not the kind of feedback that is constructive, nor is this the way to motivate and influence employee's behavior.

When we were children, our mothers gave us bad medicine in orange juice. Criticism can be bad medicine and needs to be wrapped up in a nice compliment so we are prepared to hear what we need to change.

Patricia Moody

Nevertheless, when you go to work, you are most likely to receive both positive and negative feedback. The secret is to grow from both types of feedback. Before you give or receive feedback, think about these points:

☑ Ask yourself, "What did I do well?" because we need to hear good things first even if the comments are coming from within.

☑ When providing negative feedback, we shouldn't just sandwich it in between positive feedback to make it more palatable. The objective is to provide balanced feedback. "This is what you did well, and this is what needs to be improved." Sometimes negative feedback can be rather difficult, but if the relationship is good, it is easier to hear and to digest.

☑ Then ask yourself, "What do I need to change about how I handled a particular situation?" In this way, you are providing yourself a balanced perspective. Ideally, your supervisor will use this kind of delivery of good news and information that provides reasons for you to improve.

The best feedback is balanced with some compliments and some constructive ways to improve. You can learn and grow from both if you hear feedback in a balanced way.

SOLUTION 56 ALWAYS BE CUSTOMER ORIENTED

Customer service has suffered greatly in the past few years. It seems that many people don't get the connection between customers and their paychecks. If you will go out of your way to help customers, you will be successful because sooner or later, happy customers will tell your boss. You need to know that people are much more likely to tell everyone who will listen—including other potential customers—if they are unhappy about service. But there are a few good souls who will go out of their way to report exemplary customer service.

If a customer comes to you with a complaint, thank the person. Sometimes this disarms an irate customer and he or she settles down and listens to reason. Never argue with disgruntled customers and try to tell them why they are so dead wrong. Here are some pointers on being customer oriented:

☑ First of all, listen very carefully and attentively. Stop what you are doing and look at the person. Smile when it is appropriate.

☑ Remember, customers pay your paycheck. Don't look at them as an interruption; rather, look at them with this attitude: "Here comes my meal ticket right through that door." If your company doesn't have customers, they won't need you.

☑ If someone complains, thank them for sharing the information. Tell them, "I really appreciate your sharing this information with me. Now we can fix it!"

☑ If a customer is irate, don't take it personally. Chances are the person has just had a bad day and needs someone on whom to take out the frustrations.

☑ Try to exceed your customers' expectations. Underpromise and overdeliver!

> Remarkable leaders set the pace in creating a mind-set that is focused on customers and meeting/exceeding their needs.
>
> Kevin Eikenberry

Sometimes we forget we also have internal customers. These customers are our colleagues with whom we work everyday and who we need to do our jobs. It is very smart to learn to get along with all kinds of people within your company because they can have a great deal to do with your success on the job.

Here are some ways you can build solid relationships with internal customers:

☑ Be courteous. Thank people when they do something that helps you. Write a note; send a card. If they do something really noteworthy, purchase a little gift.

☑ Be thoughtful. Remember birthdays with a card, taking the person to lunch or some other thoughtful gesture.

☑ Help your colleagues when you can. First, be sure you do your own job, but if you have time to support someone who is overworked and stressed, offer to help.

☑ Be empathetic. If someone is having a bad time, perhaps a difficult family situation, offer assistance.

☑ Be a good listener. If someone confides in you, keep this information confidential.

☑ Congratulate people when they are successful. Perhaps someone makes a big sale or earns a promotion. This is a good time to write a note, call the person, or send a card. People tend to remember written remarks, and they make a lasting impression.

☑ A great part of being customer-oriented, both with internal and external customers, is simply being a nice person and treating others as they want to be treated.

In your words, define "Underpromise, overdeliver:"

_____

_____

_____

_____

PUTTING IT ALL TOGETHER

Many important points for your future success were addressed in this chapter. To summarize, we send messages about who we are and who we intend to become by what we wear, how we conduct ourselves, how we dine, how we treat others in the workplace, and the confidence we display. People tend to judge us on these messages that we ourselves communicate; thus the image you present is very important to your success. Likewise, our manners, customer service, and internal and external communications all play a prominent role in our success.

REFERENCES

Heathfield, S. M. (2007). "Play Well with Others: Develop Effective Work Relationships." Available at http://humanresources.about.com/od/workrelationships/a/play_well.htm. Retrieved August 16, 2007.

Larson, B. (2000, Summer). "Dressing for the Interview at a Business Casual Environment." Republished from the New Jersey Staffing Alliance's *Staffing News.*

Laskowski, L. (1996). "Overcoming Speaking Anxiety in Meetings and Presentations." Available at http://www.ljlseminars.com/anxiety.htm. Retrieved March 16, 2007.

Malloy, J. (1988). *The New Dress for Success Book.* New York: Warner Books.

McKay, D. R. (2007). "Inappropriate Dress and Conduct May Send the Wrong Message." Available at http://careerplanning.about.com/cs/dressingforwork/a/inapprop_dress_2.htm. Retrieved March 11, 2007.

Quintessential Careers. (2007). Available at www.quintcareers.com/dress_for_men. html. Retrieved March 3, 2007.

Seitz, V. (2000). *Your Executive Image: The Art of Self-Packaging for Men and Women.* Madison, WI: Adams Media.

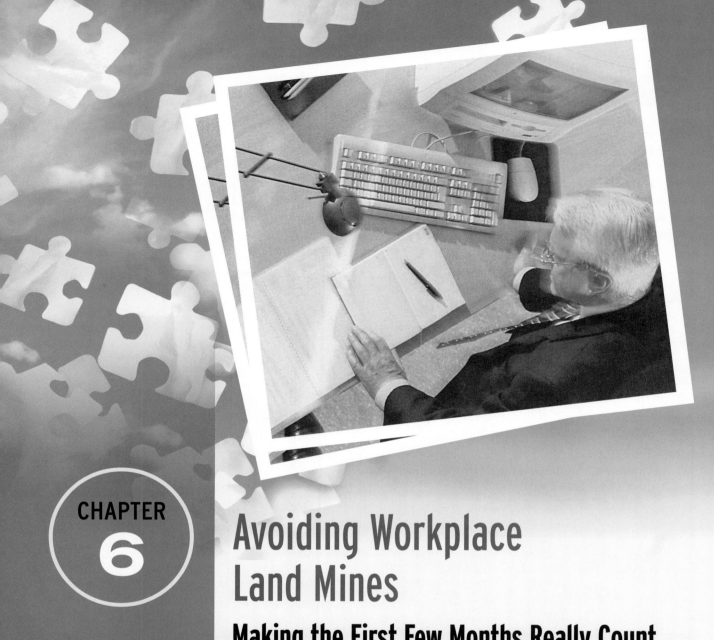

Avoiding Workplace Land Mines

Making the First Few Months Really Count

WHY?

is time management important? Why do I need to avoid workplace romances? Why can't I join in the gossip like everyone else? Why shouldn't I talk negatively about a former boss?

After you read this chapter, you might feel like you will spend all your time at work navigating through a field of land mines, and in some ways, work can feel that way, especially during your first year when you are still finding your direction. It is very important to perform in an outstanding manner and convince your bosses that they made a very good decision to hire you. From day one, you need to perform at your highest level and be willing to learn. Sometimes this means a willingness to do the dirty work that no one else wants to do. It means arriving early and staying late if necessary. In some cases, you will be on probation for a certain period of time, usually ninety days, so it is imperative that you perform at the top of your game during this time.

You will be assigned specific duties, and you need to excel in those areas. If you can, perform your assignments in such a way as to exceed what people expect. Always do more than just get by. In the first weeks and months of your new job, you will be establishing a reputation that might follow you for a long time. You want to be known as a hard worker, one who works smart, who can be depended on, and who gets along well with colleagues.

Right away you need to listen closely to your boss and observe his or her work habits and expectations of employees. Your boss will have several top priorities. You need to know what they are and focus some of your attention on helping get them accomplished. If your boss gives you an assignment, give it top priority, even if it doesn't seem very important to you. Many times the boss only knows how well you are doing based on your performance as it relates to what he or she has assigned.

The majority of companies conduct formal performance appraisals. Ask for a copy of the evaluation instrument, study the items on which you will be judged, and be sure you are performing all of them at a very high level. You don't want any surprises when your boss evaluates you. It is not unusual for employees to think they are doing what the boss expects, only to learn at evaluation time that they have missed the mark. Sometimes a boss can be slack about evaluations and may fail to conduct yours on time. In a very tactful manner, ask when you will be evaluated because it is important to your professional career, and often raises are tied to evaluations.

Although doing your current job exceedingly well is key, it is also important to be looking toward a promotion and your next career opportunity. Learn everything you can about the company, the goals and objectives, the mission statement, and vision statement. Observe people in leadership roles who have done well and are respected by colleagues: What is their educational background? How do they communicate? What do they do that sets them apart? Study the trends in your industry. Read good books and business journals. What can you learn from these books and journals that you can apply to your own work and perhaps do a better, more creative job?

Not only do you have to know how to do your job, you have to manage your time and stress, set priorities, avoid gossip and people who participate in it, try to be positive, and watch out for office politics that might get you in trouble. Then there are the backstabbers, romantic temptations, attendance at parties, and looking out for sexual harassment, not to mention people who are abusing alcohol and other substances. So work is not just being able to do the job. It also includes public relations, interpersonal relationships, building a network of people who can help you, and making good decisions, all the while perhaps trying to continue your education and spend time with family. If people ever say building a career is easy, they're lying.

So it isn't easy all the time! But if you are in the right job, building a career can be very rewarding. In this chapter, we offer you some tips for dodging the land mines and successfully navigating the path to an outstanding career.

SOLUTION 57   GET A HANDLE ON YOUR TIME AND PRIORITIES

Do you feel like you are one of those people who never has enough time? Do you envy people who seem to do it all and do it all well? Do you find yourself making bad grades or not doing well at work because you don't manage your time well? Well, the truth is, you have all the time there is! You have the same amount as everyone else, so if your life is a mess because of lack of time, chances are you are not managing your time very well or you are simply trying to do too much. More than likely, you are juggling some things you need to drop while you focus on priorities in your life as it is right now.

You might be surprised at where you really spend your time. We suggest you track how you spend your time for one week. Write in a daily log exactly what you are doing every fifteen minutes during your waking hours. Use the daily time sheets in Figure 6.1 as a model.

> Once you have done this, analyze how you are spending your time. What do you need to do differently? In the space provided, name five items on your time log you could have handled better:
>
> _____
> _____
> _____
> _____
> _____

One of the most effective time management tools is making a list. Every day before you go home from work or school, make a list of everything you have to do. Then put numbers by each item according to how important the task is, when it is due, who assigned it, and how much time it takes. If you just do this one simple exercise, you will be amazed at how much better you are using your time. This is an

FIGURE 6.1 Daily Time Sheets

Monday		Tuesday		Wednesday	
6:00	6:00	6:00	6:00	6:00	6:00
	6:15		6:15		6:15
	6:30		6:30		6:30
	6:45		6:45		6:45
7:00	7:00	7:00	7:00	7:00	7:00
	7:15		7:15		7:15
	7:30		7:30		7:30
	7:45		7:45		7:45
8:00	8:00	8:00	8:00	8:00	8:00
	8:15		8:15		8:15
	8:30		8:30		8:30
	8:45		8:45		8:45
9:00	9:00	9:00	9:00	9:00	9:00
	9:15		9:15		9:15
	9:30		9:30		9:30
	9:45		9:45		9:45
10:00	10:00	10:00	10:00	10:00	10:00
	10:15		10:15		10:15
	10:30		10:30		10:30
	10:45		10:45		10:45
11:00	11:00	11:00	11:00	11:00	11:00
	11:15		11:15		11:15
	11:30		11:30		11:30
	11:45		11:45		11:45
12:00	12:00	12:00	12:00	12:00	12:00
	12:15		12:15		12:15
	12:30		12:30		12:30
	12:45		12:45		12:45
1:00	1:00	1:00	1:00	1:00	1:00
	1:15		1:15		1:15
	1:30		1:30		1:30
	1:45		1:45		1:45
2:00	2:00	2:00	2:00	2:00	2:00
	2:15		2:15		2:15
	2:30		2:30		2:30
	2:45		2:45		2:45
3:00	3:00	3:00	3:00	3:00	3:00
	3:15		3:15		3:15
	3:30		3:30		3:30
	3:45		3:45		3:45
4:00	4:00	4:00	4:00	4:00	4:00
	4:15		4:15		4:15
	4:30		4:30		4:30
	4:45		4:45		4:45
5:00	5:00	5:00	5:00	5:00	5:00
	5:15		5:15		5:15
	5:30		5:30		5:30
	5:45		5:45		5:45
6:00	6:00	6:00	6:00	6:00	6:00
	6:15		6:15		6:15
	6:30		6:30		6:30
	6:45		6:45		6:45
7:00	7:00	7:00	7:00	7:00	7:00
	7:15		7:15		7:15
	7:30		7:30		7:30
	7:45		7:45		7:45
8:00	8:00	8:00	8:00	8:00	8:00
	8:15		8:15		8:15
	8:30		8:30		8:30
	8:45		8:45		8:45
9:00	9:00	9:00	9:00	9:00	9:00
	9:15		9:15		9:15
	9:30		9:30		9:30
	9:45		9:45		9:45
10:00	10:00	10:00	10:00	10:00	10:00
	10:15		10:15		10:15
	10:30		10:30		10:30
	10:45		10:45		10:45
11:00	11:00	11:00	11:00	11:00	11:00
	11:15		11:15		11:15
	11:30		11:30		11:30
	11:45		11:45		11:45
12:00	12:00	12:00	12:00	12:00	12:00

(continued)

FIGURE 6.1 Continued

Thursday		Friday		Saturday		Sunday	
6:00	6:00	6:00	6:00	6:00	6:00	6:00	6:00
	6:15		6:15		6:15		6:15
	6:30		6:30		6:30		6:30
	6:45		6:45		6:45		6:45
7:00	7:00	7:00	7:00	7:00	7:00	7:00	7:00
	7:15		7:15		7:15		7:15
	7:30		7:30		7:30		7:30
	7:45		7:45		7:45		7:45
8:00	8:00	8:00	8:00	8:00	8:00	8:00	8:00
	8:15		8:15		8:15		8:15
	8:30		8:30		8:30		8:30
	8:45		8:45		8:45		8:45
9:00	9:00	9:00	9:00	9:00	9:00	9:00	9:00
	9:15		9:15		9:15		9:15
	9:30		9:30		9:30		9:30
	9:45		9:45		9:45		9:45
10:00	10:00	10:00	10:00	10:00	10:00	10:00	10:00
	10:15		10:15		10:15		10:15
	10:30		10:30		10:30		10:30
	10:45		10:45		10:45		10:45
11:00	11:00	11:00	11:00	11:00	11:00	11:00	11:00
	11:15		11:15		11:15		11:15
	11:30		11:30		11:30		11:30
	11:45		11:45		11:45		11:45
12:00	12:00	12:00	12:00	12:00	12:00	12:00	12:00
	12:15		12:15		12:15		12:15
	12:30		12:30		12:30		12:30
	12:45		12:45		12:45		12:45
1:00	1:00	1:00	1:00	1:00	1:00	1:00	1:00
	1:15		1:15		1:15		1:15
	1:30		1:30		1:30		1:30
	1:45		1:45		1:45		1:45
2:00	2:00	2:00	2:00	2:00	2:00	2:00	2:00
	2:15		2:15		2:15		2:15
	2:30		2:30		2:30		2:30
	2:45		2:45		2:45		2:45
3:00	3:00	3:00	3:00	3:00	3:00	3:00	3:00
	3:15		3:15		3:15		3:15
	3:30		3:30		3:30		3:30
	3:45		3:45		3:45		3:45
4:00	4:00	4:00	4:00	4:00	4:00	4:00	4:00
	4:15		4:15		4:15		4:15
	4:30		4:30		4:30		4:30
	4:45		4:45		4:45		4:45
5:00	5:00	5:00	5:00	5:00	5:00	5:00	5:00
	5:15		5:15		5:15		5:15
	5:30		5:30		5:30		5:30
	5:45		5:45		5:45		5:45
6:00	6:00	6:00	6:00	6:00	6:00	6:00	6:00
	6:15		6:15		6:15		6:15
	6:30		6:30		6:30		6:30
	6:45		6:45		6:45		6:45
7:00	7:00	7:00	7:00	7:00	7:00	7:00	7:00
	7:15		7:15		7:15		7:15
	7:30		7:30		7:30		7:30
	7:45		7:45		7:45		7:45
8:00	8:00	8:00	8:00	8:00	8:00	8:00	8:00
	8:15		8:15		8:15		8:15
	8:30		8:30		8:30		8:30
	8:45		8:45		8:45		8:45
9:00	9:00	9:00	9:00	9:00	9:00	9:00	9:00
	9:15		9:15		9:15		9:15
	9:30		9:30		9:30		9:30
	9:45		9:45		9:45		9:45
10:00	10:00	10:00	10:00	10:00	10:00	10:00	10:00
	10:15		10:15		10:15		10:15
	10:30		10:30		10:30		10:30
	10:45		10:45		10:45		10:45
11:00	11:00	11:00	11:00	11:00	11:00	11:00	11:00
	11:15		11:15		11:15		11:15
	11:30		11:30		11:30		11:30
	11:45		11:45		11:45		11:45
12:00	12:00	12:00	12:00	12:00	12:00	12:00	12:00

important point for all employees but especially for a new one: Get to work on time, be a colleague whom others know they can depend on, demonstrate an outstanding work ethic, and you will get ahead.

One of most people's biggest time problems is simply procrastination. We do what we like to do and put off difficult tasks. Of course, you would rather go to a movie with friends than write a paper or a work report, but you could enjoy that movie so much more if you did your work first and then played. You have to put a plan into action for it to work. "Life rewards action" (McGraw, 1999).

Here are some clues to avoiding procrastination, which will help you in planning and organizing for school and work:

- Break up big jobs into small ones.

- Allow yourself a certain amount of time to complete a task.

- Set up a regular time to study and stick to it.

- Set reasonable goals that you can meet in 20- to 25-minute blocks.

- Take short breaks; get up from your computer and move around. Leave your desk for lunch and breaks. You'll come back refreshed.

- Allow yourself longer than you think you need for a project so you don't have to stay up all night.

- Avoid having to cram for school or work projects.

- Don't get too involved with outside organizations and commitments.

- Start on the most difficult, boring jobs first.

- Weed out personal belongings; get rid of clutter that takes your time.

- File things as you go; don't pile them up into stacks.

- Handle paperwork immediately.

- Organize your work space and designate a specific place for your supplies.

- Prepare to be successful at work or school by getting ready the evening before. Decide what you are going to wear; press your clothes if they need it; polish your shoes.

- Keep a Rolodex file, Palm Pilot, or iPod for important phone numbers and addresses you use frequently.

- Organize as effectively at home as you do at work.

- Plan a rotation schedule for housework.

- Organize your closets and dresser drawers.

- Fill up your gas tank the night before to avoid stress in the morning.

- If you are a perfectionist, get over it!

- Take time for activities you love and create a healthy balance in your life.

- If you have children, schedule at least an hour a week with each one. Make this a happy, special time.

- Make family meals enjoyable. Sit down together at least three times a week.

- Put fun days on your calendar and keep them sacred.

GRADUATE QUOTE

The most important thing I learned about transitioning from college to the world of work is that you must follow through. By this, I mean that no one is going to find the job for you and most likely, no one is going to come looking for you. *You* have to be the one to send the résumé, make the phone calls, meet with contacts, etc. I learned that looking for a position is a full-time job itself.

MEGANN PRATT, Graduate!
Colorado Mountain College,
Carbondale, CO General Studies

CAREER: College Administrative
Assistant Colorado
Mountain College

AVOIDING PROCRASTINATION
An Exercise in Time Management

Look at the points detailed in Figure 6.2. Replace these procrastination failures with steps that should have been followed to get the job done and to earn the boss's approval:

1. _____
2. _____
3. _____
4. _____
5. _____
6. _____
7. _____

FIGURE 6.2 A Day in the Life of THE PROCRASTINATION TRAP

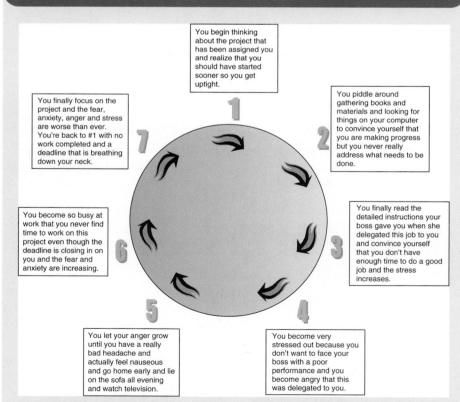

(Adapted from Sherfield, R., Montgomory, R., and Moody, P. *Cornerstone: Discovering Your Potential, Learning Actively, and Living Well,* 5th Edition, 2008, Pearson Prentice Hall.)

Not using your time well causes extreme stress, and stress can be very damaging to your health over a period of time. Stress causes heart attacks, high blood pressure, and other high-risk health problems. Get a handle on your time management!

 SOLUTION 58 DON'T BE A PART OF THE WATER COOLER GOSSIP CIRCLE

There are very few people who don't like to gossip. You will find the workplace no exception to this rule. Rumors fly around all the time, many of which have no real substance whatsoever; in fact, some people love to take a little tidbit of information and embellish it beyond belief. The problem with this little exercise is that it damages and hurts the people who are the subjects of this unfounded gossip. The other problem is that everybody knows who the rumormongers are, and nobody trusts them. It's not hard to tell who goes up and down the halls spreading malicious gossip. A sure way to damage your personal reputation is to become one of these people.

Avoid, at all costs, becoming a part of the rumor mill. This may sound like an easy thing to do, but in reality it is human nature to want to be in the know. To do this, however, you must engage in gossip, and a gossip is never trusted. One of the quickest ways to lose your credibility is to be seen keeping company with the corporate busybody, and every company has at least one. Build a reputation with your peers and supervisors of outstanding integrity and professionalism.

Avoiding known gossipers is not in and of itself enough to avoid the rumor mill. There still will be ample opportunity to engage in gossip during your everyday interactions with co-workers. If you are present when a conversation based on speculation or rumor begins, we suggest you either remove yourself quickly or state that, because the topic in question has not been substantiated, the conversation should not continue. You might ask a question like this, "How do you know that? Did you see that happen or is this just a rumor?" Or you might say, "Does John know that you are saying things like this? I'm sure he would like to know you are defaming his character." It will not take too many such circumstances, in which you either leave or put a stop to the conversation, before your position about gossiping is well known and people will not include you. Most people will respect your character and integrity. Stepping on one's feelings is as painful as stepping on one's toes, and it lasts a lot longer.

Never go to bed at night wondering if you were a conversational gun in the slandering of a person's character or the endangerment of his/her future.

Letitia Baldridge

 SOLUTION 59 NEVER SPEAK NEGATIVELY ABOUT YOUR BOSS OR FORMER EMPLOYER

Think about this quote: "If you work for a man, work for him, or find another job." This is good advice whether your boss is a man or woman! Although some bosses absolutely won't earn your respect or deserve your loyalty, nevertheless, he or she is the boss. All bosses are not good supervisors, but they are still the boss. You will be very fortunate if you get a boss who is visionary, fair, honest, ethical, caring, and one who tries to help all employees have a chance to grow and to learn. Even if you have a terrible boss, if you are going to take the paycheck, you need to give a good day's work for a good day's pay.

You will no doubt hear some grousing about your boss when you go to work because some people just naturally decide not to like a person in authority, no matter how nice or talented that person might be. Some people are jealous because they

POSITIVE HABITS

WORK

Do everything possible to make your boss look good. Avoid getting involved with the gossipers and naysayers.

BIGGEST INTERVIEW BLUNDER

Marie Hanson went on a job interview and was asked to describe her current boss. She proceeded to blast him with a stream of negative comments. She didn't get the job.

wanted the position. Some will complain about a woman boss; others will complain about a male boss. Don't participate in this kind of conversation. You might say, "Well, she's been pretty good to me so far, so I think I need to give her a chance."

Most bosses will tell you that the number-one quality they value is loyalty. This doesn't mean you can't disagree with the boss. It just means you disagree with him or her in person and you do it respectfully. Should you choose to disagree with your boss, you need to choose your words carefully and say something like this: "Mrs. Brown, I know you have so much more experience than I do, and I may be way off base, but it seems to me that the decision to close that branch might be a little premature. Are you aware that XYZ company is getting ready to build a big plant within a half mile of that branch?"

Never make the boss look bad in front of anyone to show how smart and clever you are. If you have a boss who truly encourages speaking up and disagreeing in meetings—and these are rare—be sure that even then you use a respectful tone of voice and you don't say or do anything that causes the boss to lose face.

Figure out what is near and dear to the boss's heart, and work hard to make it happen. This is not being underhanded; it's just using good sense. Don't let your boss hear bad news from someone else if you know about it. Bosses don't like surprises. They especially don't like to hear about it from their own boss.

If you talk negatively about your boss, someone is going to tell the boss either because they are loyal or because they want to score points or perhaps they don't like you. Unless your boss is doing something illegal or unethical, be as loyal as you can.

When you go for an interview, never say anything bad about the company or your boss. Even if the person deserves to be attacked, the interviewer will assume you will be negative when you go to work with the new company, and most likely, you won't get the job offer.

Observe supervisors carefully while you are learning and growing in a new position. What characteristics do you want to develop? Which ones do you want to avoid? You can be learning to lead even while you are a very new employee.

SOLUTION 60 BE AWARE OF WORKPLACE POLITICS

Politics are rampant in the workplace! You will see lying, bullying, exaggerations, people taking credit for others' work—the list goes on and on. The secret is to know what is going on but not to be a participant in the negative aspects of office politics. Most people know who the colleagues are who spread the rumors, attack others, or play up to the boss. You can't stop politics, so don't waste your time trying. The only way you can avoid them is to go to work in the middle of a forest and never see anyone else.

The good news is that not all politics are bad. You don't have to change who you are to be successful at office politics. Nice guys do finish first most of the time. J.W. Marriott, CEO of Marriott Corporation, made this statement: "The closer you get to the top, the nicer people are." You can be thoughtful, sincere, considerate, and interested in others, and your chances of succeeding are far better than those who choose to use dirty politics. The best way to earn recognition is to do a good job and to be a good colleague to everyone.

In the not-too-distant past, people played politics to get ahead. Power appeared to be more important to that era than it is today. Young people in today's workplace want to learn more skills, have time for their families and friends, and make a difference in their communities. They value people who help them improve and grow.

Some people believe office politics are only played by people who can't get ahead by any other means but, truthfully, most people are involved in politics. You don't have to be an underhanded person to make politics work for you. You can demonstrate strength of character, integrity and fair play and become known for these traits. Real political power is based on the ability to put forth new and visionary ideas and to get other people excited about helping you make those ideas happen.

You can always count on the fact that there will be always a grapevine. Someone has said that 80 percent of what comes down the grapevine is true. If you are the boss, you need to put the truth down the grapevine as often as you can. If you hear a rumor and you know it is not true, simply say, "That's not true. I was in that meeting, and Mr. Carter didn't say that. What he said is this."

Politics will always exist. Know what is going on around you at all times, but refuse to be a player in underhanded dirty politics. Practice honesty, integrity, fairness, and decency, and if you are good at your job you will succeed. Take time to get to know people on a personal level; don't judge them based on what anyone else says. Just because one person has a problem with a colleague doesn't mean you have to.

What does this statement mean?

Never judge another person through someone else's eyes.

_____

_____

_____

_____

 SOLUTION 61   AVOID BACKSTABBING AND TRAMPLING ON OTHERS

There are many ways to trample on others' feelings, and you will probably encounter or observe most of them. You must avoid participating in such behavior. Some of the typical behaviors that people hate most are these:

- Taking credit for someone else's work

- Not doing your work well and on time so someone else falls behind and looks bad

- Unfounded rumors such as accusing a person of having an affair

- Schmoozing those at the top and scorning those below them

- Spreading enough rumors about people so they hate each other with the idea that the gossiper will come out on top

- Resisting requests for information that a person needs to do his or her job

- Bullying by loud, intimidating colleagues

- Laughter at some offcolor or inappropriate joke that hurts another colleague

- Being left out of the loop on things that should be common knowledge

QUOTE

One in five employees reports being bullied at work.

Valerie Cade

Just as these behaviors hurt you, they also hurt other employees. You will be respected if you refuse to participate in these games. If someone mistreats you, gather your courage, go to his or her office, and say something like this: "I was told that you were spreading a rumor about me that isn't true, so I decided to ask you if you did this. Did you say I was having an affair with Mr. Kendall?" Because most people who trample on others and backstab their colleagues are intimidated underneath their loud exteriors, the person will probably deny having said it and probably won't say it again. You can respond, "Well, I didn't think you were that kind of person, and I'm glad to know you aren't doing such a despicable thing. So we don't have a problem."

These kind of behaviors are unavoidable. But you can refuse to participate in the games. The only person you can control is *you*.

SOLUTION 62 USE GOOD JUDGMENT IN WORKPLACE ROMANCES

Getty Images-Stockbyte

Is it something in the air? Or is it the music that plays constantly in many offices? Or is it the close proximity of office cubicles? No one seems to know what causes so many office romances, but "almost half of us have been romantically tied to someone from work, and many more would like to find amour in a neighboring cubicle" (Vault.com. 2001). Office romances seem to be rather common today. They are not as taboo as they once were, but for best results, cupid is best left out of the office.

What does your company's policy say about office relationships? Read this as soon as possible before an office romance is even remotely possible.

Before you jump into a romantic relationship with a co-worker, think about it carefully. This may seem like the love of your life right now and may appear to be the soulmate you have longed for. But what happens if this romance goes sour? What have you got to lose if it doesn't work out? Or even if it does work out? In a worst case scenario, you could lose your job. Some companies' corporate regulations forbid romantic relationships. You could damage your professional reputation and, in some cases, even be charged for sexual harrassment if you get your life tangled up with the wrong one. Certainly, you know by now that everyone is not honest and ethical, much less responsible. If you have a relationship that doesn't work out, naturally, it would be much easier if it took place somewhere outside your office.

According to Joni Johnston (2002), president and CEO of WorkRelationships.com, "Most dating relationships end. Think of the number of people we date and the number we end up marrying—the odds are not good." Is this relationship worth the gossip that will surely go on around you? Remember, there are very few secrets at work. Could you become involved in some kind of jealous triangle? Are the quarters too close for comfort to keep an office romance going? You have heard the old expression, "Look before you leap." This is one of those times when you really need to weigh all the consequences before jumping in and getting way over your head.

All that said, and even if it is not a good idea, it is virtually impossible to stop love from happening. Because you obviously have similar work interests, it stands to reason that you might share other mutually rewarding hobbies, sports, movies, and so on. You might even have a group of friends to which you both belong, and perhaps you all go out together after work. One thing leads to another, and you find yourself in an office romance.

Although we highly recommend not getting involved romantically at work, it would be wrong to say that everything is negative about a workplace romance. Because you work with the person, you can observe his or her behaviors frequently and determine if this person is a good match for you. You could have the opportunity to go to lunch or work out together in the company exercise facility. You can get an idea if this person is a good love interest or simply a wolf in sheep's clothing.

You need to maintain a good balance between romance and work. Here are some pointers that might help you as you deal with office relationships—the romantic kind.

QUICK FACT

Roughly a quarter of workplace relationships result in either a long-term relationship or marriage.

Vault.com study, 2001

- *Never* have a relationship with your boss or a subordinate! You increase the risk of a sexual harrassment lawsuit, you damage morale in the office, and you might get accused of preferential treatment. If you are a collegue competing for promotions, salaries, and other perks, naturally people will say you are receiving better treatment. What about evaluations? How can a boss be unbiased in evaluating a love interest? "Just don't date anyone in your direct chain of command. Just don't do it," according to Dave Taylor (2005). Even if none of these things are true, people are going to talk, and both your careers are going to be damaged.

- Never get involved with a married person—at work or anywhere else. You will quickly ruin your reputation. If this person will cheat on his or her spouse, he or she will cheat on you.

- If you sense a work relationship is getting too serious, spend less time working and more time doing things that take your mind off the person. Go to places where you might meet someone with similar interests; spend more time working out; look up old friends. Give yourself a chance to have a good life without an office romance.

- If you fall in love and you think you absolutely must have this person, one of you needs to move to another department or even to another company. Is this person worth giving up your job?

- If you become involved with a colleague, move very slowly into a serious relationship. It takes very mature people to handle a romantic relationship in the office.

- Johnston (2001) offers good advice: "Once you enter into a relationship, there are two people contributing to the way you are perceived in the company. It doesn't matter if you're being professional, if that other person is not it's still going to impact you." What if your love interest shares intimate information with a colleague and it gets out around the water cooler?

- Do your homework. Does your company forbid interoffice dating? Are there unwritten rules that eveyone seems to follow? What is the policy on harrassment? Does your relationship with this person provide situations that may be harmful to the company? Are there any older, long-term employees in relationships with colleagues? Are other peers dating, and how has this impacted them with their colleagues and bosses? If you were discussed in the same way as they are, could you live with it?

If you get involved, make some hard-and-fast rules you both will follow: no contact at work, no discussion of dating, no talk of love, and how you will treat each other if the relationship doesn't work out. Of course, there is no guarantee that either of you will live up to these promises. Can you be sure all of this will happen if things don't turn out well? In extreme cases, one person or the other can't let go of their love interest, and it creates a bad scene at work and can even result in violence.

 Don't fall in love and get all starry-eyed and stop paying attention to your job. You need to go to work, be prompt, meet deadlines, and handle your assignments conscientiously so your work doesn't suffer. Avoid e-mailing on company computers, and don't spend lots of time text messaging when you should be working. If this prince or princess doesn't work out, you still need your job and your reputation.

 If you break up—and you most likely will, according to statistics—handle it with maturity. Don't say bad things about your love interest; don't jump into another relationship at work right away; cool off. No one gets over a broken heart easily, but this is one of those times when you must deal with it very maturely.

Although office romances may bring happiness, they have the potential of bringing just as much sadness and, at the same time, damaging your career. Try very hard to avoid compromising situations. Proceed with caution, maturity, and wisdom.

> **QUOTE**
>
> There is no greater hatred than the hatred between two people who once loved.
>
> Sophocles

SOLUTION 63 DON'T PARTY AT THE COMPANY PARTY

Don't party at the company party! Arrive a little late and leave a little early. If everyone else is staying very late and drinking too much, excuse yourself and leave. Never drink more than one drink at a company function. Nurse that drink as long as you are there, and refrain from drinking simply because the liquor is

free. This is not the place for you to have too much to drink and make a fool of yourself. In this case, free is *never* good because you might be tempted to drink too much.

Wear something in good taste. This is a work function, not a laid-back social gathering with your best buddies. Women certainly want to look attractive but not overly sexy. Wives of upper management are not likely to dress in skimpy tight clothes. You want to fit in with them. Men should dress like the company executives do. They won't have on jeans and T-shirts.

If you are attending a swim party, don't swim. You will look like a drowned rat while everyone else is still fresh and attractive. Don't parade around in a swimsuit even if you look like a movie star. Neither men nor women will win friends by insisting on showing off a great body. This is not the place!

If you are playing golf or tennis at a club, you need to know the rules and dress the part. Look like *somebody*. Learning to play golf reasonably well is worth the effort for men and women alike. Many important discussions take place on the golf course. If you are entertaining clients or participating in a company golf outing, take your attire seriously. Executives do pay attention.

QUOTE

At every party there are two kinds of people—those who want to go home and those who don't. Trouble usually follows those who don't.

Unknown

As a businessperson, you probably will attend cocktail parties. Consider them an extension of work. You are there to make a good impression, network, expand your client base, and generally represent your company positively. In other words, work the room. Here are some basic tips for working a room:

- Don't be the first one to arrive unless you are hosting the party.

- Survey the room before you enter.

- If you have a drink, hold it in your left hand so your right hand is free.

- Avoid eating at the party. It is difficult to talk, eat, and shake hands. Eat before you go! You are there to do business, not eat. The worst thing you can do is to load up your plate and act like this is your last meal.

- Don't cluster in the corner with the only person you know! Move around the room, offering to shake hands and introducing yourself. Take the initiative. Most people will be glad you did.

- Focus on the other person. Smile and be friendly.

- Sell yourself with a sound bite, something interesting about yourself. For example: "I'm John Martin, the new admissions coordinator at Marion Hospital."

- Don't look around the room while you're talking to a person. Look at the person as though he or she is the most interesting person in the room. Use the person's name.

- Don't talk about politics, make fun of a state, or tell religious or ethnic jokes. You never know whom you might offend.

- Don't talk about your health.

- Converse a few minutes, excuse yourself, and move on.

Treat business parties, receptions, and cocktail parties as an extension of work. Look your best, present yourself well, and consider these events as a great opportunity to network.

SOLUTION 64   PUT A STOP TO SEXUAL HARASSMENT

The most important fact about sexual harassment is that it is illegal. The federal government defines sexual harassment as deliberate or repeated unsolicited verbal comments, gestures, or physical contact of a sexual nature that is considered to be unwelcome by the recipient, man or woman.

Some examples of sexual harassment are verbal abuse or harassment (e.g., dirty jokes, unwanted letters, e-mails, sexually explicit pictures, telephone calls, or written materials); unwelcome sexual overtures or advances, pressure for dates or to engage in sexual activity; remarks about a person's body, clothing, or sexual activities; personal questions of a sexual nature; touching of any kind or referring to people as babes, hunks, dolls, honey, boy toy, and so forth.

If you are the perpetrator, you will most likely be fired. If someone is harassing you, you don't have to put up with it. The law requires a supervisor to investigate any claims of sexual harassment.

Here are some steps to protect yourself from sexual harassment:

- Make a conscious effort to keep interactions between you and the person harassing you as impersonal as possible.

- Avoid being alone with the person harassing you. If that person is your professor, bring a friend with you to meetings and arrange to meet in a classroom either right before or right after class.

- Keep a record of the harassment in case you have to bring formal charges—the date, what was said, and what happened.

- Tell the harasser that you believe he or she is harassing you and you want the behavior to stop. Be very specific, so the person knows what you perceive as harassment.

- Tell your academic adviser or a campus counselor about the events if the harassment occurs at school. If it happens at work, tell your supervisor. If your supervisor is the one who is harassing you, tell the supervisor's boss.

- See a lawyer if necessary. Sexual harassment is against the law, and you may have to bring legal charges.

THINK ABOUT IT

How could one incidence of sexual harassment in which you were charged as the instigator ruin your career?

SOLUTION 65   DON'T ALLOW SUBSTANCE ABUSE TO RUIN YOUR CAREER

One of the overriding purposes of this book is to help you with decision making. We want you to make wise choices about relationships, finances, automobile purchases, use of your time, career choices, and so on. Although it is not up to us to tell you how to spend your life, we can tell you with great certainty that substance abuse of any kind can ruin your life and the lives of those who care about you.

It is disturbing to read that "nearly half of America's 5.4 million full-time college students abuse drugs or drink alcohol on binges at least once a month," according to a new study that portrays substance and alcohol abuse as an increasingly urgent problem on campuses across the nation. Alcohol remains the favored substance of abuse on college campuses by far, but the abuse of prescription drugs and marijuana has increased dramatically since the mid-1990s, according to a study released recently by the National Center on Addiction and Substance Abuse (CASA) (2007) at Columbia University.

The CASA study found that

[C]ollege students have higher rates of alcohol or drug addiction than the general public: 22.9% of students meet the medical definition for alcohol or drug dependence—a compulsive use of a substance despite negative consequences—compared with 8.5% of all people 12 or older. Nearly half of the students surveyed by CASA said they drank or used drugs to relax, reduce stress or forget about problems. Nearly 40% of students reported that they had participated in binge drinking during the previous two weeks.

Students who said they had abused painkillers such as Percocet, Vicodin, and OxyContin during the past month rose from fewer than 1% of students in 1993 to 3.1% in 2005, a reflection of how the rising number and availability of prescription drugs has increased abuse. (Leinwand, 2007)

People abuse substances such as drugs, tobacco, and alcohol for many complex reasons, but our society pays a terrible price because of these abuses. People harm themselves and others, work suffers, families are adversely affected by it, relationships are ruined, and many people end up in prison because of substance abuse. There is a strong correlation between drug dependence and crime. Although the use of cocaine has declined, use of other drugs such as heroin or "club drugs" has increased (Daly & Richards, 2007).

Friends, family, and co-workers may see some of the following signs of substance abuse:

- Giving up hobbies and sports the person used to enjoy
- Showing a decline in grades or work performance
- Becoming aggressive or hostile
- Appearing rundown, hopeless, depressed, or suicidal
- Using room deodorizers and incense to hide odors
- Using drug paraphernalia such as baggies, pipes, and rolling paper
- Getting drunk or high regularly
- Lying about how much he or she is consuming
- Avoiding friends and family to get drunk
- Hiding alcohol; drinking alone
- Getting in trouble with the law
- Drinking and driving
- Getting suspended from school or work because of substance abuse–related incidents. (Daly & Richards, 2007)

Although we cannot go into great depth on the issue of substance abuse in this book, suffice it to say it is an increasingly serious problem among college students and American workers. Many students are not well educated on the potential harmful effects of substance abuse. Many college students, for example, have the mistaken idea that marijuana is harmless and non-habit-forming. According to Hoffman and Froemke (2007), "The odds of marijuana dependence in adulthood are six times higher for those who start using pot before the age of 15 than for those

QUOTE

The estimated number of users of illicit drugs in the United States is about 13 million. About 10% of the population is dependent on alcohol and 25% of Americans smoke cigarettes.

National Household Survey

IF YOU WERE IN CHARGE

SOLVE THE PROBLEM

Ron has been getting to work late, his work is not up to par, and he has been getting into arguments with his co-workers. You have reason to believe he is abusing alcohol. If you were in charge, what would you do?

who begin after 18." Residual damage from substance abuse includes unwanted pregnancies, sexually transmitted diseases, driving fatalities, and accidents. Cooper (2002) reported that 61 percent of men who binge drink practice unprotected sex as compared with only 23 percent who do not binge drink. Forty-eight percent of women who participate in binge drinking practice unprotected sex compared with eight percent of women who do not practice binge drinking.

A substance-abuse dependency started in college is very likely to carry over into the workplace. Many companies today require a drug test before they will hire you. We offer the concerned advice of being very careful not to develop a substance abuse problem that can impact you for the rest of your life. If you have a problem or know of someone who does, get help at your earliest convenience.

PUTTING IT ALL TOGETHER

Avoiding workplace land mines can be quite tricky, but it's just a part of going to work everyday. If you go to work with the right attitude, give your best, support your boss, and build a network of people who have goals and dreams like yours, you will be able to navigate the minefield.

Another way to avoid the many minefields you may encounter at work (and in your personal life) is to review *and practice* the Six Levels of Ethical Decision Making found in Chapter 2 of this book. Those six levels are solid indicators of whether a decision or action is just, ethical, and/or moral.

REFERENCES

Cooper, M. (2002). "Alcohol Use and Risky Sexual Behavior among College Students and Youth." *Journal of Studies on Alcohol* 63 (2): 101.

Daly, K., & Richards, J. (2007). "Substance Abuse." eMedicine Health. Available from http://www.emedicinehealth.com/substance_abuse/article_em.htm.

Hoffman, J., & Froemke, S. (2007). *Addiction: Why Can't They Just Stop.* New York: Rodale Press.

Kersten, D. (2002). "Office Romances Can Be Risky, Rewarding" *USA Today.* Available from http://www.usatoday.com/money.jobcenter/workplace/ relationships/ 2002-11-12-office-romance.

Leinwand, D. (2007). "College Drug Use, Binge Drinking Rising." National Center on Addiction and Substance Abuse Study. Available from http://www.usatoday.com/news.nation/2007-03-15-college-drug-use-N.htm.

McGraw, P. (1999). *Life Strategies.* New York: Hyperion.

National Center on Addiction and Substance Abuse (CASA). (2007).

Taylor, D. (2005). "The Intuitive Life Business Blog." Available from http://www.boulderinnovationcenter.com/images/2005.10.25.05_Solving_ the_University_to_Industry.pdf.

Vault.com: The Thrilling Scoop on Workplace Romance (2008). Available from http:vault.com/nr/printble.jsp?ch_id=402.

Leading with Passion, Power, and Promise

Finding the Leader in You

 WHY?

do I need to know about leadership strategies? Why do I need to learn about creative problem solving? Why is learning to lead meetings so important? Why do I need to be able to manage conflicts and deal with difficult people?

Everyone recognizes good leadership and strong leaders. Sometimes we refer to leaders as having "the right stuff." We observe outstanding leadership in dynamic corporate presidents, in good teachers, in football stars, and in well-known politicians. Leadership qualities can be found in class presidents, in military platoon leaders, or in officers of organizations. At times we can almost see leadership. We certainly feel the presence of a great leader, but leadership remains somewhat intangible.

Thousands of books have been written about leadership. Companies try to develop leadership in their employees; teachers try to instill leadership qualities in their students; parents encourage their children to become leaders. For many people, the characteristics of leadership appear to be elusive and hard to define. Some people think leaders are born, not made, and in some cases it may be true that certain people are born with personalities that seem better suited for becoming leaders. Today, however, most people tend to think that leadership can be developed if one has the desire and the willpower to become an effective leader.

Before we go further, we need to define leadership. Among the many definitions the one we like best is this one: Leadership is the ability to establish a culture in which people can make contributions, use their unique talents, and feel they have been part of something bigger than they are. The influence potential of leaders is determined largely by how well they get other people to do what they want them to do willingly and enthusiastically.

So how does one become a leader? In his book *Leadership Jazz,* DePree (1992) makes this statement: "One becomes a leader, I believe, through doing the work of a leader. It's often difficult and painful and sometimes even unrewarding, and it's work. There are also times of joy in the work of leadership."

Leadership is not playing a role, acting a part, wearing a uniform, or holding an office. Leadership is caring about people and an organization, putting others' needs ahead of your own, giving more of yourself than just enough to get by, and working as hard on "dirty work" as on "glory work." Leadership is knowing when to follow, sharing successes, understanding peoples' innate needs to achieve and to feel good about themselves and helping others develop their potential.

We have included this chapter on leadership to help prepare you for your future leadership roles. Those roles may be as simple as leading a small team in developing a sales strategy or as paramount as helping your company emerge from bankruptcy. Make no mistake, however, a leadership role, big or small, will be in your future, and understanding the legal, moral, and ethical issues, as well as the power of your role, will help you lead with outstanding qualities.

SOLUTION 66   EMBRACE OUTSTANDING LEADERSHIP QUALITIES

The leader's job is to secure the cooperation or a group of followers, stimulate them to work together for common goals, guide them using previous experience, encourage them to become a dedicated member of the team, and set such a positive example that people willingly do what the leader wishes. Leadership should never be confused with power, adoration, and seizing recognition for oneself. Although good leaders come in many shapes and sizes and rise from a multitude of backgrounds, they share common characteristics.

Win McNamee/Reuters/Corbis/Bettman

Although some leaders are born with the innate ability to get people to follow them, most people can learn to lead. Major points for becoming an outstanding leader are listed next.

Outstanding Leaders

- Understand the importance of being able **to shape a vision** that is compelling enough to make other people believe in it and clear enough that they can see themselves participating in making this happen.

- Must be **goal oriented** and demonstrate direction in their own lives. Leaders must never allow their personal goals to supersede the goals of the organization, nor should an organization be used as a vehicle to serve the leader's personal ambitions. Goals must be jointly shared by the leader and the people.

- Have the ability to establish **a climate of success** in which people feel they can achieve and find fulfillment. This climate is inviting, encouraging, and rewarding to individuals. They are able to involve all people and make them feel a part of an organization.

- Must have a **strong system of values and morals.** As a leader, one must be an example for others to follow, meaning that one must be a decent, ethical, honest, and trustworthy person.

- Are **great communicators.** They are outstanding listeners as well as talkers. They know how to communicate up and down the chain of command.

- **Help others feel good about themselves** and assist others in sharing in successes and in being a part of something bigger than themselves. A good leader is a diplomat who can navigate through the difficult situations that leaders and decision makers confront.

- Know the basic underlying truth of leadership: **Leaders serve others.** They meet the needs of others ahead of their own. Albert Schweitzer, Mother Teresa, and Martin Luther King are all recognized as great leaders. These famous leaders met the needs of others often enough that people began to seek their leadership. Recognition and honor are almost always accorded those people who lead by serving.

● Understand that leadership is caring about people and an organization, putting others' needs ahead of your own, giving more of yourself than just enough to get by.

● Know that **they must step aside and let others lead** sometimes. They realize that they may be leaders today and followers another day. They know they must first be good followers and good teammates to become a leader.

● **Must be courageous, decisive, bold, imaginative, creative, and strong.** They must be able to develop plans that are daring and different and then they must have the strength to make them happen. Good leaders are can-do people.

● Must **display confidence** in themselves and others. They must look, act, and speak like leaders. The ability to speak well is a great asset to anyone trying to lead.

● Must be courageous and **able to stand adversity.** They must be able to look at a bad situation and find a way to capitalize on it.

● **Do what they say they will do.** Good leaders "keep their promises and follow up on their commitments" (Berko, Welvin, & Ray, 1997).

● Know they **must compromise** on some issues. We cannot always get everything we want. People who are unyielding, unbending, and uncompromising accomplish very little. The leader's job is to get the group to reach a consensus and then to implement the plan.

● Must be **open minded** and able to hear competing viewpoints and separate the good ideas from the bad. Leaders must be able to keep arguments from getting personal. No members should be allowed to attack other individuals. The leader's job is to give everyone a forum in which to express ideas and opinions, bring the group to a satisfactory conclusion, get disagreeing members to accept the compromise, and not take criticisms of an idea too personally.

● Must always **share the victory!** This can be accomplished by celebrations that involve everyone and by making statements such as, "I could never have done this without such a great team of people working with me. This is a victory for all of us." Praise people and present awards publicly. Make people feel good when they have worked hard and made outstanding contributions. Winning nobly and with class is a must for great leaders.

● Must be able to **lose gracefully.** No one likes to lose, but it happens to everyone at some time or other. They must make a statement such as "We lost to a better team, and we congratulate them on their victory." Good losers, although losing gracefully, are already preparing for their next victory because they have learned from defeat.

● **Are cheerleaders.** Leaders write notes of personal congratulations; they thank people sincerely in front of groups; they tell people, "I appreciate you." Leaders spend a great deal of their time cheering others' accomplishments and no time cheering their own.

QUOTE

Remarkable leaders never build pyramids in their own backyards.

Wess Roberts

- **Get along well with all kinds of people** and see the best in all people. They don't judge people by their race, religion, color, ethnic background, sexual orientation, or level of education. Good leaders cherish diversity! A great team requires a very diverse group of people; if they are all just like you, the organization will not be successful.

- Must be **passionate about their vision**, their followers, and their goals.

- Know how to "**make a difference in the lives of others**—and liberate the leader in everyone" (Berko et al., 1997).

Consider each of the following topics and write your thoughts in the space provided. Later your instructor may ask you to join a small group and discuss your thoughts with others.

Topic 1:

    What values and morals do leaders need? _____

_____

_____

Topic 2:

    What do you personally look for in a leader? _____

_____

_____

Topic 3:

    Name some ways that leaders can develop other leaders. _____

_____

_____

Topic 4:

    What leadership characteristics do you think you have? _____

_____

_____

GRADUATE QUOTE

The biggest mistake I made when searching for a position was that I thought my skills and past experiences would carry me through the interview. I did not do my homework for the interview, such as researching the company or preparing questions to ask. I did not get the position. That one interview taught me the paramount importance of being prepared to go on an interview.

C. STEVEN SPEARMAN, Graduate! Belmont Abbey College - Charlotte, NC College of Business Administration

CAREER: Vice President and Program Manager, J.P. Morgan / Chase Bank

SOLUTION 67   UNDERSTAND THE CATEGORIES OF LEADERSHIP POWER

Many people confuse management with leadership, just as many confuse power with force. Real leadership power must be earned. It cannot be bought, inherited, or bestowed on someone. The strangest thing about power is that the less you use it, the more you seem to have. Power is a precious commodity that few people know how to use. Conversely, if you have power, you must use it at times when a hard decision has to be made or people will lose their respect for you, and along with that, you will lose your power. The weakest leaders are those who use their power for trivial reasons or personal gain. Weak leaders use force rather than leadership. Remember, leadership is the ability to get people to follow you voluntarily. Good leaders use their power to develop other leaders and take pride in seeing people whom they have led become successful.

Categories of Leadership Power

Power comes to us through a variety of means. Specifically, we can view the acquisition of leadership power in six categories, illustrated in Figure 7.1. Each category is numbered in order of significance in acquiring power for a leadership role. Category 1 is the weakest and most short lived, whereas category 6 is the strongest and most long lasting. However, categories 1 through 5 are actually part of category 6. Each one builds on the other and strengthens category 6.

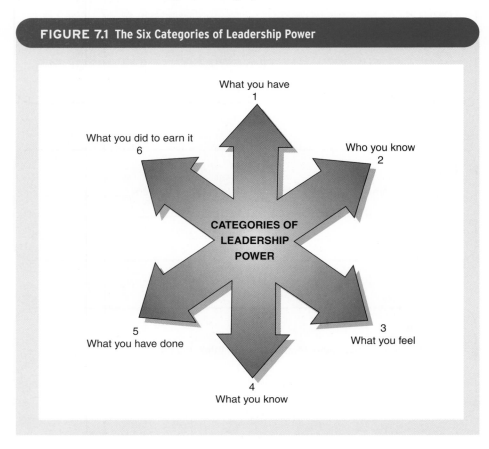

FIGURE 7.1 The Six Categories of Leadership Power

Category 1: What You Have

Standing alone, category 1 is the weakest category for acquiring power for a leadership role. Many people are drawn to materialistic goods, and they place people who have a variety of these goods on a pedestal. Some people who are wealthy and have valuable property, spacious homes, or other commodities viewed as "important" use these objects to attract and gain temporary power. Unfortunately, some people are swayed by such things and step back and let wealthier people make all the decisions.

Most people have worked hard all of their lives for their possessions. As a tool for acquiring lasting power, however, possessions are weak tools. They can be lost or stolen, and if your power base is built only on material objects, your power base will soon crumble.

Category 2: Who You Know

You probably have heard the expression, "It's not *what* you know but *who* you know." In today's workplace this often is true. Networking and making contacts are of ultimate importance to most employees today. Nevertheless, a power base built only on "who you know" is weak. Managers, supervisors, and leaders who acquired their position because they "knew the boss" are familiar to us. Many people who acquire power this way rise to the occasion and quickly learn that the boss or the owner can make you a supervisor or assign you to a leadership role, but that person cannot give you real power. Those who acquire power in this fashion and fail to realize that power is earned through the respect of the people they lead usually do not succeed in a leadership role. This is not to say they lose their job or even their role, but they do not have true power. They may have a title but not the respect of the people they are trying to lead.

Category 3: What You Feel

What you feel is much more abstract than what you have or who you know. Acquiring power by what you feel can be summed up as "leading with a soul." People respect leaders they see as reflective and thoughtful. When leaders make decisions with their soul, those who are being led know the difference. This is the beginning of earned power. People begin to respect and appreciate that the leader has taken the time to look at every option, explored many solutions—and taken the human side of matters into consideration. Earning true power begins with soul leadership. This category includes the fact that leaders care about the people they are leading; they feel their pain and frustrations and try to help them overcome their problems. Leaders who care also try to help people get promoted and find their strengths, so they, too, can become leaders.

Surround yourself with the most brilliant, talented, and optimistic people possible.

Steve Brannon

Category 4: What You Know

Sometimes older people have difficulty being led by younger people. The younger person feels threatened and sometimes uses too much force, and the older person sees the younger leader as a hotshot fresh out of college with no real life experience, just book knowledge. To a large extent, leadership power is gained through competence and expertise. When the workforce knows that the leader is intelligent, bright, studious, resourceful, and clever, respect and earned power follow. Be cautioned, however, that real leaders with real power are knowledgeable students, too. They continue to learn from their surroundings, and they learn from the people they lead. If you are a young leader, it is wise to ask older people for their advice and suggestions. What people are not up on, they are down on.

Category 5: What You Have Done

Life experience, properly used, is one of the most powerful tools in leadership and can earn you great respect and power. Leaders should be careful, however, not to rely too heavily on the past and thus overlook current trends and new options. Using what you know is one of the strongest tools for gaining respect and acquiring power. People like working for leaders they believe have experience, knowledge, background, and training. They also like working with leaders who know how to use past situations to offer solutions to current problems. It is very difficult for a young leader with a weak résumé and little experience to be given much respect by colleagues. If you have power and feel secure within yourself, it is easy for you to tap into what other people know by including them in decisions and plans.

Category 6: What You Did to Earn It

Coming full circle, true power is always earned. Power may come from what you have, who you know, what you feel, what you know, and what you have done, but, ultimately, true power is earned. Here are some ways that power can be earned:

- Respecting other people
- Appreciating the work that people do
- Appreciating what people know
- Demonstrating a genuine interest in colleagues and their families
- Appreciating and calling on others' life experiences
- Being courageous and making fair decisions
- Giving power to others to help themselves (empowering)
- Remaining calm and getting the facts in the face of crisis
- Being a positive, optimistic force
- Using creativity and asking for help
- Providing employees with the tools, support, and training to help them do the best job possible
- Living the motto "I am a part of a bigger picture."

Powerful leaders enable others to be the very best they can be. They encourage others to explore options and to create new paths. Last, powerful leaders are not challenged or threatened by people who excel, but they learn from them, too.

IF YOU WERE IN CHARGE

SOLVE THE PUZZLE

Jack and Robert are always late to meetings and disruptive when they come into the room. During the meeting, they whisper and talk while the chair of the committee is trying to conduct the meeting. If you were in charge, what would you do?

SOLUTION 68   LEAD WITH VISION

A vision portrays how the future is supposed to look. It provides people with a framework to help them understand. A leader's vision gives direction and asks, *What* should we be? *Where* should we be? *When* should we be there? *Why* should we be there? *Where* will we concentrate our resources? *How* will our lives be changed?

"Vision, quite simply, is a way of spelling out for your listeners the big picture, to help them understand the effort in which they are engaged, and to win their buy-in" (Barnes, 2005). A good leader must be able to paint a picture that is compelling for the people who are following. The vision must be something worth working for together and something that will challenge people to work for a common goal.

Good leaders understand there can be no leadership without followers. Leaders and followers ideally bring out the best in each other. A visionary leader must capture the imagination of followers by painting a picture of some worthy achievement. Leaders are the kind of people who draw others to them; many times this is because of the vision a leader lays out.

Followers are not likely to get excited about a plan that accomplishes very little or that is not much different from what they have always done. In other words, they don't want a leader who "majors in the minors." Leaders must often develop a vision statement with their followers. Being able to comprehend, design, and sell a challenging vision is one of the hallmarks of a great leader.

A BRAVE NEW WORLD

An Activity for Creative and Constructive Thought

Think about the United States today. There are many wonderful things about America, but our country also faces some serious and mind-boggling challenges. If you were a powerful leader in this country today, with real power, describe one bold vision that you would implement for America.

Remember, true leaders are innovative, optimistic, and sometimes outrageous.

My Vision

_____

_____

_____

_____

Reasons for Selecting This Vision

_____

_____

_____

_____

SOLUTION 69   **THINK BEFORE YOU ACT**

At times a leader must make a quick decision. This decision could mean life and death, or it could involve a piece of equipment needed right now, or it might be necessary to bring a halt to something an employee is doing. Most decisions, however, can wait until you have had time to think about the end results and the process needed to accomplish an objective.

Here are some points to consider before you act:

- Can it wait? (But don't let decisions sit on your desk forever).
- Do you have all the facts?
- Have you asked another leader how that person would handle this situation?
- How does your decision impact everyone concerned?
- Have you heard from everyone the decision might impact?

The best advice to be offered here is simply, "Stop and think!" Don't make rash decisions that can come back to haunt you. Sometimes, you may not have much time to make a decision before you act. You can't hear opposing viewpoints; you can't take a vote; you can't read a good book—you simply have to act. Stay calm, think, and make the best decision you can make. Remember, however, that *no* decision *is* a decision.

 SOLUTION 70   **MAKE GOOD DECISIONS USING CREATIVITY AND LOGIC**

 QUOTE

Nothing is more difficult, and therefore more precious, than to be able to decide.

Napoleon

The word *decision* comes from the Latin word *decidere,* meaning to "cut off." In other words, you have decided on something, and all other options have been canceled. If you decide to take a job in New York instead of Atlanta, you won't ever know how it might have worked out in the other position. In many, if not most, cases, decisions are final, and we have to live with the results. Life is a series of choices, and the ones we make impact our lives in many different ways; therefore, we need to make good, logical, and creative choices.

Decisions mean letting uncertainty enter your life because the results usually happen somewhere in the future. For example, you could decide suddenly, without thinking the decision through, to drop out of school. The results might be that you can't get a good job or you aren't earning the salary you had hoped for. If you had taken time to think about this decision and weigh all the possible results, you might have decided not to leave school. We all make poor decisions at one time or another, but we can learn to make good decisions most of the time by using the right strategies. The leader's job is to make the hard decisions, the decisions that can't be delegated, and to make the right decisions. Some decisions are amazingly smart; others are painfully ridiculous. The scary part of leadership is that we don't have a crystal ball to see how our decisions are going to turn out.

As you lead and make decisions, approach difficult problems as though you are trying on a new pair of glasses. Try to see things you have never seen before, look beneath people's hidden agendas and fears and try to find their strengths, and be sensitive to others' feelings. Consciously, try to see things in a new light, and you might be able to devise a new solution.

Here are some suggestions to consider when making decisions:

- Set high standards and have big expectations.

- Surmount your anxieties (Useem, 2005).

- Create an atmosphere in which information flows freely.

- Use logic to solve problems. Think through your decisions step by step. Analyze the potential outcome and impact on other people. Weigh all the information. Look before you leap if you have time to study the situation.

- Use creativity to solve problems. Just because it has never been done before doesn't mean it isn't a good idea. Remember that people resist change, even good change.

- "Don't put paint on a rotten board." That is, glossing over a difficult problem is only going to cover it up temporarily; it won't solve the problem. Address the problem, not the symptoms!

- Get other people's ideas and tap into their creativity—but you make the decision. You don't have to take a vote or get a consensus if you are the decision maker. The leader makes the call and bears the responsibility.

- When possible, make decisions transparent.

- Quit worrying about being a perfectionist because you can't be.

- Understand that you cannot please everyone. Do what you know in your heart is right.

- Don't become paralyzed with indecision until the decision is made by lack of a decision.

- The decision you are making should match with the overall goals of the organization or with your personal goals if the decision is personal.

- Remember that decisions are very much about "who" rather than "what" (Collins, 2005).

- Once a decision has been made, execution becomes crucially important.

- Forgive yourself when you make a bad decision and move on!

Ho Old/Corbis/Reuters America LLC

QUICK FACT

In 1955, Ruth Handler and her husband Eliot, Mattel Toys co-founders, bet their company on advertising toys like Barbie on television when they signed on with ABC's *Mickey Mouse Club* for the sum of $500,000, the net worth of the company at that time. They had only a few hours to make this monumental decision.

Fortune magazine, June 27, 2005

MAKE A DECISION
An Activity in Creative Problem Solving

Assume you are in a leadership role and faced with solving this problem: You have just been told that the regional manager is arriving three days from now. This manager is very demanding and authoritative and known for his critical reviews. This is an unexpected visit, and no one is prepared. Your boss has asked you and the people you supervise to make a PowerPoint presentation at the beginning of the meeting on the new products you are about to unveil. How would you solve this problem creatively and logically and make your boss, yourself, and your employees look good?

_____

_____

_____

_____

_____

SOLUTION 71   KNOW HOW TO PARTICIPATE IN AND LEAD EFFECTIVE MEETINGS

Kate Cook/Allyn & Bacon

Perhaps you have already had to lead meetings at work or at school. If you haven't already done so, sooner or later, you will find yourself at the head of the table in a leadership role. There is a true art to leading (and participating in) an effective meeting. Productive meetings do not just happen. Good meetings take planning, research, and careful preparation. It is doubtful that anyone would say, "I love sitting through long meetings, especially boring, unproductive ones." If you can lead a good meeting in which people can honestly say, "I really got something out of that meeting," you will shine.

Here are some tips for both participating in a meeting and leading one.

Participating

Before the Meeting

● Prepare to do well by developing a folder with agenda, supporting documents, minutes, and handouts for each committee or group with whom you have meetings.

● Before the first meeting, read previous minutes so you will be prepared.

● Bring all necessary supplies to the meeting (pen, paper, personal calendar, highlighter, and supporting folder).

During the Meeting

- Take good notes, highlighting any items that require your personal action.

- Participate in the meeting if you have relevant information.

- Ask a thought-provoking question to enable your committee to think through critical decisions.

- Listen twice as much as you talk.

- Don't make commitments for something over which you have no authority.

Follow Good Meeting Manners and Established Protocol

- Arrive at least five minutes early. Late arrivals irritate some bosses greatly. In any case, it makes you look slack.

- Never smoke or eat in a meeting unless everyone is eating.

- If refreshments are served, choose only items you can eat inconspicuously, and don't talk with your mouth full. Place a coaster under your glass.

- Choose your seating carefully. The seat to the right of the leader is usually reserved for the next in command. Sit close so you can hear. Avoid sitting by people who talk to each other during the meeting. This behavior is rude, and the boss—and everyone else—will notice.

- Never use inappropriate language in a meeting.

- If you have to leave early for any reason, inform the chair prior to the meeting. Leave as quietly as you can. Call the committee chair during the day to determine what you missed.

- Leave your seat and work area free of debris. The committee chair is not your mother and will be irritated if he or she has to clean up after you.

After the Meeting

- Read your notes to ensure you understand them. Transfer highlighted items that you need to do to your personal planner so they become a part of your to-do list. Develop an action plan that enables you to complete your tasks prior to the next meeting.

- Provide an overview of the meeting for your superior either in writing, through e-mail, or through a meeting.

Leading a Meeting

First, always consider this: Do we *need* a meeting? If you are leading or chairing a meeting, here are several questions to ask yourself to assist you in your task:

1. Do I need the group to accomplish the task, or is this something I could handle by phone or e-mail with a few key people?

2. Will a meeting save time by allowing us to accomplish more faster?

3. Do I need the group to meet to allow me to gain their commitment?

QUOTE

A stream of decisions over time, brilliantly executed, accounts for great outcomes.

Jim Collins, *Fortune* magazine author

BIGGEST INTERVIEW BLUNDER

Evelyn wrote on her résumé that she spoke Spanish fluently. The interviewer asked several questions in Spanish to test her proficiency. Evelyn's Spanish was mediocre at best. She did not get the job because the interviewer quickly found that she had not been truthful on her résumé.

4. Do I have everything I need to conduct this meeting properly (time, answers to questions, supplies, handouts)?

5. Do my committee members have the time to meet?

6. Will my committee members have enough time to prepare adequately for the meeting?

Before the Meeting

- Set goals and objectives.

- Plan and disseminate an agenda to your committee members in time for them to study and prepare.

- Secure meeting space and supplies.

- Notify members of the meeting and inform them of when, where, what, how, and why.

- Arrive early for the meeting to be sure everything is ready.

- Conduct the meeting in an organized way. Own the meeting!

- Review decisions and assign tasks to members with deadlines.

- Determine the committee's next meeting time.

- End the meeting on time—preferably no longer than an hour.

Have someone transcribe the minutes of the meeting and disseminate them as soon as possible. Minutes should include a comprehensive action plan that describes an overview of important discussion items, action items, responsible parties, and due dates. Participating and leading impressive meetings gains positive recognition with your bosses and colleagues.

POSITIVE HABITS

@

WORK

When your boss appears to be stressed and overworked, ask if you can help; volunteer to go get lunch; be willing to stay late and help him or her catch up. Come in early and say, "I know you're under the gun to get this done. Is there anyway I can help?"

SOLUTION 72   LEARN HOW TO DELEGATE EFFECTIVELY

If you cannot delegate, you cannot lead! Many leaders have a very difficult time giving up control. You simply cannot hold everything close to yourself, and you must trust others to help get the work done. When you delegate, you simply hand work over to someone else, usually someone who reports to you. The opposite of delegation is dumping, the process of giving bad jobs to someone who has no choice in the matter. Delegation, done properly, should be considered an opportunity to assume more responsibility and to develop leadership skills that will prepare a person for promotion. If you view delegation as job enrichment, the chances are good that the person to whom you are delegating will be motivated to do a good job because people like responsible jobs over which they have control. If you have responsibilities delegated to you, appreciate the opportunity and learn from it. Someone had to have confidence in you to decide to delegate to you.

Many people use this excuse not to delegate: "By the time I could teach someone else to do this, I could have done it twice." That may be true, but the next time you need it done, you already have someone trained to do the task, and a simple review of the steps is all that is required.

People need clear goals. They need their managers to sit down with them periodically and help them understand what is expected of them. Many employees don't have a clue. They may be doing what they think the boss wants, and it may not even be close. If your employees don't know where you want them to go, any road will be fine. You have to lay out the path, especially when you delegate.

Here are the steps to take in delegating work to someone else:

1. First, remember you are still responsible for getting the work done. If it doesn't happen, the responsibility is still yours. Likewise, if it is done poorly, your boss will hold you accountable.

2. When you delegate a task, delegate authority to get it done along with the responsibility. For example, if you ask someone to collect data from all your colleagues, you have to make this known that you, as the boss, have asked this person to collect data.

3. When you delegate a task to someone, begin by telling the person you have a job you need help with and you need him or her to help get this done.

4. Tell the person you trust the employee and believe he or she has the skills to do the job well. Be positive.

5. Let the person know that you look on this as an opportunity for him or her to grow and expand abilities and that these tasks are the kind he or she will need to be able to do to move up the ladder. In other words, you are grooming this employee to be promoted. Be careful, however, not to go overboard on this idea because promotion may not be imminent and may not be your decision.

6. Once you have described the task, work with the employee to set realistic goals and deadlines. Set intermediate steps to achieve deadlines, and checkpoints.

7. It may be necessary to provide training to ensure the person is able to do the job according to your expectations. Discuss the quality you expect.

8. If the employee is not meeting deadlines and not doing quality work, constructive criticism and more direction needs to come as soon as you are aware of the problem.

9. Discuss how the goals can be achieved and the steps to achieving the assignment.

10. Establish a timeline. Set an ending date that allows you time to recover if the assignment is not completed or done to your expectations. Remember, your name is on the line!

11. Establish intermediate checkpoints to be sure the person is on target, especially if this is a big, time-consuming task.

12. Encourage the delegatee to ask questions if concerns arise.

13. Evaluate the project and provide feedback to the person who did the job.

14. When the job is completed, give the person the credit for doing the job. Praise him or her openly in front of other colleagues.

QUOTE

Everybody wants to be *Somebody*.

Patricia G. Moody

SOLUTION 73   LEAD WITH RESPECT INSTEAD OF CONTROL

Most people want to do a good job, and they want to be a part of something big. They want to be in on things and have a voice in what is going on that impacts them. Leaders who know this and practice good leadership techniques usually earn their subordinates' respect. People need to trust their managers and to believe they will be fair to them and stick up for them. They need to believe that workloads are being distributed evenly and fairly and they don't have to carry someone else. They need to believe that the organization will deliver what is being promised and that their hard work and dedication will be rewarded. Employees need to know that what they are doing makes a difference and that someone recognizes the fact that they are contributing.

But employees do not like to work for controlling supervisors who micromanage them. Managers who practice a philosophy of "my way or the highway" rarely get people to follow them unless they are looking right at them all the time. The mark of a good leader is that people do their jobs whether the boss is there or not. They work because they respect the boss and their colleagues and they want to do a good job.

As you assume more leadership responsibility in your position, consider the following leadership tips and rewards that earn respect from employees:

- The opportunity to work for an effective, knowledgeable manager.

- Having a job that allows the person to think for himself or herself and to make decisions.

- Being able to see the end result of their work and to have a good job celebrated and praised.

- Interesting work. Employees can live with doing some tedious, boring jobs if they sometimes get interesting tasks.

- Information that keeps them informed whether the news is good or bad.

- A boss who listens and pays attention to what they are doing.

- Respect from their boss and their colleagues.

- Challenging work that helps them grow and learn.

- Training and education that gives them an opportunity to get better and perhaps get a raise and/or a promotion.

 SOLUTION 74   LEARN TO MANAGE CONFLICTS EARLY AND EFFECTIVELY

QUOTE

If you are patient in one moment of anger, you will save yourself a hundred days of sorrow.

Chinese Proverb

We've all felt it before. It creeps up on us like the flu. We never expected it to happen, but before we know it, in a moment of anger, during a misunderstanding, dealing with a difficult colleague, or in a jealous rage, we lose control, and the door to conflict has been opened. Conflict can happen between anyone, even the best of friends. Learn to look on conflict as a normal part of life. Conflict can actually help you learn and grow if you manage it properly.

The word *conflict* is derived from the Latin *conflictus,* meaning "to strike together with force." There are many causes of conflict. What causes one person to go off the deep end may only slightly irritate another person. Sources of conflict may be deep-seated and can be related to situations that happened previously that were unpleasant and bring back bad memories.

As a result of being forced to work through a situation, good things can actually occur:

- As a result of being forced to work through a situation, the relationship may become more viable.

- A discussion might clear the air.

- People might examine the issues and develop new strategies and solutions that lead to growth and progression.

- Perhaps both people can compromise and get most of what they want.

- Talking together can provide a better understanding of each other.

- Communications in the future might be improved.

- Stress can be reduced if the conflict is resolved.

Billy E. Barnes/PhotoEdit Inc.

Conflict resolution is a way of settling disputes and disagreements in a peaceful manner through discussions that lead to an understanding of the cause of problems. Ideally, conflict resolution resolves the problem without name calling, violence, fights, or long-term hostilities. Although some conflicts are easy to resolve, others may take months. As a leader, you will be called on to resolve conflicts and disputes.

To resolve conflicts, you need to understand some of the causes:

1. Failure to understand and respect an individual's needs, background, culture, sex, age, values, and so on.

2. Killing someone's ideas without giving them an opportunity to sell his or her thoughts.

3. Failure to provide clear jurisdiction, job responsibilities, territory.

4. Change that is constant and unnecessary can create friction.

5. Interpersonal conflicts. Sometimes people just clash, and they simply don't get along. Interpersonal communication is complicated.

6. Harsh criticism and lack of appropriate feedback.

THINK ABOUT IT

How will it help you as a leader if you can mediate disagreements between difficult people even though it may not be the most pleasant task?

When resolving interpersonal conflict and incompatibility, you will need to discover ways that all parties can win at least some measure of satisfaction. This is not easy! If you have to resolve a conflict, these suggestions should be helpful whether it is with two other people or with you and someone else:

- Conflict just won't go away. Putting your head in the sand and ignoring it is the wrong thing to do. The quicker you face it, the better.

- As the mediator, you need to be objective and show no favoritism. Don't attack either person or let them attack each other.

- Define the conflict. Get to the root of the problems, not the symptoms. Is this a people argument or an issue conflict?

- Try to set up an ending scenario in which an agreement can be reached.

- If you are the boss, let them know you expect them to resolve their differences and be able to work together. The workplace cannot be disrupted by constant conflict.

- Ask them to state their opinions in respectful language. Don't let the parties get off track, accuse each other in threatening tones, or use improper language to each other.

- Try to avoid having a winner and a loser. Try for win-win if possible. Both parties will more than likely have to compromise.

- Diffuse anger with humor if possible, but don't make light of the situation.

- Never make a decision without hearing both sides. There are always at least two sides.

- Provide constructive criticism and feedback to both parties. Avoid accusing and finger pointing. State feedback positively.

- Your goal is to reach a mutually desirable end. Suggest some possible solutions that do not favor one over the other.

- You cannot change either party; you can only try to get them to see the other person's side.

- Sometimes you have to get people to make tradeoffs.

- Occasionally, you have to allow for a cooling-off period before people are able to settle down and perhaps reach an agreement.

- Don't expect someone else to read your mind. State your opinions in a modulated, even voice. Avoid yelling and shrill-pitched words. Stay cool!

- Allow both parties to save face. Humiliation is never a good tactic in any circumstance!

- Try to end the meeting in a positive manner.

> **QUOTE**
>
> A leader is needed who can listen to both sides and propose a model for a problem-solving session in which both sides come together and mediate a solution.
>
> Warren Bennis and Joan Goldsmith

Resolving conflicts is never easy. It takes a level-headed person who is able to see all sides of a situation and who can use strategies for diffusing the situation and reaching a mutually satisfying conclusion.

The following assessment on conflict management will help you determine how well you manage conflict at this point in your life.

CONFLICT MANAGEMENT ASSESSMENT

Read the following questions carefully and respond according to the key provided. Take your time and be honest with yourself.

1 = *Never* typical of the way I address conflict

2 = *Sometimes* typical of the way I address conflict

3 = *Often* typical of the way I address conflict

4 = *Almost always* typical of the way I address conflict

1. When someone verbally attacks me, I can let it go and move on.   1 2 3 4

2. I would rather resolve an issue than have to "be right" about it.   1 2 3 4

3. I try to defuse arguments and verbal confrontations at all costs.   1 2 3 4

4. Once I've had a conflict with someone, I can forget it and get along with that person just fine.   1   2   3   4

5. I look at conflicts in my relationships as positive growth opportunities.   1   2   3   4

6. When I'm in a conflict, I will try many ways to resolve it.   1   2   3   4

7. When I'm in a conflict, I try not to attack or abuse the other person verbally.   1   2   3   4

8. When I'm in a conflict, I try never to blame the other person; rather, I look at every side.   1   2   3   4

9. When I'm in a conflict, I try not to avoid the other person.   1   2   3   4

10. When I'm in a conflict, I try to talk through the issue with the other person.   1   2   3   4

11. When I'm in a conflict, I often feel empathy for the other person.   1   2   3   4

12. When I'm in a conflict, I do not try to manipulate the other person.   1   2   3   4

13. When I'm in a conflict, I try never to withhold my love or affection for that person.   1   2   3   4

14. When I'm in a conflict, I try never to attack the person; I concentrate on their actions.   1   2   3   4

15. When I'm in a conflict, I try to never insult the other person.   1   2   3   4

16. I believe in give and take when trying to resolve a conflict.   1   2   3   4

17. I understand *and use* the concept that kindness can solve more conflicts than cruelty.   1   2   3   4

18. I am able to control my defensive attitude when I'm in a conflict.   1   2   3   4

19. I keep my temper in check and do not yell and scream during conflicts.   1   2   3   4

20. I am able to accept "defeat" at the end of a conflict.   1   2   3   4

Total number of 1s _____

Total number of 2s _____

Total number of 3s _____

Total number of 4s _____

If you have more 1s, you do not handle conflict very well and have few tools for conflict management. You have a tendency to anger quickly and lose your temper during the conflict.

If you have more 2s, you have a tendency to want to work through conflict, but you lack the skills to carry this tendency through. You can hold your anger and temper for a while, but eventually it gets the best of you.

If you have more 3s, you have some helpful skills in handling conflict. You tend to work very hard for a peaceful and mutually beneficial outcome for all parties.

If you have more 4s, you are very adept at handling conflict and do well with mediation, negotiation, and anger management. You are very approachable; people turn to you for advice about conflicts and their resolution.

SOLUTION 75   UNDERSTAND, RELATE TO, AND LEAD DIFFICULT PEOPLE

If you are a leader or an employee, you will deal with difficult people. Most likely, we can all be difficult at times and under certain situations, but some people excel at being difficult. They resist everything; they think every rule is made to get them; they can't get along with their colleagues; they won't carry their loads; they don't get paid enough—on and on the list goes.

As you try to motivate all people and to give everyone a fair chance, remember this one important principle: Reinforce the behavior you want. When someone performs well—even if it's for a day—recognize and praise them. Many people have never had praise at work or at home. Having you notice them can be enough to get some people to change their behavior. For example, say, "I really appreciate your staying late to help Jack today. You were a real team player." "I'm very impressed with the way you handle irate customers on the phone. You are making a great difference in helping us resolve problems." Catch people doing something right, and tell them about it!

If they don't do well, don't ignore the behavior. Bring the behavior to their attention as close to the time it is committed as you can. If a person is late, for example, let them know you know as soon as it happens. Certainly, everyone has a problem sooner or later but if this becomes a habit, everyone notices they are getting away with it. If they need training to perform their duties, get it for them. If they are having personal problems and you can provide company counseling, recommend it. Do everything in your power to help the difficult person be successful. First, you try to salvage difficult people, but you need to know that you can't save every one of them. Sometimes you have to perform surgery; in other words, you may have to follow company policy, document unacceptable behavior and work performance, and fire the person.

Difficult people come in all shapes and sizes, all ages and backgrounds. They may have a Ph.D. or they may have a middle school education. They may be loud and obnoxious or sly and underhanded. Regardless of what their tactics and habits may be, they are a disrupting force in the workplace and cannot be ignored.

How to Deal with Difficult Employees and Help Them Improve

- Create a climate in which people feel they are heard.

- Assess the situation. Identify difficult people, study their behavior, and see if you can determine why they are causing trouble.

- If someone tells you about the problem, get the other side before making a decision or an accusation. Remember, some people are very cunning and underhanded, and everyone does not tell the whole story. They usually omit their own wrong behaviors. Don't jump to conclusions. Nothing is ever exactly as it seems at first glance. Never react—act!

- Don't sit around and wish they will change. Chances are difficult people have been acting this way for a long time and getting away with it. Wishing for a different behavior will get you nothing and provide no relief. You *must* confront the person and be very specific about the behavior and your expectations.

- If this is a personal difficult person, ask for a time to discuss the situation. Try to resolve it by calling it to the person's attention, letting the person know you want to get along with him or her and to be a good colleague.

- If it is an employee under your supervision, develop a plan that includes exactly what the offensive behavior is, what needs to be done, and what you expect.

- If a difficult person has been getting away with offensive behaviors for a long time, the other employees will appreciate having a boss who takes care of it, and they will respect you for doing so.

- Confront the employee in a private setting. *Never* embarrass or humiliate anyone in public. They will never forget or forgive you. Tell him or her in a strong, assertive, forceful voice that this behavior has been documented, and it has to stop *now*. Remember to address the criticism to the behavior, not the person.

- Stick to the one behavior you are discussing. Don't load up the employee with all kinds of criticism.

- Let the person explain his or her feelings and reasons. Tell the person how you feel. "I am disappointed you would say that to your colleague."

- Stay in control of the meeting. If the person gets loud and obnoxious, ask him or her to quiet down and to treat you with respect. Don't let the meeting deteriorate into a gripe session. Explain that the person needs to work more and complain less.

- Try to include the employee in designing a solution. Ask the person to stop the offensive behavior.

- If a formal disciplinary action is necessary, state the action in writing, following your company's policies. Inform the person you are summarizing this meeting and placing a copy in the personnel file.

- Monitor the effectiveness of your meeting. Pay close attention to the employee's behavior.

- If you see positive results, praise the employee. Your goal is to salvage the employee, not isolate him or her.

When discussing Generation Y, Nadira Hira made this statement: "This is the most high-maintenance workforce in the history of the world. The good news is they're also the highest performing."

Fortune magazine, May 28, 2007

SOLUTION 76 BUILD A PROFESSIONAL NETWORK

In the book *The Career Fitness Program* (Sukiennik, Bendat, & Raufman, 2001), the term *network* is used as both a noun and a verb. As a noun, a network is defined as a group of individuals who are connected to and cooperate with one another. As a verb, "to network" is to develop contacts and exchange information with other people for the purposes of developing business or expanding one's career opportunities. The verb form is action oriented. To build a professional network, you have to be actively engaged in meeting people. Begin to develop your professional network during your college years and continue through retirement. *Networking* became a buzzword in the 1990s, but it entails more than just being able to name people. It is far more than name dropping. Successful professional networking is the result of a carefully developed plan and consistent daily attention to that plan.

A successful professional network also is a two-way street. Although the motivation for developing a network is somewhat self-centered, it requires giving something back. Just as a mentoring relationship must involve give-and-take, so should networking relationships. People will be more willing to assist you in your networking activities if they realize you are willing to assist them in their goals and objectives as well. "There is a reason sheep, buffalo, prairie dogs, and even lions live in groups: Working together is safer and more effective than working alone" (Finnigan & Karasu, 2006).

Before you embark on a professional networking plan, assess your current relationships to ascertain the extent to which you have already established a network. Many people overlook the reality that they have spent most of their life networking. Make a list of people with whom you currently are in close interaction. These people might be roomate(s), people who live in your residence hall, apartment complex, or housing development, family members, or friends you have made in college. Next list people with whom you have less intimate relationships. These might be classmates, professors, people with whom you commute to campus, people with whom you work. Finally, list people with whom you have less contact but who have some impact on your life, such as college or university administrators and employers.

Having assessed your current relationships, develop a vision for your network. What goals do you have for your professional life? What people will you need to help you meet those goals? Develop a list of goals and objectives for your network.

Now look carefully at your own personal qualities. Do you have a healthy outlook on your chosen career? Do you realize everything that happens in your career begins with you? Do you recognize you can control a great deal of your professional growth by your own actions and decisions? Do you realize the people with whom you choose to associate, both personally and professionally, will greatly impact your future?

Understanding you are in control of your future is empowering. Today the world is full of individuals who blame their circumstances on anyone but themselves. Granted, fate plays a bad joke on people in some instances, but for the most part we have great control over our lives, especially our professional lives. Therefore, you must not merely hope you will become successful. You must deliberately plan and cultivate success, and you can accomplish this in part by choosing your associates.

If you are not already part of a professional association through a student chapter in your college, start researching in your career field. Every career is associated with at least one professional association. Call to find out about student memberships. Even if you are within months of graduation, it is not too late to join. Many associations allow student memberships to continue for up to two years after graduation. Because this membership usually carries a much reduced membership fee, it will save you money in the long run. Start attending local meetings and become active in the association.

As you start meeting new career contacts, keep meticulous records. Create a file for each professional association you belong to. Keep contact information on the association, its leaders, and everyone with whom you have contact. After each meeting or contact with professionals in the association, write a brief note indicating how much you appreciated their help or your conversation with them.

Place notes regarding the important contacts you make in a tickler or file-card system that reminds you periodically to send a note just to keep the relationship fresh. A good way to keep your name in front of people is to keep a record of their specific interests and send them articles that might be of interest to them, along with a brief note. This is a great networking practice.

If you have a mentor, ask him or her to help establish your professional network. Ask to be included in professional association meetings. Offer to work the registration table so you meet people attending the meeting. Take minutes or serve in some capacity that will enable you to meet more people. Be willing to help your mentor in return for assistance given you.

BUILDING YOUR PROFESSIONAL NETWORK

Consider the people you know at school, work, and your community. Who would you include as the top-ten members of your personal network? Think about who can help you the most, and conversely, who can you help and how? Brainstorm all the places you might have network members: class, places of worship, professional organizations, work, friends, neighbors, relatives, and professors.

1. _____
2. _____
3. _____
4. _____
5. _____
6. _____
7. _____
8. _____
9. _____
10. _____

It's never too early to start getting serious about your professional network. Get to know as many people as you can while you are still in college. You never know when one of them may be a key to your personal success.

In her book *Turning Points,* Diane Ducat (1999) suggests seven ways your professional network can assist you. A carefully developed professional network provides:

1. Experts from whom you can seek advice.

2. A guide to assist you in learning new skills or tasks.

3. Access to people who are "in the know" within your professional community.

4. Someone to offer solace during difficult times in your life.

5. Someone to motivate you.

6. Someone who will give you honest, truthful advice.

7. Necessary introductions to enable you to grow professionally.

Understanding the results you wish to obtain from a professional network in the early stages will enable you to cultivate a network that is well rounded and productive. Always be on the lookout for ways in which you can be of service to those in your network. Successful networking must be a two-way relationship. Offer to assist those in your network with activities associated with professional associations, charity events, informal work events, and the like. Although you may not have the knowledge or contacts to bring to a networking relationship, you do have a valuable commodity in the form of your time.

After reading this chapter, you can see why it is important to study leaders and learn what it takes to be a great leader. Leadership is not always easy, but it can be rewarding if your heart is in the right place and you are committed to helping colleagues become outstanding employees.

PUTTING IT ALL TOGETHER

You may be thinking at this moment, "Leadership? I'm just trying to find a job and survive." That may be true, but never doubt that your superiors are continually evaluating you, your talents, your communication skills, your conflict management skills, and your overall decorum.

Effective, fair, honest, and hardworking leaders will always be needed in the workplace. *You* may be the next leader of a team, a department, a division, an entire shift, or even a company. It is never too early to begin thinking about your leadership abilities or about honing your leadership skills.

REFERENCES

Barnes, J. (2005). *John F. Kennedy on Leadership: The Lessons and Legacy of a President.* New York: AMACON/American Management Association.

Berko, R., Welvin, A., & Ray, R. (1997). *Business Communications in a Changing World.* New York: St. Martin's Press.

Collins, J. (2005, June 27). "Jim Collins on Tough Calls." *Fortune,* 89.

DePree, M. (1992). *Leadership Jazz.* DTP Trade Paperbacks.

Ducat, D. (1999). *Turning Points: The Career Guide for the New Century.* Upper Saddle River, NJ: Prentice Hall.

Finnigan, D., & Karasu, M. (2006). *From Learning to Earning.* New York: Sterling.

Sukiennik, D., Bendat, W., & Raufman, L. (2001). *The Career Fitness Program: Exercising your Options* (6th ed.). Upper Saddle River, NJ: Prentice Hall.

Useem, J. (2005, June 27). "Decisions, Decisions." *Fortune.*

Taking Care of Business
Manage Your Personal Finances Wisely

 WHY?

do I need to know about the perils of credit card debt? Why is my credit score so crucial? Why should I understand tax laws? Why do I need to learn about buying a car and a home? Why is planning for retirement important to me at this stage of my life?

"Where does all my money go?" "I thought I would get more money in my paycheck!" "I never realized how much money went to pay taxes, insurance, social security, and investments." "How will I be able to pay all my bills and have any money left over?" "How did I get this deep into credit card debt?" "What is a FICO score, and why is it so important?" These are typical questions and feelings expressed by new college graduates.

Many college students are surprised, if not shocked, when they get their first real job and begin to fully understand how many expenses they have and how much is deducted from their paychecks before they even get their earnings in hand. Such topics as automobile insurance, 401(k)s, credit card debt, student loans, house payments, and many other relevant financial topics suddenly become very important. Other surprises sometimes come when graduates try to buy a car or house or get a cell phone and find that their FICO score is too low to qualify.

Managing your personal finances efficiently cannot be overemphasized regardless of what profession you enter. For the first time, you may become aware of the importance of maintaining a good credit score, the significance of credit card debt, and how difficult it is to repay college loans. You will begin to realize how expensive taxes and other deductions are to your bottom line. The good news is that you can learn to manage your money well and still have many of the things you want and need.

You may say to yourself, "I've suffered and sacrificed for several years now, and I'm ready to have a new car, move to a nicer place, and finally get a new wardrobe because I deserve it all." Most college students can't wait to get a real job and buy everything they could not afford as students. In the frenzy of buying because of pent-up purchasing desires, however, many new graduates dig themselves into a financial hole and find it very difficult to recover.

It is not unusual for college graduates to accumulate significant college loan and credit card debts, as well as car loans and other financial obligations by the time they finish school. Therefore, learning to manage your money and pay off financial obligations are vital components of your overall education. Even if you are one of the fortunate ones who graduate with no debts or financial obligations, financial management will be very important to your future happiness, success, and well-being.

 SOLUTION 77   DEVELOP THE DISCIPLINE TO SAVE AND INVEST RIGHT NOW

You will work hard to earn your salary, and it is easy to let it slip away from you on frivolous items and poor decisions. However, you can decide to manage your money and become financially secure. If you make up your mind to retire comfortably—even to be wealthy—you can do so by reading, researching, questioning, making wise decisions, and disciplining yourself to save and invest on a regular basis.

Discipline is extremely important to your financial success because it is much easier to spend than to save and much more gratifying to purchase clothes, jewelry, and cars now than to struggle to save 10 percent or more of your income. If you can focus on the following statements, however, it might help you develop more discipline: If you save now and invest wisely, the time will come when you can have almost anything you want! You can retire early and travel, you can educate your children, you can live in a nice home and drive luxury cars, and you can spend money without worrying about every dime. Delayed gratification is the first key. Starting early is the second step to developing financial discipline and, ultimately, security.

 QUOTE

I've been rich and I've been poor. Rich is better.

Sophie Tucker

If you earn the typical starting salary and are totally on your own, you will find you can't buy everything you would like. Before you rush out and buy a new car or a new wardrobe, give yourself time to understand your total financial picture to avoid making huge mistakes that are not easily resolved. You've waited this long; be patient a little longer until you have had time to evaluate your income, debts, and other financial obligations. If you have never had to manage a budget, financial management may be more difficult than you imagined. Keep in mind that you have to be able to pay household expenses, taxes, insurance, medical bills—on and on the list goes. And many students *must* begin repaying thousands of dollars in student loans.

> In the space provided, list the things you purchase daily that are wasteful or frivolous.
>
> _____
>
> _____
>
> _____
>
> _____
>
> _____
>
> List three strategies that you can use—starting tomorrow—to avoid this spending behavior.
>
> _____
>
> _____
>
> _____
>
> _____

SOLUTION 78   UNDERSTAND THE FINANCIAL LINGO

Your first step in financial management is to decide to become knowledgeable about finances—your finances. If you have the opportunity, take a personal-finance course or if that is not possible, you can educate yourself in other ways. Continue your financial education by enrolling in financial management seminars and by reading financial publications such as *Fortune, Forbes, Money, Successful Investing,* and others. The more you read and study, the more likely you are to become a successful financial manager and investor and the more comfortable you will become in making financial decisions. It is never too early to start learning about personal finance, and no amount of money is too small to save or invest.

Although it is fine to listen to your friends' advice and the counsel of financial managers, you need to be able to make your own decisions and to plan your own strategies for investments, savings, and debt reduction. You may overhear a supposedly hot tip in the elevator at work, but chances are slim that acting on it will be a wise decision. Successful saving and investing require discipline, reading, research, and planning.

As you begin learning about financial management, you will need to understand the following terms:

POSITIVE HABITS

WORK

Talk to a human resource specialist about any benefits that you do not fully understand before making a decision to enroll or not.

After tax	Money left over after taxes are paid.
Annual percentage rate	The amount charged on your loans and mortgage. Commonly known as APR.
Bond	Bonds allow companies to borrow money from investors. Investors buy bonds and earn interest on their investment until the bond matures.
Collateral	Items of financial value that you put up as security for a loan. For example, you may finance a boat, and you put your car up as collateral. This means you could lose your car if you default on your loan for the boat.
Compound interest	Method of figuring interest that allows you to collect interest on your investment. This interest is added back to your investment, enabling you to collect interest on interest. This principle is what makes it possible to earn large amounts of money on investments over a number of years.
Default	Failure to pay back a loan that you have committed to by a certain specified time.
Discretionary income	Income that you can choose how to spend; it does not have to be spent on recurring budget items such as rent, mortgage, car payments, or student loans.
Dow Jones average	A long-established gauge of the stock market that closely follows thirty large-cap stocks and serves as a benchmark of how the market is performing.
401(k)	A tax-deferred plan that enables you to save for retirement while putting off paying taxes on your earnings. Your company may use this type of program to allow you to save. Many companies have matching programs that allow you to contribute a certain percentage of your salary.
Grace period	During the grace period, you pay no interest charges from the time between the end of your billing cycle and the day your payment is due. There is no grace period on charges that are carried forward from previous months. If you have student loans, you usually have a grace period of six to nine months before you are expected to begin paying back the loans.
Installment loan	An installment loan is made on items such as cars, boats, and large appliances. The loan is paid back in monthly payments with interest for a specified period of time. For example, a car installment loan might be for four years.
IRA	An Individual Retirement Account that allows certain people to invest pretax funds in a tax-sheltered program depending on income. *Tax sheltered* means you don't pay taxes on the money until you withdraw it, usually at retirement.
Money market	Type of investment that pays interest based on the current prime rate.

Mutual fund	A pool of stocks managed by a professional. You invest in a mutual fund by buying shares. These shares entitle you to a portion of the fund's earnings, depending on how many shares you own. Many people prefer to invest in this manner because they don't have to select the stocks, nor do they have to make decisions about when to buy and sell. The professional manager makes these decisions. In the beginning, this is probably the best choice for inexperienced investors.
Nasdaq	Stock exchange made up typically of smaller, newer companies.
NYSE	New York Stock Exchange, which is made up of older, well-established companies.
Penalty	Money charged to your credit card bill if you are late with a payment. Late payments can cause your interest rate to go up in addition to being assessed a penalty.
Portfolio	All the stocks and bonds you own are known as your portfolio.
Pretax	Your earnings before taxes are deducted.
Profit sharing	A program that many companies offer to their employees, enabling them to share in the profits by investing in the company. If your company has such a plan, take advantage of it, although it usually is not required. As a rule, you must be with a company for a specified length of time before you are eligible for profit sharing. Increasingly, companies are using profit sharing as a retirement program, meaning you will have no other company-contributed funds when you retire. If this is the case with your company, profit sharing is immensely important to you.

(continued)

GRADUATE QUOTE

As my studies were coming to a close, there was a tendency to relax and coast to the end. My self-discipline kept me on track, and I learned that this was the key to the finish line. I was nervous to begin my internship but realized that my studies had more than prepared me to succeed. I also learned that using my design skills to create my résumé was an excellent opportunity for me to express my style and creativity. A well-designed résumé always gets attention.

SONIA ARMFIELD, Graduate! The Art Institute of Las Vegas, Las Vegas, NV Bachelor of Arts in Graphic Design

CAREER: Freelance Graphic Artist

Monica Graff/The Image Works

Rollover	This is a process in which you roll money over from one account to another. For example, if you leave one company, you can usually roll over the money you had accumulated to the new company or to another fund. If you want to move money from a traditional 401(k) to a Roth, you must first move it to a rollover IRA and then to a Roth.
Roth IRA	To be a Roth IRA, the account must be designated as such when it is opened. Roth IRAs are set up with after-tax money. The difference between Roth IRAs and traditional IRAs is that qualified distributions are tax free. In other words, a Roth IRA allows you to invest after-tax money, and this account is never taxed again if you satisfy the requirements; the fund continues to grow untaxed. Some financial investors think the Roth IRA is a very good idea for young people who aren't making large salaries because their taxes are less now than they will be later at the time of withdrawal.
SEP-IRA	Tax-deferred plan designed for self-employed people. SEP stands for Simplified Employee Pension. You may do extra work such as designing, consulting, or computer work in addition to your regular job, perhaps using a home office, or your major source of income might be through self-employment. In some cases you can contribute to a SEP-IRA, which gives you an additional way to invest for the future. SEP-IRAs allow you to invest in the same types of investments as other funds.
S&P 500	Index that tracks 500 large-cap stocks and is considered an excellent measure of how well the stock market is performing.
Stock	Share of a company. The more shares you own, the more your investment is valued. Ace Machine Company sold 5 million shares, and you own 200 of those shares. The value of your shares of stock can go up and down.
Stockbroker	Person who earns a living by trading stocks for clients and giving them advice regarding stocks, mutual funds, and bonds.

IF YOU WERE IN CHARGE

SOLVE THE PUZZLE

You are aware that several new employees don't fully grasp all the details about benefits, payroll taxes, and deductions, but they are embarrassed about asking questions.
If you were in charge, what would you do to help these new employees?

SOLUTION 79 IDENTIFY, UNDERSTAND, AND REDUCE YOUR PERSONAL "LATTE FACTOR®"

In his book *The Finish Rich Notebook,* David Bach (2003) states, "How much you earn has no bearing on whether or not you will build wealth." The typical person fits this rule: The more we earn, the more we spend. Today many people spend far more than they make and subject themselves to stress, exorbitant debt, fear, and an ultimate future of poverty.

Bach uses what he terms the Latte Factor® to call our attention to how much money we carelessly throw away when we should be saving and investing for our future. He tells the story of a young woman who said she could not invest because she had no extra money. Yet almost every day, she bought a large latte for $3.50 and a muffin for $1.50. If you add a candy bar here, a drink there, and a special energy shake at the gym, you could easily be spending $10 a day that could be invested.

If you take that $10 per day and invest it faithfully at 10%, in 34 years you will have $1 million. This is the power of compound interest! If you are a relatively young person, you will probably work that many years and more, so you could retire with an extra $1 million in addition to any other savings you might have accumulated.

The point is that most of us have the ability to become rich, but we either lack the knowledge or the discipline to do so. Remember the Latte Factor® as you go through your college career and practice it, along with other sound financial strategies, if you want to become wealthy.

CALCULATE YOUR OWN LATTE FACTOR®

An Exercise in Financial Awareness

Consider what you spend on a "personal specialty item every day." For example, if you buy one large drink each morning at $1.81 and a ham biscuit at $1.25, then your Latte Factor® is $1113.84 per year ($1.81 + $1.25 × 7 days × 52 weeks/year).

My daily "have to have it" is ———————————————————

My personal Latte Factor® is ———————————————————

SOLUTION 80   AVOID CREDIT CARD DEBT

The worst kind of debt is credit card debt! Why? Because it carries the highest interest rates; penalties for late payments are exorbitant; late payments affect your overall credit score; and hidden costs detailed in the fine print can make a shambles of your financial future. It's in a credit card company's best interest to keep you in debt—after all, that's how they make their real money (Daskaloff, 1999).

The credit card trap has ensnared millions of hard-working Americans. So if you find yourself in the credit card debt swamp, you are not alone. It is so easy to use plastic with the idea that you will pay off this debt soon. Usually this doesn't happen, and the debts begin to mount quickly, especially if you continue to use credit cards frequently.

Be aware that credit card companies have implemented new strategies to charge you exorbitant rates. In some cases, the payment window has been shortened. If you are late, you may see your rate go from 12 to 21 percent, and you might notice late charges added to your bill. Pay attention! If you notice something like this on your statement, call the number on the bill and complain and ask that your rate be changed back to 12 percent. If the person you are talking to says he can't make that decision, ask to speak to a supervisor. Tell the supervisor you want to be sure this is not going to impact your credit rating. Also, it is a good idea to call the credit card

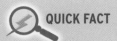

company and ask for a lower rate if you have been a good customer. Ask to speak to a supervisor when you do this because they have the authority to make the decision.

Before accepting a credit card, check the following items carefully:

- ☑ Look for the lowest permanent interest rate.

- ☑ Look for credit cards with low or no annual fees.

- ☑ Don't accept a credit card simply because you can get it or if you are offered a high credit limit. Avoid having too many cards. The more cards you own, the more likely you are to get in credit card trouble. Also, if you own a large number of cards, it impacts your credit rating negatively and increases the possibility of identity theft.

- ☑ Read the terms of the credit card offer as well as the disclosure statement that comes with a card. Check for annual fees, late payment fees, over-the-limit fees, account setup fees, cash advance fees, and the method they use to calculate balances.

- ☑ Be careful of low introductory rates. These special rates can last for short periods of times and then skyrocket once the introductory period is over if you are late with a payment.

Adapted from State of New York Banking Department, 2007.

QUICK CHECK

An Exercise for Credit Card Assessment

Examine each of your credit card bills for last month. Complete the exercise based on your findings.

NAME OF CARD	INTEREST RATE	ANNUAL FEE	LATE FEE ASSESSMENT	MONTHLY PAYMENT	BALANCE
1. _____					
2. _____					
3. _____					

Which card is the worst for you and your financial future? _____

Why? _____

How can you begin reducing or eliminating your credit card debt? List five to seven solid strategies to begin this task. _____

_____

_____

_____

_____

You may have already received several credit cards and accumulated sizable debts. You may have several credit cards on which you have charged the limit. Thinking that you will pay off their credit cards when you get a full-time job, you have been making the minimum payment most of the time. If this is the case, you now have two problems: a substantial debt with a high interest rate and, if you have been late with payments, a poor credit record.

Making late payments only two or three times can reflect negatively on your credit rating. A poor credit record (the FICO score is discussed later) can keep you from being able to buy a house or a car or get a loan. A low FICO score certainly affects your interest rate on any loan. Credit card debt is the worst kind of debt you can have! So the first financial move you need to make is to pay off these debts.

To understand how important getting rid of this kind of debt is, consider this: If you have a debt of $1,000 and make only minimum payments, it will take more than 15 years to pay off this debt at a cost of more than $2,000 in interest, assuming you don't charge anything else. If you are late with payments, you will be penalized heavily and might legally be charged a higher interest rate.

Another point to understand is the bad news about making minimum payments. If you make a minimum payment and the amount goes down the next month, you are paying less in interest so you are not addressing the principal. In some cases, you are not even covering the interest from the previous month. Daskaloff (1999) says, "You should never pay less than the previous month's interest charge." Pay as much as you can because paying more than is owed is the only way to end the credit card trap.

Another pitfall that impacts many people is the ploy used by credit card companies to allow you to skip a month without making a payment because "you are such a good customer." The credit card company is taking care of themselves, not you. The interest keeps accumulating while you enjoy this so-called free month, and you are losing, not saving. While addressing pitfalls, you also need to be very much aware that transferring balances to those cards that promise you a low rate of interest for several months or a year may not be the gift they appear to be. If, for example, you owe money on that card already, the money you send to the credit card company will be applied to the part of the debt you already owe at the higher rate of interest; you could pay for a year and never reduce the debt you transferred if you are not paying attention to the fine print. Remember: Credit card companies don't want you to know the real truth.

If you are charged late fees or other hidden fees, call the company's customer service number that is on your bill and argue to have these fees removed. Many times they will remove them with little or no argument because they realize they are exorbitant.

So what should you do if you have accumulated large credit card debts?

- ☑ Cut up all your credit cards except one that requires you to pay the balance every month.

- ☑ Keep the card that carries your lowest interest rate.

- ☑ Make a decision to use this card only in case of dire emergencies.

- ☑ Always pay more than the required monthly payment.

- ☑ Never charge things you can't afford to pay for at the end of the month.

- ☑ Pay off your balances each month and avoid instant gratification spending that makes you exceed your financial limits.

If you already have a job and your company has a credit union, try to borrow the money at a much lower rate of interest to cover all your credit card debts. Instead of making several small payments at 21 percent interest, you can consolidate your debts and make one large payment at an interest rate about half the one you are paying on credit cards. This will relieve some of your stress and help you reduce your debt much faster.

 When you get out of debt, promise yourself that this will never happen to you again, and design a budget to make sure you are in control of your spending.

Getting this credit card business straight is so important to your future. If you face reality and learn to avoid this quicksand trap, you will have a much better chance of accumulating wealth. We highly recommend that you take time to read some of the references listed at the end of this chapter and take steps to reduce credit card debt immediately. Start today!

SOLUTION 81 RUN FROM AUTO TITLE LOANS, PAYDAY LOANS, AND CHECK-CASHING CENTERS

> **QUOTE**
>
> He that is of the opinion money will do everything may well be suspected of doing everything for money.
>
> Benjamin Franklin

Don't even think about an auto title, a payday loan, or a check-cashing service! If there is anything worse than credit card debt, it's these services. This is highway robbery but is legal in many states. To the credit of some state legislatures, they have made these loans and services illegal or have put severe constraints on them.

First, let's look at automobile title loans. What happens in the case of an automobile title loan is that you literally use your car title to secure a high interest loan, usually no longer than 30 days. This means that if you as the borrower cannot repay the loan within 30 days, the lender can take your car and sell it to get the loan money back. Many title lenders will not make the loan if you owe anything on your car.

Auto title lenders often target people with bad credit, low-income individuals, members of the military, and elderly people—in other words, people who are desperate to borrow money. They make money from high interest loans and by selling cars they have repossessed from customers who cannot repay their loans. If you are desperate for cash, an auto loan may seem like a good idea, but the solution is very short term and the effects can be devastating (South Carolina Appleseed Legal Justice Center, 2004).

If the borrower can't pay the loan on the due date, many lenders will roll it over, which compounds the problem because now the high rate of interest is continuing to build. The paperwork may show that you borrowed the money at 25 percent (which is exorbitant), but this rate over a year is actually 300 percent.

To show the deal is a high-interest loan, the lender must have this notice on the paperwork in some states:

This is a high-interest loan. You should go to another source if you have the ability to borrow at a lower rate of interest. You are placing your vehicle at risk if you default on this loan.

Unless you are willing to pay the highest kind of interest rates and to risk losing your car, avoid these loans at all costs.

Payday loans are more bad news! These loans are extremely expensive cash advances that must be repaid in full on the borrower's next payday to keep the personal check required to secure the loan from bouncing. The average Payday loans cost 470 percent in annual interest. Cash-strapped consumers run the risk of becoming trapped in repeat borrowing owing to triple-digit interest rates, unaffordable repayment terms, and coercive collection tactics made possible by check holding. In one state almost 60 percent of the loans made are either same-day renewals or new loans taken out immediately after paying off the prior loan. Payday lenders use coercive tactics to collect their money in many cases. They might threaten negative credit ratings on specialized databases and credit reports. Consumers can lose their bank accounts if they have a record of bouncing checks used to get Payday loans. Some lenders threaten criminal charges or court martial if military personnel fail to cover their loans (PayDay Loan Consumer Information, 2007).

Just as bad—if not worse—are Internet payday lending businesses. By borrowing money on the Internet, you run the risk of security and fraud. In some cases, loans are directly deposited into the borrower's bank account and electronically withdrawn the next payday. Many of these loans are structured to renew automatically every payday, with the exorbitant finance charge electronically withdrawn from the borrower's bank account. Be aware that these loans are often offered with a clever rebate scheme to circumvent states' laws regarding this type loan (PayDay Loan Consumer Information, 2007).

Check-cashing services are also bad news. They charge you a high fee to "hold a check" until payday comes around. We know that may times your money may not last until the end of the week or month, but getting involved in this vicious cycle only means losing more of your hard-earned, much-needed money. Check-cashing services charge astronomical fees.

Payday loan and check-cashing centers may charge as much as $16.50 or more to hold a check for $100 for *one* week. Therefore, after one week, the amount owed would be $116.50.

That doesn't sound too bad, but if something happened and you had to have them hold the check for a while (that is to say that you had to wait a month or two to pay them back), this really becomes a "loan" and the $16.50 actually represents an annual percentage rate (APR) of *430%*! The highest APR for even the most expensive credit cards averages only 21 to 30 percent. Again, we use the word *astronomical*.

If you need extra cash until payday, try, at all costs, to borrow it from a friend or family member. In the long run, this will cost you much less. Payday loans, auto title loans, and check-cashing services are highly controversial companies that continue to face many legal battles as well as negative perception by the public. The reason they operate is a simple fact: They are highly lucrative businesses that make money by preying on people who are desperate and can't get money anywhere else. If at all possible, avoid these services.

41% of workers often live paycheck to paycheck. More than half said they would need $500 more per paycheck to live comfortably.

CareerBuilder.com, 2007

SOLUTION 82 KNOW WHAT AFFECTS YOUR CREDIT SCORE

You need to know the score—the FICO score! Financial guru Suze Orman (2007) says, "Just about every financial move you will make for the rest of your life will be somehow linked to your FICO score. Not knowing how your score is calculated, how it is used, and how you can improve it will keep you broke long past your young-and-fabulous days. The way the business world sees it, your FICO score is a great tool to

David Young-Wolff/PhotoEdit Inc.

size up how good you will be at handling a new loan or a credit card, or whether you're a solid citizen to rent an apartment to." If you have a high FICO score, you will get better interest rates. Your FICO score can impact everything from your ability to finance a house to being able to get reasonable automobile insurance premiums.

Your FICO score is connected to about everything you will deal with in the financial world and is extremely important to your future. So what is the FICO score? FICO is the acronym for the Fair Isaac Corporation, creator of the score.

"A credit score, sometimes referred to as a FICO score, is a three-digit number based on a borrower's bill-paying history and is an important component of your overall financial profile. Although most scores fall in the 600 or 700 range, "the median score is 725. If your score falls below 660, its time for concern" (AuWertin, 2008). Your credit score is calculated by using mathematical models that analyze your creditworthiness and compare your history to thousands of other consumers to arrive at a credit score. The three major credit scoring companies in America are TransUnion, Equifax, and Experian.

According to Wikipedia (2007), a credit score is a numerical expression, based on a statistical analysis of a person's credit files, to represent the creditworthiness of that person, which is the likelihood that the person will pay his or her debts. A credit score is primarily based on credit report information, typically sources from credit bureaus/credit reference agencies. Your credit score will be based on several criteria, including how much debt you have, how many credit cards you have; how many credit cards you have with balances, how long you have had outstanding debt, what is your debt-to-income ratio, how many late payments you have made, how much credit you have available, and what is your overall history of paying your debts on time. One of the most important factors in your credit score is how much available credit you have (Consumers Union, 2007).

Your credit score will be checked when you try to purchase a car or a house and, increasingly, for a variety of other reasons. So it is important, first of all, that you know your score, and secondly, that you take steps to build an acceptable credit score. If your credit score falls in the low 600s, you might be considered for a loan with a higher rate of interest, sometimes known as a subprime loan, if you are considered at all. You will be required to pay a higher rate of interest, assuming you are approved for a loan, because you would be considered a higher risk. If you are turned down for a loan, you are entitled to get a free copy of your credit report, provided you ask for it within six months of being rejected (State of New York Banking Department, 2007).

If you have already done things that cause you to have a low credit score, you can rectify that by beginning now to change your habits. We highly recommend that you request a copy of your credit report to determine your FICO score, to see if you may have a problem and to determine the concerns. In fact, we recommend that you get a credit report from all three of the credit bureaus listed earlier. Different companies report to different agencies, and you need to get the entire big picture.

Getting the best FICO score possible is very important to your bottom line and can be the difference in paying $100 more a month on your car payment or getting a 6 percent mortgage rather than a 7 1/2 percent loan. Here is the contact information for the companies mentioned earlier where you can obtain a credit report.

Equifax
P.O. Box 740241
Atlanta, GA 30374-0241
800-685-1111
http://www.equifax.com

Experian
P.O. Box 2002
Allen, Texas 75013
888-322-5583
http://www.experian.com

Transunion
P.O. Box 1000
Chester, PA 19022
800-888-4213
http://www.transunion.com

SOURCE: Consumers Union, 2007.

Write a letter or go online to one of the companies listed and request a credit rating. If you find erroneous information or reports that damage your credit, call the reporting company to see what you can do about it. You can receive one free credit report per year by logging onto **www.annualcreditreport.com.**
    Summarize the findings:

_____

_____

_____

_____

_____

_____

After obtaining a copy of your credit report, determine how you can improve your FICO score or keep it high.

_____

_____

_____

_____

_____

According to Orman (2007), there are several key ways to improve your FICO score:

  Pay your bills on time (to show you are responsible).

  Manage your debt-to-credit-limit ratio (the sum of what you owe compared with what banks think you can afford to borrow).

☑ Protect your credit card history. (Rather than canceling credit cards where you have a good history of paying, just destroy the cards and stop using them; you have not destroyed the history.)

☑ Create the right credit mix. (Lenders want to see a reasonable mix of credit cards, retail cards, and installment loans. This does not mean you should accept every credit card offered to you!)

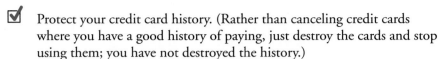

SOLUTION 83   REPAY YOUR STUDENT LOANS ON TIME

The high cost of college makes tuition out of reach for many families. For many students, if not most, the only way they can attend college is via student loans. If this is the only way you can go to college, borrow the money, but borrow no more than you absolutely must. According to Watson (2002), the median student loan debt is at record levels because of rising tuition costs—$17,000 versus $2,000 when baby boomers were in their 20s. If you are one of the many students who have borrowed money to go to college, you may be concerned about your ability to repay the loans. Before you graduate or transfer, find out everything you need to know about your loan, and determine your options. Some of the most pertinent points about student loans are as follows:

☑ You have a legal obligation to repay your student loans with interest.

☑ Bankruptcy will not eliminate your obligation to repay any student loans.

☑ Get the addresses and phone numbers of lenders before you leave college. Certain circumstances, such as graduate school, allow you to defer your payments. A deferment allows you to postpone your payments, but you will still have to pay these loans with interest.

☑ Learn all the options you have for repaying your loans. Based on your salary, expenses, and budget, decide which one is best for you.

☑ If for some reason you cannot make your payment, let the lender know immediately. This is not something that will go away. You do not want to default on your loan, which will cause you to have a bad credit rating, prohibit you from holding a government job, and prevent you from getting a tax refund while the loan is repaid.

DOs

☑ Get the lender's policies in writing and read them carefully.

☑ Consolidate your loans if possible, and go with the lender that offers you the most benefits other than the ones required by law.

☑ Learn what kind of protection you have if you are late with a payment.

☑ Use the FFELP Lender Authentication Search Tool to determine if a company is an authorized federal lender.

☑ If possible, consolidate your loans while you are in your grace period (six months after you graduate) because the interest rate will be lower.

☑ Complete your consolidation application and send it in before June 30 if possible because interest rates are most likely to increase on July 1.

DON'Ts

☑ Don't consolidate with anyone but a bona fide lender, not a marketing company.

☑ Do not use the U.S. Department of Education as a lender with which to consolidate your loans because they offer a very poor benefit package.

☑ Avoid consolidating with marketing companies, and be aware that many will use terms that sound like government terminology.

☑ Be careful about being hooked by a lender promising a cash rebate. The odds are favorable that a reduced rate will save you much more money than a rebate.

☑ Avoid companies that offer free gifts to get your consolidation package. This practice is prohibited by federal law. If a company is using this tactic, they are a marketing company and not a bona fide lender.

☑ If a lender does not state all the terms of benefits in writing, do not sign up with them.

SOLUTION 84 PROTECT YOURSELF FROM IDENTITY THEFT

The FBI calls identity theft one of the fastest growing crimes in the United States and reports that 500,000 to 700,000 Americans are victims each year. Identity theft is a federal crime that happens when someone assumes another person's identity. This occurs when someone's name, social security number, or any account number is used for unlawful activities (Federal Reserve Bank of Boston, 2007).

Identify theft is divided into four major categories: financial identity theft (using another's name and social security number to obtain goods and services); criminal identity theft (posing as another person to avoid criminal prosecution); Identity cloning (using another person's information to assume his or her identity in daily life); and business/commercial identity theft (using another's business name to obtain credit) (Wikipedia, 2007).

Identity thieves frequently open new accounts in someone else's name. They often apply for new credit cards using another person's information, make charges, and leave the bills unpaid. It is also common for them to set up telephone or utility services in someone's name and not pay for it. Some victims have found that identity thieves applied for loans, apartments, and mortgages using their information. They may also access your existing accounts and take money from your bank accounts, make charges on your credit cards, and use your checks to make down payments on cars, furniture, and houses.

Your identity is arguably your most valuable possession. A clean legal record and credit history opens the door for work, mortgage loans, and other day-to-day privileges that most people take for granted. Stains on those records can take years to erase, but most people pay more attention to securing their car than protecting personal data. That's why identity theft last year struck 9.9 million Americans, costing businesses and individuals $53 billion, according to a survey commissioned by the Federal Trade Commission.

David McGuire, *Washington Post*

One of the most recent popular forms of identity theft is for thieves to use your information to apply for tax refunds. They also apply for government benefits including unemployment insurance (Federal Reserve Bank of Boston, 2007).

Thieves have many ways of accessing your information, including your mailbox, trash, and directly from postal workers. Home computers can be affected with viruses that transmit your data to thieves. Group identity has become a major problem for consumers. This happens when a thief gains access to a place that keeps records for many people. Targets can be car dealerships, schools, hospitals, stores, fitness centers, and even credit bureaus. Thieves may use the information themselves or sell it to other criminals (Federal Reserve Bank of Boston, 2007). They may even copy your personal information from courthouse records.

As you can tell, identity theft is a very serious problem for the victims. Here are some ways to prevent identity theft:

- ☑ Carry only the credit cards and identification information you need at any given time.

- ☑ Never carry your social security card or birth certificate in your wallet or purse.

- ☑ Sign all new credit cards immediately and write across the back of the card in permanent ink, "Check ID."

- ☑ Do not make Internet purchases from sites that are not secured (check for a padlock icon to ensure safety).

- ☑ Do not write your pin number, social security number, or password on any information that can be stolen or that you are discarding.

- ☑ Try to memorize your passwords instead of recording them on paper or in the computer. Never give anyone access to your passwords no matter how much you trust them.

- ☑ Get someone you trust to check your mail in your absence.

- ☑ Destroy all copies of documents you don't need.

- ☑ Be aware of "shoulder surfers." Shield your numbers when using an ATM.

- ☑ Avoid providing your social security number to any organization until you have verified their legitimacy.

- ☑ Check your credit card file periodically by requesting a copy of your report.

- ☑ If you lose your driver's license, notify the state office of the Department of Motor Vehicles, and place a fraud alert on your license number.

- ☑ Request a new driver's license with a new number.

- ☑ Until you know people very well, such as new roommates, colleagues, and neighbors, protect your personal data.

- ☑ Shred all mail that has your name and address on it.

Adapted from "Identity Theft and Fraud," 2005.

SOLUTION 85 RESEARCH YOUR OPTIONS WHEN BUYING A CAR

Most of us enjoy a new car, and many love fancy expensive cars. Unfortunately, this is not one of the best places to spend your money. However, unless you live in a big city with good transportation services, a car is a necessity for getting back and forth to work and for recreational purposes. Buying a car can be a very confusing and frustrating experience for anyone, especially someone who knows very little about the lingo and sales techniques used by many auto salespeople.

Tom McCarthy/PhotoEdit Inc.

First, make up your mind that you aren't going to fall in love with a car and buy it until you have done your homework. If you know very little about buying a car, comparing one brand to another, finance charges, and so on, take someone with you who does.

Here's a smart money tip: Never buy a new car! Buying a new car is a very poor use of your money. As soon as you drive the new car off the dealership lot, the value plummets. Rather than buy a new car, search for a very good used car that is one to three years old. You can usually purchase an extended warranty on a preowned car. You will get a car that most likely looks like the current model, and you will save lots of money. Not only will the price be less, so will the taxes, insurance, and payments. Buying a house is much more important than buying a new car. If you buy a very expensive car, this decision may impact your credit score to the extent that you cannot afford a mortgage on a house.

Buying a car is a major purchase that requires a lot of thought before making the decision. Don't be pushed by an overzealous car salesperson into buying a car that is not right for you. Unfortunately, there are some unscrupulous people who will sell you a lemon and never lost a minute's sleep over it. Thus you have to search until you find a reputable dealer you can trust. The Internet provides considerable information that will help you as you begin to consider your purchase of a car.

Here are some major points to consider when buying a car:

  Do your homework! This is too important a decision to take lightly.

  Should you buy or lease? A deal that allows you to lease a new car for $160 a month may sound good, but what is the residual fee at the end? What happens if you go over the allowed 12,000 miles? Can you live within a prescribed number of miles? If you lease, you will typically have a lower down payment and a lower monthly payment, and you can drive a newer car every two to three years. *But* you don't own the car and you don't accumulate equity. Leasing is usually more expensive in the long run. Wear and tear on the car can change the residual value (what the car is worth at the end of your lease) and cost you more money when it is time to turn the car into the dealership. Study *Consumer Reports* or automotive magazines that compare the different brands and models.

> QUOTE
>
> The more confused you are, the better chance the auto salesperson has at making a fat profit off of you. Auto dealers are kings of creating confusion.
>
> Suze Orman, Author and TV Host

☑ Depending on your family needs and your budget, should you buy a sport utility vehicle, a sedan, a subcompact, or a compact?

☑ What is the EPA (Environmental Protection Agency) rating? This is a good indicator of how much gas your car will use. Gas usage is a major consideration today, especially if you have a long commute.

☑ How much are the insurance and taxes? If you buy a hot car, your insurance premiums will cost you more!

☑ For what kind of interest rate do you qualify?

☑ Should you consider a hybrid?

☑ How well does each model retain its value?

☑ What kind of service charges can you expect? Some are very high, so find out.

☑ If you are buying a used car, have your mechanic inspect it carefully.

☑ Set your price before you start looking.

☑ Negotiate! Don't ever take the first price offered to you.

☑ Credit union financing is often better than many others.

☑ If you don't understand the terminology and contract, keep asking questions. Take someone with you who does understand if you need to. Don't sign anything until you understand everything!

Adapted from "Ten Tips for Buying a Car," 2007.

Based on the points just discussed, describe the car you think you should consider buying. Include price, costs of insurance, taxes, description, model, and year.

_____

_____

_____

_____

_____

_____

_____

SOLUTION 86   UNDERSTAND TAX LAWS

Many new college graduates are not prepared for the amount of taxes deducted from their paychecks. Unless you have worked and paid taxes, you may be in for a big surprise. You will have deductions made for federal and state taxes, FICA (Federal Insurance Contributions Act; social security and Medicare taxes), as well as other deductions for benefits to which you must contribute.

When you begin a new job, you will be asked to complete paperwork that details the number of deductions, or the number of individuals you are supporting, that you want to claim. If you have only yourself, you might want to claim none. This will help ensure that enough taxes are deducted from your paycheck so you don't owe money on April 15; instead, you might be fortunate enough to get a refund. The more deductions you take, the more money flows to you with each paycheck.

Most likely you will want to get a qualified, certified public accountant (CPA) to complete your tax forms, although you may be able to do this yourself. Set up a file at the beginning of each fiscal year and keep your documentation for expenses. Have file folders for medical bills, insurance, taxes (cars and house), charity, home office (if you declare one), and any other areas that you might need for taxes. If you keep your papers filed and organized all year, it will take you much less time to get your tax information together. You will want to have everything done that you can because CPAs typically charge by the hour.

There are many ways to save money if you understand the tax laws. Take time to study and understand the basics of tax accounting.

SOLUTION 87 TAKE TIME TO PLAN A BUDGET AND STICK TO IT

Most people do not budget. They have a reasonable idea of what they can spend and how much they require to make the house payment, car payment, food, utilities, and the like, but it is just a guess. They have never sat down and decided to live within their income and to use their money wisely. Nor have they really determined exactly where their money is being spent. As a result, they are often strapped for money, late with payments, and have little or no savings and investments. In this section, we help you create a spending/savings budget.

Many people do not use their discretionary income wisely. This is the difference in being financially secure and being broke. The information in this chapter is intended to help you choose how you spend your money and to instill in you the belief that money management is an everyday process. If you are going to be financially secure, you cannot afford to live day to day and hand to mouth with no plan for accumulating wealth.

As a new graduate, you will be wise to establish a budget and live within your means because you are not likely to have a great deal of disposable income for a while. Some of your expenses will vary, depending on whether you have a roommate or a spouse or whether you live alone.

In this scenario, we will assume you live alone, you make $30,000 a year, and you are contributing 10 percent to your company's tax-deferred profit-sharing program so you will be taxed on only $27,000. Let's also assume you have company benefits that provide you full coverage for your personal health insurance and 1.5 times your salary in life insurance so you don't have to spend any of your salary on those items. This type benefit is becoming less and less available in many companies and is one of the things you should consider when accepting a job. When you consider a new job, find out about benefits. Good benefits may offset a lower salary and actually be a better deal for you.

For purposes of this exercise, let's assume you are in the 28 percent federal income tax bracket and you live in a state that has a 7 percent state income tax. In addition, FICA taxes (social security and Medicare) will be deducted before you

THINK ABOUT IT

How will making and following a budget impact your ability to buy a house?

> The only way not to think about money is to have a great deal of it.
>
> Edith Wharton

receive your take-home pay. These will amount to about 7.65 percent of your salary (this figure is subject to change).

When you deduct your federal taxes of $7,560 plus your state income taxes of $1,890 plus your FICA taxes of $2,065, your annual take-home pay is now $15,485, assuming you have no more deductions taken from your salary. Dividing this amount by 12 months, you have $1,290 a month to budget. This exercise helps you understand why you can't afford a $50,000 car, for example, and why you should be very careful to avoid credit card debts.

Because costs vary greatly from one part of the country to another, estimating expenses is difficult, but for purposes of this exercise, assume the following monthly expenses:

- ☑ Housing—$500
- ☑ Car payment—$250
- ☑ Car insurance (this varies widely from state to state, especially if you have traffic violations)—$50
- ☑ Gas—$100
- ☑ Utilities (heat, electricity, water)—$80
- ☑ Student loans—$175

You have only about $310 left for food, clothes, entertainment, telephone, cable TV, and so on. Right away it becomes apparent that having someone with whom to share expenses might be an advantage. Complete the other items of this budget with amounts you would allocate if this were your personal situation:

- ☑ Food—
- ☑ Internet provider—
- ☑ Home telephone—
- ☑ Cell phone—
- ☑ Entertainment—
- ☑ Clothes—
- ☑ Credit cards—
- ☑ Miscellaneous (shampoo, deodorant, magazines, etc.)—

Savings (you probably think you won't have any need for this, but you really do need to have money in a savings account for emergencies; financial experts use a figure of three months' salary).

This exercise can be painful, but is a valuable lesson to learn as early as possible. The good news is that you can increase your income and lessen the pressure on your budget, provided you realize that no matter how much money you make, it is easy to spend it unwisely on frivolous items that are soon forgotten.

Although you are urged to make wise financial decisions, you are encouraged to enjoy life and not be so thrifty that you don't allow yourself to spend money on things and items that bring you pleasure and enjoyment. If you learn early to budget and save, in time you should gain the ability to spend more freely on enjoyment and entertainment items.

SOLUTION 88   PLAN TODAY FOR TOMORROW'S RETIREMENT (REALLY! IT'S NEVER TOO EARLY!)

While preparing to graduate from college and immediately after you graduate, you will be faced with many decisions. If you have not done so already, you will have to make a decision about which job to accept, what area to live in, what kind of home you can afford, whether you should keep a car you own now or purchase a new one, whether to get married now or in the near future, whether to have a roommate or to live alone—the list goes on and on.

Most college graduates deal with this list of decisions, and most make reasonable decisions. This list, however, does not include one of the most important priorities: financial management. Most people fail to give the same kind of attention to financial matters that they do to other major areas of their lives. The average person spends more time deciding which programs to watch on TV than on which financial choices to make. Young college graduates often assume they do not have enough money to manage and these decisions will be important only when they are much older. Nothing could be further from the truth. The first day you go to work is the day you should start planning for retirement and financial security!

Before you accept a job, find out what options you have for retirement. Does the company offer a guaranteed pension—not many companies do anymore. Do they offer a 401(k), do they offer any matching funds based on the amount you are saving yourself? Planning for retirement is one of your most important decisions. Start immediately when you get that first permanent job. This decision is much too important to ignore or put off until later!

QUOTE

Money *does* grow on trees—the trees of patience.

Proverb

BIGGEST INTERVIEW BLUNDER

John interviewed with ACE Design Company and accepted the job without asking anything about the retirement plan. Later he learned that ACE offered neither a guaranteed retirement plan nor a 401(k). The Design It Right Company, in contrast, offered a guaranteed pension and a 401(k). Too late John realized that he turned down a better job even though the salary is higher at the job he accepted.

PUTTING IT ALL TOGETHER

Many of the major points mentioned throughout this book will have a major impact on your life and your lifestyle, but none will be more important than making wise financial management decisions. These decisions include daily budgeting, credit card choices, retirement options, savings programs, and benefit packages. Making the right financial decisions requires taking time to educate yourself about the options. You cannot afford not to prepare yourself to make wise financial decisions!

REFERENCES

AuWerten, Stephanie. "Keeping Score." February 28, 2008. Retrieved April 20, 2008, from http://www.smartmoney.com/nowwhat/index.cfm?story=20020876.

Bach, D. (2003). *The Finish Rich Notebook: Creating a Personalized Plan for a Richer Future.* New York: Broadway Books.

Daskaloff, A. (1999). *Credit Card Debt: Reduce Your Financial Burdens in Three Easy Steps.* New York: Avon.

Federal Reserve Bank of Boston. (2007). "Identity Theft."

"Identity Theft and Fraud." (2005). *Money Matters* 101: 9.

Orman, S. (2007). *The Money Book for the Young, Fabulous, and Broke.* New York: Riverhead Books.

PayDay Loan Consumer Information. Retrieved August 5, 2007, from http://www.paydayloaninfo.org/facts.cfm.

South Carolina Appleseed Legal Justice Center. (2004). "Auto Title Loans and the Law." *The Greentree Gazette*, Federal Student Loan Consolidation Program, May 2007.

Ten Tips for Buying a Car. Retrieved April 2007, from http://www.howtojoinacu.org/services.ten_tips.cfm.

Watson, N. "Generation X—Generation Wrecked." Fortune.com. November 4, 2002.

Wikipedia. "Credit Score." Retrieved April 2007, from http://en.wikipedia.or/wik/Credit_score.

Wikipedia. "Identity Theft." Retrieved April 2007, from http://en.wikipedia.or/wik/Identify_theft.

Enriching Your Personal Life

Maximizing Your Potential in All Aspects of Your Life

 WHY?

do I need to love, value, and respect myself? Why is finding meaning in my personal life relevant to my overall development? Why do I need to understand how to manage stress and time? Why are friends and family so important to my overall happiness and success?

D o you sometimes find yourself wondering, "What's it all about? What is life really supposed to be?" Many people spend their entire lives rushing from one thing to another, grabbing at the next "great thing," seeking more and more, but never quite feeling OK or seeing the beauty around them or realizing they may indeed "have it all" right now.

Many people live their lives with one of these mantras: "I'll be happy when I make more money." "I'll be happy when my children are grown, and I can focus on myself more." "I'll be happy when I get this house or this car." They are so focused on the "next great thing" that they fail to see this great day for what it really could be.

One Thursday afternoon, an older professor visited the office of a young woman who was very driven. As he watched her scurry around her office, rushing to get things done, and almost being rude to him because she had no time, he offered her some advice. He said to her, "Young lady, you can work here at this university for forty years and the day you decide to leave, they will find someone else to take your place, and in a few days, they will never know you were here. This university will drink your blood if you let it. The important thing for you to ask yourself is, *Did I enjoy Thursday?*"

Perhaps this chapter is about just that: Did you do something today that made it worth exchanging a day of your life? Did you do something today with friends and family who really matter? Or did you fritter the day away with stress and time crunches on things that have no lasting value in your life?

One of the main reasons people have a hard time finding meaning in their lives is they don't discover their purpose in life. Sometimes people who have spent their entire lives in high-pressure corporate jobs find that teaching brings them the greatest satisfaction they have ever experienced. Others may find meaning in moving to the country or the mountains or the beach and, for the first time, paying attention to nature and their surroundings. Some may find their purpose in some charitable organization that allows them to give to others.

To maximize your potential in all aspects of your life, you must first know and value yourself. You have to identify and come to grips with your signature talents, core values, basic assumptions and beliefs, guiding principles, and great passions. If you are still struggling with this—and many people spend years struggling—review Chapter 1 of this book and begin to read other books on self-esteem, human potential, and maximizing your talents.

One of the important parts of maximizing your potential is to find a life's work that makes you happy, fills you up, and leaves you wanting to get up and go back to work the next day. Many people work all their lives in jobs they hate. They tolerate whatever they have to endure for a paycheck and watch their lives slowly slip by.

Many people live their lives in quiet desperation, afraid of making a mistake, afraid of taking a chance, afraid of pursuing their dreams. "Afraid" and "fear" are important words that act like twin goblins in our lives. If you can get beyond your fears—and everybody has them—you can truly realize your potential to become who you were meant to be.

In this chapter, we offer suggestions for living your life to the fullest. We encourage you to build a foundation based on who you are, what you believe in, and what you are meant to do. We share strategies for leaving behind your fears and maximizing your potential.

> **QUOTE**
>
> Few people know what it is to live without fear—but beyond fear lies joy, as the meaning and purpose of existence become transparent.
>
> David R. Hawkins, M.D., Ph.D.

SOLUTION 89   LOVE AND VALUE YOURSELF

No lesson in this book—or any book, for that matter—is more important to your overall success and happiness than this principle: **Love yourself, believe in yourself, value yourself, and nurture yourself.**

No matter who you are or how successful you have been or will become, there will be days when you really don't like yourself. Most of us suffer at times from unhealthy self-esteem, stressful problems, and low self-worth. We put unrealistic demands on ourselves and carry around negative events that happened to us in the past. You have to learn to deal with those things and move on toward a more positive outlook.

Before we discuss enriching your personal life and the journey you are on, think about the end of your life. This may seem strange, but we want you to think about the end of your life and what you hope to have accomplished when that day comes.

Gerard Brown @ Dorling Kindersley

The Obituary: An Exercise in Thinking Ahead

The end of your life—not a pleasant thought, is it? You are graduating from college, and we are talking about your death. There is method to our madness, however. If you have ever read an obituary in the newspaper, you know the typical content: date of birth, age, family members, career, religious affiliation, community involvement, and achievements. If you think about it, an obituary is really nothing more than a brief synopsis of a person's life. "So," you say, "what does this have to do with my life? I'm not dead yet." True. But one day you will be, and the overriding question is this: What do you want your obituary to say? How will the words and pages of your life read?

If you don't think about what you really want to accomplish and who you want to become, you face the possibility of living your entire life one day at a time and never getting anywhere. Many people race around in circles chasing vague and hopeless dreams. A dream is only good if it becomes a goal with steps for achieving that goal.

Before you read any further, pretend for a moment you have lived to age 90. Treat your obituary as a goal statement, and jot down some of the things you would like to have people read about you at the end of your life.

That was hard, and maybe a little sad, wasn't it? The end of your life is not pleasant to think about, regardless of your current age. The reason we ask you to do this exercise is that, like any goal, if you don't know what you are striving toward, how will you ever get there? If you don't know what you want the end of your life to look like, how will you ever achieve the words and statements you would like to have said or written about you at the end of it? This is the purpose of beginning with the end in mind.

At times you will beat yourself up and wonder how you could have done something so stupid. But these feelings shouldn't be regular occurrences. For the most part, you should be able to look in the mirror and like and respect who you

> QUOTE
>
> The worst loneliness is not to be comfortable with yourself.
>
> Mark Twain

are and who you are becoming and feel good about yourself. You cannot achieve true happiness until you accept yourself and turn loose all the negatives and the people who drag you down. All these things add up to respect for yourself.

Your brain is a powerful computer, far more powerful than any mainframe in existence. What you tell yourself about yourself is fed into your brain, and your body carries out those thoughts. Therefore, it is very important to feed good thoughts about yourself to your brain.

You need to learn to celebrate this wonderful human being you are today and the one you will become. You have many wonderful qualities, abilities, and talents. No other person in the world is exactly like you.

Strive daily to feed positive thoughts into your brain, and try very hard not to let negativity slip in. Psychologists and self-esteem experts say, "If you are focusing enough on how good you are, your talents, and what you have to offer to the world, you should be able to name 15 positive things about yourself."

How do you start loving yourself and taking care of yourself? First, forgive yourself for anything that you don't like about yourself. In the beginning, most people can only name three or four good things about themselves, but they get better after thinking about their good points. Make a decision to put the past behind you, regardless of how bad it might have been or how many mistakes you may have made. Learn to celebrate all the good things about yourself and others!

Think about three big mistakes you have made in your life. List them in the space provided.

THREE BIG MISTAKES I HAVE MADE

1. _____
   _____
   _____
   _____

2. _____
   _____
   _____
   _____

3. _____
   _____
   _____
   _____

Everyone makes mistakes. In some cases, mistakes defeat people. In most cases, however, mistakes teach us something and can become the springboard that propels a person to success.

In the space provided, discuss what you learned from your biggest mistakes. Perhaps it is not to get too deep in credit card debt. Maybe you have learned better time management as a result of living under too much stress. You might have learned that certain people in your life are toxic, and you have moved away from them toward friends who make you feel good about yourself.

THINGS I LEARNED FROM MY MISTAKES

_____

_____

_____

_____

_____

_____

_____

_____

_____

_____

The point of this exercise you just completed is simple. As long as you live, you will make mistakes. You should get to the point where you make fewer and smaller mistakes, but you will always make mistakes. What is important is that you learn from those mistakes and let them make you better. Forgive yourself for the mistakes you made in the past, and resolve to start living in a different way today.

 SOLUTION 90 SEEK MEANING AND PURPOSE IN YOUR PERSONAL AND PROFESSIONAL LIFE

Personal and business success starts with answering the question: "What should I do with my life? By analyzing yourself and discovering your life signature, you can focus your power to coordinate spirit, mind, and body in living your purpose. Sooner or later, we all yearn to break out of our secure harbors. The heart moves beyond the familiar and convenient into more adventurous realms of possibility" (Agno, 2007).

If you want to do something worthwhile with your life, then your life will have purpose. If you want to help others who are less fortunate and actually follow through with your wishes, your life will have purpose. If you want to leave a legacy to those who follow after you, you will find purpose in your life.

Your purpose might be something you have always wanted to do, and you might set goals to attain this desire. Or you might discover your purpose quite accidentally by being in the right place at the right time when something happens that resonates with you and perhaps changes your life's direction.

One person with a purpose and a drive to accomplish something worthwhile will most likely accomplish more than ten people who hate what they are doing and have no purpose in life. Unfortunately, many people get up every day and go to a job they hate, and their lives are unfulfilled and meaningless. We hope you have decided on a career that will bring you fulfillment and happiness. In this section, we discuss some strategies for finding purpose and joy in your life.

The first step toward finding purpose in your life is to take care of basic needs such as security, belonging, and self-esteem. Women have sometimes been taught

to ignore their own needs while taking care of everyone else. Perhaps you need to heal some inner wounds left from childhood. It is not only appropriate but important that you first take care of your own personal needs. If you are living a life that is stressful, hectic, and chock-full of boring tasks that take up all your time and leave no room for joy breaks, you may need to put stability in your life before trying to find purpose. You may have to give up something or someone. You may have to find a way to live more simply and less expensively to find happiness.

Throughout the process of finding your purpose in life, "it is important to get emotional support and encouragement from friends, family, and others in your life. It is very helpful to regularly connect with others who understand your desire for a meaningful life and career and who may be working toward the same ends themselves. . . . It is especially helpful to have people who are good listeners, and who won't rush you into thinking about practical issues or making decisions too quickly" (Early, 2008).

You might begin this search for your life's purpose by responding to the questions in the space provided. But realize that searching for your purpose and meaning in your personal and professional life may take some time. In this book, we primarily want to introduce you to the concept of having a purpose in your professional and personal life and to help you start focusing on this important aspect of your life. Finding your purpose answers the question, "What's it all about?"

LIFE'S PURPOSE QUESTIONS

An Exercise in Finding Purpose and Position

1. What activities do I like best?

_____

_____

_____

2. Do I like to work with technology?

_____

_____

_____

3. Am I a people person?

_____

_____

_____

4. In what part of the country do I want to live?

_____

_____

_____

5. Do I like to live in the city or a rural area?

_____

_____

_____

6. What kind of people do I like?

_____

_____

_____

7. What are my special talents, gifts, and skills?

_____

_____

_____

8. What values are important to me?

_____

_____

_____

9. What kinds of environmental and social issues concern me?

_____

_____

_____

10. What am I passionate about?

_____

_____

_____

11. In what ways am I already making contributions that are personally rewarding to me?

_____

_____

_____

12. What kind of organization fits my needs and talents best?

_____

_____

_____

13. Am I driven by money, titles, fame, inner peace, recognition?

_____

_____

_____

14. Is there a voluntary project that interests me and might lead to a fulfilling purpose for my life?

_____

_____

_____

(continued)

15. Am I focused on what I want to accomplish in my personal and professional life?

_____

_____

_____

Adapted from Early (2003).

As you continue to gain insight into who you really are, what you value, what you hope to become and achieve, your life's purpose will emerge. Today all of this may seem to be encapsulated in a fog surrounded by barriers that make it impossible for you to enter, but as time goes by, and if you keep searching for the answers to the questions just listed, you will determine how and where you want to spend your life.

SOLUTION 91 EMPLOY A VARIETY OF STRESS AND TIME MANAGEMENT TECHNIQUES

We live in a very fast-paced society with many pressures and demands on our minds and bodies. Most people can go for a few days with heavy stress and handle it reasonably well, but prolonged stress can wreak heavy damage on your body. Diseases such as heart attacks, high blood pressure, and lung diseases can be caused or aggravated by prolonged stress.

It behooves all of us to take care of our bodies by practicing stress management techniques. In today's fast times, however, we tend to forget the importance of taking care of our bodies. *Stress* is such a common word that many people do not take it seriously, and few understand the dynamic effect that stress can have on the body—not to mention the mind and soul.

The word *stress* comes from the Latin word *strictus,* which means "to draw tight." Stress is your body's reaction to the world around you. Everyone experiences some type of stress. Medical research shows that a certain amount of stress is not bad;

Corbis Royalty Free

in fact, it may even be helpful. Our reaction to stress is what determines if it is good stress (eustress) or bad stress (distress).

As you have worked toward your college degree, you probably have had some physical reactions characteristic of distress such as:

dry mouth	fatigue
tension	impotence
coughs	suicidal thoughts
loss of appetite	insomnia

Distress can have an adverse effect on memory as well. The release of a hormone called cortisol can make you forget things you know you should know (Friend, 1998). "The findings can sometimes explain why the mind goes blank before a key business presentation, a test or an acting debut." This research suggests it is important to learn how to deal with stress in the body before it becomes overwhelming or does permanent damage to your body.

You probably have gone through some positive reactions or eustress as well. Here are some signs of eustress:

heightened awareness	energy boost
excitement	increased sensitivity
happiness	optimism
liveliness	

As you enter the world of work, no doubt you will experience a plethora of stressful situations. Usually, one, or a combination, of these three elements is causing the stress in your life:

situational stress

psychological stress

biological stress

Situational Stress

Situational stress is the type of stress that comes from the physical or social environment. A change in physical environment, such as moving away from college to accept a job in another region of the country, can cause a great degree of stress. A change in residence, change in work responsibilities, change in living conditions, and revision of personal habits all appear on the Holmes-Rahe Scale (1967), which measures life-event stresses. (The Holmes-Rahe Scale can be found at http://www.geocities.com/beyond_stretched/holmes.htm.)

Social-environmental stress is a result of people around you changing. You probably will experience this as you complete your degree and move on to the world of work. You will have new friends, colleagues, and neighbors. Completing school, change in living conditions, and change in social activities appear on the Holmes-Rahe Scale.

QUOTE

Stress can cause severe health problems and, in extreme cases, can cause death.

Mind Tools Website, www.mindtools.com

BIGGEST INTERVIEW BLUNDER

Mary was taken to lunch on her interview. Because she was nervous, she asked her interviewer if she could smoke and was told it was her choice. Mary smoked several cigarettes and later learned this was part of the interview and the company would hire no smokers.

Psychological Stress

As you begin to look for a job, prepare a résumé, get ready for graduation, rent a moving truck, and buy airline tickets for job interviews, you may begin to feel psychological stress. This is stress caused by events.

Biological Stress

Biological stress is caused by new physical demands on your body. While in college, you may have opted to take classes that began after 10 A.M. Your new job may require you to be at work by 8 A.M., and you may have to stay after 5 P.M. This can cause stress on your physical body.

Designing a Stress Management Plan for Your Body

Instead of letting stress get the best of your body, you can use some strategies to prevent or alleviate stress. We suggest trying one, or a combination, of the following:

1. **Relaxation Techniques**   Relaxation techniques can be as simple as closing your office door or looking away from your computer for five minutes, closing your eyes, taking deep breaths, or listening to soothing music. You don't have to be an expert in yoga to relax, which may be something you want to explore also.

2. **Exercise**   You don't have to belong to an expensive gym to get enough exercise to reduce stress in you body. Exercise can be as easy as walking around the office building or stretching at your desk. Some people use part of their lunch break to do moderate exercise.

3. **Massage Therapy**   Many people think they have to be on vacation to enjoy the benefits of a massage. This is not true. Although it may be hard to find the time or money to go to a formal massage therapist frequently, you can reward yourself for a job well done. If you know you are going to be involved in a stressful project, you may want to prearrange one or more massages during the project span. In the meantime, you may find relief in a simple neck, shoulder, or back rub from your spouse, significant other, or friend.

4. **Aroma Therapy**   Millions of dollars are spent yearly on various aromas that elicit emotions or feelings. We've all had a moment when we caught a whiff of some perfume or cologne that brought back memories of something or someone pleasant. Aroma therapy works much the same way. You don't have to have expensive equipment or a lab to mix formulas. You can practice aroma therapy in your office, your car, or your home.

5. **Healthy Eating Habits**   Sometimes one of the hardest things to do when we get into a new situation is to maintain a healthy diet. It can be as easy as stopping to think about your food choices. Grabbing a fast-food snack at lunch or dinner may seem like a handy solution, but it may represent a meal loaded with fat, cholesterol, and calories.

THINK ABOUT IT

How will being able to manage stress in your personal and professional life impact your chances for success in the workplace? How will this affect your life at home?

6. Holistic Care   Just as it would be difficult to achieve balance and harmony without considering the body, mind, and soul together, it probably will be just as difficult to maintain a healthy body by following just one of the preceding tips. With the demands of today's workplace, you may have to practice a variety of the techniques presented in this chapter.

Consider some other good techniques for reducing stress:

1. Maintain a positive attitude.

2. Set goals and have a positive direction in life.

3. Implement a plan for regular physical exercise.

Managing Priorities and Time: Twin Stress Demons

Stress management and time management can be double demons in your life if you don't manage both of them. Stressing out over poor priority and time management decisions is very common in most people's lives.

If you were to ask most people in today's workplace, they would tell you they simply do not have enough time to get everything done that is required in one day. Some would tell you that the phone, computer, Internet, faxes, mail, and meetings converge to fill up all their time. Others would tell you they are able to accomplish all that has to be done. Still others, if they are honest, would tell you that they simply don't know how to set priorities. The truth of the matter is that priority management is a personal and independent skill. No one priority management plan fits every person.

Some priority-management experts suggest you list your priorities and check them off as you go through the day. This works for a great many professionals. Others buy day planners to manage their days. This, too, works for some. Other experts suggest you let your assistant plan your calendar and activities. Again, this plan works for some, but everyone doesn't have an assistant, and many people prefer to manage their own schedules and priorities.

A study of top executives and their daily work habits and priority-management efforts revealed that "most of their time wasn't planned in advance" (Deutschman, 1992). It was found that they spent 76 percent of their time talking to others. "The country's top executives walk into the office in the morning with only a vague sense of what the day will bring." Almost all of us could manage our time and priorities better if we did advance planning.

When it comes to managing your priorities, you have to sort out what style best fits you, your company, and your life. The following tips on priority management may help you develop your own management plan:

Tips for Developing a Time Management Plan

- Instead of writing memos, use the telephone or e-mail whenever possible.

- Learn to say no.

- Avoid scheduling meetings whenever possible. Will a phone call or e-mail do?

- Clean off your desk daily.

- Never handle correspondence twice.

- File—don't pile!

- Reply directly on memos and letters.

- Learn to delegate when possible.

- Study your work habits to find out what hours of the day you are most productive, and use that time wisely.

- Develop a daily to-do list and see if this works for you.

- Carry a small notepad with you at all times.

- Focus on completing one task at a time if possible.

- Leave your work area during lunch.

- Make your work area fit your style—make it stimulating and fun.

- Have a place for everything on your desk and inside of it.

- Work on harder projects first.

- Don't schedule back-to-back meetings if you can help it; leave time to process the previous meeting.

- Spend less time with people who waste your time.

In the space provided, list five doable, concrete activities that you can begin to employ in your life *today* to manage your time more effectively and reduce stress.

MY PLAN FOR PRIORTY MANAGEMENT

1. _____
_____
_____

2. _____
_____
_____

3. _____
_____
_____

4. _____
_____
_____

5. _____
_____
_____

 **QUICK FACT**

Most (75 to 90 percent) of visits to primary care physicians are because of stress-related problems including backaches, insomnia, anxiety, depression, chest pains, hypertension, and headaches.

Essi Systems, Designers of Award Winning Stressmap

SOLUTION 92   INCORPORATE JOY BREAKS INTO YOUR LIFE

Some people get so caught up in their work that they lose touch with themselves, their families, and their friends. They work very hard to keep many balls in the air—responsibilities like work, meetings, boss's assignments, trying to get ahead, money problems, going back to school—while they are dropping the most important things and people in their lives. Getting ahead is not worth the price of giving up movies, games, walks on the beach, backyard cookouts, playing with children, and spending special time with people who mean the most to you.

Getty Images, Inc.–Photodisc

We would be the first to tell you you have to work hard and smart to succeed, so we are not telling you not to work hard. We are suggesting, however, that you incorporate joy breaks into you daily life. Find a few minutes to look at a sunset, read a chapter in a book, watch a good television program, or sit in a swing with a person who is significant to you and listen and talk. Hard work should be rewarded with joy breaks! We encourage you to pursue joy actively!

To understand joy and motivation, we need to grasp the concept of intrinsic and extrinsic factors. Motivation is strange. It seems infectious to some and contagious to others. Sometimes it comes with great force, and other times it seems elusive. Why do some people seem to be more motivated than others to find joy? We have all been motivated by something at one point or another, but why? What causes us to have that driving force to succeed, to be more, to find joy, to be happy, to get that college degree, or to succeed in our first job? Two possible reasons are intrinsic motivation and extrinsic motivation.

Motivation that stems from factors such as interest or curiosity is called *intrinsic motivation.* When we are intrinsically motivated, we do not need incentives or punishments because the activity itself is rewarding. In contrast, when we do something to earn a grade or reward, avoid punishment, please the teacher, or for some other reason that has very little to do with the task itself, we experience extrinsic motivation (Woolfolk, 2006).

The pursuit of joy is intrinsic. We pursue joy and happiness not for a reward but, instead, for the act itself. Joy comes in as many different forms as the people who pursue it. Some find joy in work. Others find it in leisure activities, family, personal growth, or giving. Next we examine some of the activities that bring joy.

Joy in Self-Growth and Discovery

Some people find joy in learning more about themselves and their purpose in life, developing a vision, exploring their potential, strengthening their soul, or solidifying their life's philosophy. Deepak Chopra (1994) suggests that one way to begin a

> ### QUOTE
> Happiness comes only when we push our brains and hearts to the farthest reaches of which we are capable. The purpose of life is to matter—to count, to stand for something, to have it make some difference that we lived at all.
>
> Leo Buscaglia

> ### POSITIVE HABITS
>
> ### WORK
> Try every possible means to spend at least fifteen minutes per day—at work—to do something you love. Bring joy into your work day.

journey in self-growth and discovery is to practice silence: "There is a prayer in *A Course in Miracles* that states, 'Today, I shall judge nothing that occurs.' Nonjudgment creates silence in your mind." He believes that, through this silence, we can begin to access our own potential.

William James, an American psychologist, suggested that humans use only 10 percent of their brain's capacity and thus never really understand or use much of their potential. Otto (1972) found that if we were to use only half of our brain, we could learn forty languages with little difficulty. Many psychologists, sociologists, therapists, philosophers, medical personnel, and religious figures agree that we do not know the limits of human potential.

So what are some of the factors you must overcome to begin using more of your potential? At the forefront is fear—of failure, of rejection, of growth, of truth. Other factors include prejudice, lack of role models and mentors, a low self-image, comparing ourselves to others who have done more, a need for security, learned helplessness, and—to be honest—laziness.

To begin to discover more about your potential and grow as a human being, you might consider the following:

- Work to overcome your fears.
- Take positive risks every day.
- Enlist friends and family to help you.
- Stop comparing yourself to others.
- Surround yourself with people you admire and consider to be using their potential.
- Take on projects that are hard and maybe even out of your league so you can expand your knowledge.
- Learn to question assumptions.
- Strive to remove biases and prejudices from your life.
- Continue your education through graduate school, seminars, and lectures.
- Don't be afraid of change and growth; embrace it.
- Join organizations that promote growth and self-expansion.
- Read, and put into practice, self-help advice from books and professionals.

There is no such thing as luck. There is preparation meeting opportunity.

Oprah Winfrey

Joy in Work

In the play *Bent* by Martin Sherman (1979), two characters in a Nazi concentration camp are forced to carry rocks from one pile to another all day long. When all of the rocks are on one side, they must move the rocks back to the other side, one by one. One character, Horst, asks Max, the second character, "Why?" Max responds, "It's supposed to drive us crazy . . . it makes no sense. It serves no purpose . . . the work is totally nonessential. I figured it out. They do it to drive us crazy."

Work, to some, is a four-letter word, but to many, it is an essential part of who they are as a person. Some of the values of work, and some of the joys that come from work, are as follows:

A sense of accomplishment

A sense of making a contribution to the world

A sense of helping others

A healthy feeling of being in control of our personal destiny

A sense of belonging to a team

A sense of being productive

A sense of growth and developing our potential

Marianne Williamson (1994) sums up the value of work with these words: "The meaning of work, whatever its form, is that it be used to heal the world."

If you find yourself in a profession, a career, or a vocation that turns out to be drudgery and a "job," take the wisdom of Leo Buscaglia (1982) to heart:

> If you don't like the scene you're in, if you're unhappy, if you're lonely, if you don't feel things are happening, change your scene. Paint a new backdrop. Surround yourself with new actors. Write a new play—and if it's not a good play, get the hell off the stage and write another one. There are millions of plays—as many as there are people.

Joy in People

From earliest childhood, we have had an idea of what a family does. We learned it from our own parents, relatives, or from reruns of TV shows featuring the Waltons, the Brady Bunch, and Bill Cosby. Traditionally, a family consisted of a mother, father, and their children. Today's family sometimes looks quite different. There may be only one parent, or both parents may be the same sex. Some experts define a family as a group of people who love and support each other in the best and worst of times. Regardless of the biological roots of your family, you can find joy in sharing, giving, and a sense of common history.

Much joy in our lives can come from our friendships. The word itself brings feelings of warmth, comfort, and love. We can find joy in friendship because they involve enjoyment, acceptance, trust, respect, mutual assistance, confiding, understanding, and spontaneity. President Woodrow Wilson once said, "Friendship is the only cement that will ever hold the world together." In your new profession, take time to value and nurture existing relationships, and always cultivate new ones.

Comstock Royalty Free Division

Joy in Leisure

Much joy can come from leisure activities such as travel, movies, boating, sports, plays, concerts, and just sitting by the lake. Sometimes, however, vacations can be as stressful as going to work. It all depends on how well you are able to relax and let down your guard.

As you begin to seek joy in leisure, understand that different leisure activities bring joy to some and stress to others. Some people like to sit on the beach doing nothing during their vacation, and others prefer to be constantly on the move—sightseeing, camping, hiking, or going to museums. Regardless of your preference, as you begin your career, don't underestimate the power of your leisure time. Guard it, protect it, and use it to your best advantage for renewal.

Joy in Giving

One of the highest attributes of human potential is the ability to give to the world unselfishly. When we talk about giving, we do not mean material objects or money or possessions. Giving can be as simple as a smile, a compliment, a touch, or a great joke that makes everyone laugh. It is odd that giving is so simple, yet so few seem to have the skill to do so. Kahlil Gibran (1923) in *The Prophet,* says, "You give little when you give of your possessions. It is when you give of yourself that you truly give. . . . There are those who give with joy, and that joy is their reward."

It is hard sometimes to understand that each of us, without fail, regardless of age, wisdom, or contribution, are eternally woven into the fabric of this universe. If we were to die at this moment, we could not erase the fact that we played a part in human history. How the pages of that history will read is up to us.

In the space provided, make a list of special joy breaks you can take that will bring happiness and relaxation to your life.

IF YOU WERE IN CHARGE

SOLVE THE PROBLEM

Jack and Tina are going through a bad divorce. They both come to work and constantly bash each other. Their behavior is causing disruption in the area for which you are responsible. If you were in charge, what would you do?

QUOTE

In order to make your dreams come true, the first thing you have to do is wake up.

Bill Cosby

MY PERSONAL JOY BREAKS

_____

_____

_____

_____

_____

_____

_____

_____

_____

_____

 SOLUTION 93   FIND BALANCE BETWEEN WORK AND HOME

In today's world of work, new employees can spend upward of ten to twelve hours per day, and up to six days a week on the job. This expectation of employers seems to have become the norm for many industries. We highly recommend that you work hard, but we also urge you to work smart, use time management and priority management strategies, set goals, and seek balance in your life. If you get ahead at the expense of your personal life and your relationships with family and friends, you will have an empty life. If you find yourself in such a situation, you are going to have to pay special attention to your body, mind, and soul. Balance and harmony come at a price, one that many are not willing to pay. To find balance and harmony in our lives, we usually have to slow down, give up something, and spend more time with loved ones and friends. This may sound like a punishment, but the rewards from this lifestyle outweigh the sacrifices.

We know George Carlin as a comedian, but he has written a beautiful message related to balance between work and home. This message speaks to the human condition and offers us advice on slowing down and enjoying life. His timely message encourages us to take time for the people who really matter in our lives. Here is his message:

George Carlin's Message for Life

The paradox of our time in history is that we have taller buildings but shorter tempers, wider freeways, but narrower viewpoints.

We spend more, but have less.

We buy more, but enjoy less.

We have bigger houses and smaller families, more conveniences, less time.

We have more degrees but less sense, more knowledge, but less judgment, more experts, yet more problems, more medicine, but less wellness.

We drink too much, smoke too much, spend too recklessly, laugh too little, drive too fast, get too angry, stay up too late, get up too tired, read too little, watch T.V. too much, and pray too seldom.

We have multiplied our possessions, but reduced our values.

We talk too much, love too seldom, and hate too often.

We've learned how to make a living, but not a life.

We've added years to our life but not life to our years.

We've been all the way to the moon and back, but have trouble crossing the street to meet a new neighbor.

We conquered outer space but not inner space.

We've done larger things, but not better things.

We've cleaned up the air, but polluted the soul.

We've conquered the atom, but not our prejudice.

We write more, but learn less.

We plan more, but accomplish less.

We've learned to rush, but not to wait.

We build more computers to hold more information, to produce more copies than ever, but we communicate less and less.

These are the times of fast foods and slow digestion, big men, and small character, steep profits and shallow relationships.

These are the days of two incomes but more divorce, fancier houses, but broken homes.

These are days of quick trips, disposable diapers, throwaway morality, one night stands, overweight bodies, and pills that do everything from cheer to quiet, to kill.

It is a time when there is much in the showroom window and nothing in the stockroom.

A time when technology can bring this letter to you, and a time when you can choose either to share this insight, or to just hit delete.

Remember, spend some time with your loved ones, because they are not going to be around forever.

Remember, say a kind word to someone who looks up to you in awe, because that little person soon will grow up and leave your side.

Remember, to give a warm hug to the one next to you, because that is the only treasure you can give with your heart and it doesn't cost a cent.

Remember, to say, "I love you" to your partner and your loved ones, but most of all mean it.

A kiss and an embrace will mend hurt when it comes from deep inside of you.

Remember to hold hands and cherish the moment for someday that person will not be there again.

Give time to love, give time to speak!

And give time to share the precious thoughts in your mind.

And always remember: Life is not measured by the number of breaths we take, but by the moments that take our breath away.

Does any part of George Carlin's message speak to you? In the space provided, discuss one major point that struck a chord with you relative to your own personal life. Is there something you need to change to have balance in your life? Jot down a few things that need to change in your life to usher in more balance, joy, and happiness. Be honest with yourself.

_____

_____

_____

_____

_____

"When people talk about balance they often think of a set of scales with each side weighing the same. Getting our work and home lives into that sort of balance is rarely possible. But there are ways of creating a match between what our job demands and what we need to do to keep our personal lives healthy" (Kinley, 2002).

The way we determine how we live our lives may depend on the requirements of our work. Some people have very demanding jobs that require total devotion to their jobs. Many young attorneys, for example, report that they work 80 hours a week in the beginning as they are trying to establish themselves. This job has to matter greatly to them if they are willing to take this much time away from their friends and families, and only they can determine if it is worth it. Others may function better on a stable 9-to-5 job where they can close up their desks and leave like clockwork everyday.

Each of us has to determine which pace is best for us. If you are a racehorse, working at a turtle's pace will drive you mad; but, if you are a turtle and you are asked to keep pace with a racehorse, the stress will kill you. Balance between work and home is really an individual preference based on your drive, ambition, need for recognition and status, and desire for cars, houses, and other things. How much the need to be a good team member at work, a hands-on parent, a caring and concerned partner, and a lover of nature plays an important role in striking the right balance for an individual.

As you move into the workplace, consider these questions in determining the right balance between work and home for you:

> **QUOTE**
>
> Live a balanced life—learn some and think some and draw and paint and sing and dance and play and work every day some.
>
> Robert Fulghum

IS THERE BALANCE IN MY LIFE?

10 Questions for Your Consideration

- Do I have the kind of personality that loves running wide open and dealing with stress and responsibilities?

- Do I have the kind of personality that seeks a steady pace at work with regular hours and not too many decision-making responsibilities?

- Does my pace at work allow for flexibility as my personal life changes and new demands at home come into the picture?

- Can I find enough balance in my life to leave work and get to a child's soccer match?

- Does my dedication to work allow me time to take care of a sick friend or relative?

- Does my partner understand when sometimes I have to work on weekends?

- Have I determined with my partner (if this is applicable) what we value as a couple?

- Have I determined what values at work are important to me?

(continued)

● Do I have an understanding between my boss and me that there will be times when I need to leave early to take care of family needs but I will make up that time missed?

● Do I have an understanding with my partner, family, and friends that at times I will have to be more devoted to my work than others?

Finding balance between work and home is really an individual choice that must be adapted to each person's style, demands at home, and desire to excel. One thing is certain: Workaholics never find satisfaction in their personal lives. Each of us has to determine what is really important to us.

Often balance helps us nurture our souls and rid our minds of clutter. Balance can help heal our bodies and our tired minds. Finding the right balance can help free us from depression, anxiety, panic attacks, and fear. Balance can give us more optimism and a brighter attitude. Most importantly, balance can provide us the time to build strong relationships with people who really matter.

 SOLUTION 94   TAKE CARE OF YOUR SOUL AND SPIRITUAL DEVELOPMENT

As strange as it may seem to talk about one's soul, we absolutely must consider the condition of our soul when discussing balance and harmony in our life. As long as there has been recorded history, philosophers, religious figures, leaders, and lay people have labored over the meaning of *soul* and just how much attention should be paid to something that we can't see or touch. Few agree on the answers.

Thomas Moore (1992) says, "The soul is not a thing, but a quality or a dimension of experiencing life and ourselves. It has to do with depth, value, relatedness, heart, and personal substance." He suggests we can't care for our soul until we discover how it operates in each of us. For some, the soul blossoms when it witnesses beauty. For others, it flourishes when friends are near. Some are enriched by giving, and others by receiving. Each soul operates differently, and each person must care for his or her own soul in his or her own unique way.

It has been said that we are lucky if we have one or two close personal friends—soul mates if you will—over the years of our lives. Ironically, most people list friendship and relationships as one of the most important ingredients in a happy and healthy life. Medical research suggests that positive relationships with people are paramount. Evidence indicates that an absence of satisfying communication and interaction can even jeopardize life itself. For instance,

> Socially isolated people are two to three times more likely to die prematurely than are those with strong social ties. The type of communication relationship does not seem to matter; marriages, friendships, and community ties all seem to increase longevity. Divorced men (before the age of 70) die from heart diseases, cancer, and strokes at double the rate of married men. Three times as many die from hypertension; five times as many commit suicide; seven times as many die from cirrhosis of the liver; and ten times as many die from tuberculosis. The rate of all types of cancer is as much as five times higher for divorced men and women compared to their counterparts. (Adler et al., 2006)

Clearly, to achieve some balance and harmony, the soul needs other people. As we care for the soul, we should consider that every moment spent with friends and

QUOTE

We don't receive wisdom; we must discover it for ourselves after a journey that no one can take us or spare us.

Proust

significant others could be the moment we find happiness and, in all frankness, the last moment we may share with them. Deepak Chopra (1994) says,

> We have stopped for a moment to encounter each other, to meet, to love, to share. This is a precious moment, but it is transient. It is a little parenthesis in eternity. If we share with caring, lightheartedness, and love, we will create abundance and joy for each other. And then this moment will have been worthwhile.

As you work to maintain balance and harmony in your life, consider the following ways to nurture your soul:

- Develop an appreciation of, and participate in, the fine arts.
- Make time for heart-to-heart conversations with friends and loved ones.
- Take stock of your value system and work to maintain harmony with those values.
- Devote time to your own spirituality.
- Laugh often.
- Cry as much as you need to.
- Apologize when you should.
- Forgive yourself.
- Support yourself with positive, upbeat people.
- Reward yourself.
- Take long walks and enjoy nature.
- Listen to all types of music. Sing in the car. Sing in the shower.
- Play an honest, fair game in a sporting event.
- Give as much love, honesty, trust, and compassion as you can. It will come back to you.
- Spend time with yourself and develop your own life philosophy.
- Make a commitment to live by that philosophy.
- Celebrate your strengths.
- Take a positive risk each day.
- Do a good deed expecting nothing in return.

SOLUTION 95 ENJOY FRIENDS AND FAMILY

Many people spend their entire lives focused on accumulating more and more things and money while paying little attention to developing positive relationships with family and friends. These people usually end up lonely old people with no one to turn to for comfort and support. Although we strongly recommend that you build a solid financial foundation, we cannot emphasize enough how important it is to enjoy, love, and respect your family and friends.

Quite often people say they value friends and family above all else; yet, if you really examine their lives, you will find this is not true based on their actions. It has been said, "If you want to know what you value, look at your checkbook and your calendar." This is a very hard-hitting question we all need to answer. Where do you spend your time and money? Those two hot spots will answer a lot of questions about what is really important to you.

Many people say they love their children, but they don't give them the time and attention they need. When their children really need them, they are occupied with work or their own pleasures. A very important point to remember about one's children is this: Children need love, especially when they don't deserve it.

Ten Commandments for Healthy Relationships with Family and Friends

1. Love and value each person for the good things they bring to your life.
2. Forgive your family and friends when they make mistakes and perhaps they will forgive you.
3. Settle problems quickly with an open and forgiving mind.
4. Celebrate each person's unique talents and abilities.
5. Plan regular times to spend with each family member and friend.
6. Go out of your way to do something nice for family and friends on a regular basis.
7. Respect each person's private business and personal lives.
8. Be happy and upbeat when you are around family and friends and bring joy into their lives.
9. Do something extra special to honor family and friends' special occasions such as birthdays, anniversaries, and promotions.
10. Laugh often and long and cherish your family and friends.

> **QUOTE**
>
> Rings and gems are not gifts. They are only imitations of gifts. The only true gift one can give is himself.
>
> Unknown

PUTTING IT ALL TOGETHER

Anna Quindlen, well-known author, made this statement: "If your success is not on your own terms, if it looks good to the world but does not feel good in your heart, it is not success at all." Perhaps her quote sums up this chapter well. She is saying to us that no matter how much we seem to have accomplished in the eyes of the world, what is really important is how we feel about ourselves in our hearts.

Perhaps she meant that if we accumulate lots of money, and in the eyes of the world look very successful and admirable for our business skills, but in our heart, we know we got our money by being dishonest, we will not feel successful. Another scenario might be that we are held in high esteem at our work and people look up to us, but in our hearts, we know we have not been fair to our family with our time and energies so we feel like a cheater instead of someone to be admired.

The overriding theme of this chapter is simple: Manage your time, stress, money, values, and ethics in such a way as to be able to look in the mirror and like who you see. Be able to lie down and sleep at night knowing you have done no one wrong. Look at your family and know in your heart they love you because you have loved and supported them.

REFERENCES

Adler, R., Lawrence, R., & Townde, N. (2006). *Interplay: The Process of Interpersonal Communication.* New York: Holt, Rinehart & Winston.

Agno, J. (2007). "What Is Life?" Retrieved November 7, 2007, from http://home. att.net/'signatureseries/.

Buscaglia, L. (1982). *Living, Loving, and Learning.* New York: Fawcett Columbine.

Chopra, D. (1994). *The Seven Spiritual Laws of Success: A Practical Guide to the Fulfillment of Your Dreams.* San Rafael, CA: Amber-Allen.

Deutschman, A. (1992, June 1). "The CEO's Secret of Managing Time." *Fortune,* vol. 125, no. 11.

Early, J. (2008). "Steps Toward a Meaningful Career—and Life." Retrieved April 21, 2008, from http://www.lifepurposecoaching.com/steps_meaningful_career.htm.

Friend, T. "The Effects of Stress." *USA Today,* August 20, 1998, p. D2.

Gibran, K. (1923). *The Prophet.* New York: Alfred A. Knopf Publishers.

Holmes, R., & Rahe, R. (1967). "The Social Readjustment Scale." *Journal of Psychosomatic Research,* vol. II, no. 2.

Kinley, L. (2002). "Achieving a Balance Between Work and Home." Retrieved November 9, 2007, from http://www.relate.org.nz/article_000071.asp.

Moore, T. (1992). *Care of the Soul: A Guide for Cultivating Depth and Sacredness in Everyday Life.* New York: Harper Perennial.

Otto, H. (1972). *New Light on Human Potential in Families of the Future.* Ames, IA: Iowa State University Press.

Quindlen, A. (2000). *A Short Guide to a Happy Life.* New York: Random House.

Sherman, M. (1980). *Bent.* New York: Avon Books.

Williamson, M. (1994). *Illuminata: A Return to Prayer.* New York: Riverhead Books.

Woolfolk, A. (2006). *Educational Psychology* (10th ed.). Boston: Allyn & Bacon.

Surviving and Thriving in Your Career for the Long Term

Thinking About Your Future, Thinking About Your Life

WHY?

do I need to worry about staying current when I haven't even finished school yet? Why is it important for me to be involved in my community? Why do I need to be worried about building my own brand? Why should I be willing to move away and leave my family and friends?

Once you get a position and begin to prove yourself in this new job, you need to think about long-range plans, thriving in your career, and making a name for yourself as a hardworking, creative team player. There are many ways to do this. Of course, the most important thing you need to do is to excel at the entry-level job you accept in the beginning. In your heart, you may know you can do bigger and better things, and perhaps you don't like some of the tasks assigned to you that may seem menial. The fact remains, however, that if you don't do this first job well, there won't be any promotions. So you need to start strong and never let up. Do everything possible to be a good colleague who gets along well with everyone. But this doesn't mean you can't simultaneously plan and strategize to move up the ladder, get a position with more authority and higher pay, and gain recognition for your accomplishments.

As you mature and age, your priorities and interests will change. When you begin working in your first job, you may be willing to go anywhere and explore the world. At certain times in your career, you may welcome change and at others, you may just want things to hold steady. "At some stages, there are likely to be significant pressures on your career due to family commitments" (Eby et al., 2005). For now, you need to focus first on the job at hand while looking down the road at where you want your career to go. So what do you need to do besides doing a good job right out of the gate? In this chapter, we provide many ways you can make a name for yourself, find rewards inside and outside of work, build your personal brand, and continue learning and growing.

You will learn soon enough that you are responsible for you. Even if you have an excellent mentor and large network, you are still in charge of your life, and it's basically up to you to make things happen. Doing a good job is imperative, but working hard by itself may not get you ahead. Haven't you known people who worked hard all their lives and never really got ahead? Previously, we asked you to set goals and to know what you want. This chapter is about doing the extras, taking the next step, going out of your way, giving back to others, and finding many ways to grow and expand your potential so you can accomplish your goals and dreams. This chapter is designed to help you build your own personal brand and to learn to gain positive visibility that can help you earn promotions and respect.

SOLUTION 96   TAKE RESPONSIBILITY FOR STAYING CURRENT AND CONTINUAL LEARNING

Almost as soon as you enter the workforce, you are likely to hear the term *lifelong learning*. This term embraces the concept that it is never too soon or too late to learn. Because you just graduated and spent the last fourteen to sixteen years in school, you are probably not in any mood to hear about more education. You are ready to go to work, make money, and enjoy life.

Many new college graduates have the mistaken idea, "Well, I am a college graduate now, and I will never again have to study and take tests. I know all there is to know about my field." Because of the rapid changes taking place today, however, what you learn in college is simply not sufficient to take you through a work career that is likely to cover several decades.

The truth is, in many cases, you have only just begun to study, learn, and take tests. And you have just begun to learn about your field! You may have acquired a lot of book knowledge, but when you go to work in the real world, your education really begins. Not only will you have a great deal to learn about your profession, you will need to adjust to diversity, office politics, and difficult people. Nevertheless, this is an exciting time that offers you wonderful opportunities to learn and grow. You just need to get your attitude ready to keep learning because new and continuous knowledge offers your best chance to grow and be promoted. "Lifelong learning is attitudinal; that one can and should be open to new ideas, decisions, skills or behaviors. Lifelong learning throws the axiom 'You can't teach an old dog new tricks' out the door" (Wikipedia, 2007).

The world of work has changed greatly over the past few years. No longer does a person go to work for a company and stay there until he or she retires and gets a gold watch. Many people find themselves traveling internationally because companies have expanded operations all over the world. All these changes can be scary and demanding but at the same time exciting and challenging!

Very few, if any, professions are remaining static today. If you go to work and do not continually work to stay updated, you may quickly fall behind. Advances in science and technology are accelerating at an alarming rate. Innovations are being developed all over the world. Competition from global employees who can "plug and play" and compete with you while living in India or China is increasing. You simply can't afford to stop learning!

Lifelong learning is more than just education beyond your formal education. It encompasses education throughout your entire life and includes many modes of learning other than just a formal classroom. Lifelong learning might be undertaken to improve your skills in your current profession or it might be used to prepare you for an entirely new field.

So how does one go about tackling lifelong learning?

- Learn to love learning.

- Read, read, read, especially in your field and related fields. Read current business books, self-help books, current journals, and magazines.

- Take advantage of seminars and training offered in your company and locally. Internal corporate training is designed to improve the company's employee base.

- Ask permission to get more training outside the company and perhaps in other locations other than the city where you live.

- Earn certificates that add to your credibility.

- If your company pays college tuition, get an advanced degree or another degree in a complementary field; at least, take courses that prepare you for higher level responsibilities.

- If you have not had preparation on areas such as equal employment, unfair trade practice laws, budgeting, or human resource rules and regulations, seek opportunities to improve your knowledge in these areas. Such training will make your more competitive for a management position.

- Take courses via eLearning, distance education, and correspondence courses.

- Check local colleges and universities to see what is offered in continuing education courses.

- Design a lifelong learning action plan that keeps you at the forefront of your career and keeps you growing everyday; set clear goals focused on what you hope to accomplish.

- Empower yourself through knowledge that brings confidence.

- Keep learning as long as you live!

Here's an inspiring example of having a clear goal and visionary action plan:

Florence Chadwick

In 1952 on a foggy Fourth of July morning, Florence Chadwick set out to swim twenty-one miles, determined to be the first woman to swim from Catalina Island to the mainland. An accomplished swimmer, she was already the first woman to swim the English Channel.

The water was extremely cold to the point it made her numb; the fog was oppressive, making it difficult to see the boats of her training team; sharks had to be driven away with rifle shots. She swam on and lasted fifteen and one-half hours before asking to be lifted from the icy waters. Her trainer and her mother told her she was very near to the mainland and urged her not to quit. But all Florence could see was the fog, and she had been in the water for almost sixteen hours.

In truth, she was only about 25 minutes from the mainland and had quit just $1/2$ mile shy of her destination. Florence Chadwick had never quit before and was sorely disappointed in her failure.

Later as she explained her failure to a reporter, she said simply, "If I could have seen land, I might have made it."

Two months later, Chadwick tried again. The fog was still dense and the waters still icy, but this time she swam with a vision in her mind of what her goal looked like. She could see the coast in her mind even thought she couldn't see it with her eyes. Not only did she become the first woman to swim the Catalina Channel, she beat the men's record by two hours.

Florence Chadwick had a clear goal and a definite plan of what she wanted to accomplish and how she was going to do it!

Adapted from *Carr-Ruffino (1993)*.

SOLUTION 97   INVOLVE YOURSELF IN THE COMMUNITY

"Companies that encourage and support their employee's efforts to get involved in community work accomplish two goals: (1) They motivate employees, who appreciate the company's efforts; and (2) they solidify the company's good reputation in the community." Several major corporations, including Levi Strauss, McCormick and Company, Inc., ARCO, Westin Hotels, and State Farm Insurance, use creative ways of supporting their employees' efforts in community service. Levi Strauss donates funds to organizations in which their employees are volunteering. McCormick sponsors a Charity Day in which employees work on Saturday for time and half pay, which is matched dollar for dollar by McCormick and donated to a charity. Ninety percent of their employees participate. Westin Hotel awards employees who excel at their jobs and contribute to the community. State Farm gives a certain portion of funds raised in a sales competition to the Special Olympics (Positive Leadership, 2000).

Many corporate executives today believe they have a responsibility to assist their communities in staying healthy and viable. This belief presents many opportunities for employees to participate and to have the spotlight shine on them for their contributions. One way of getting positive attention, in addition to performing well on the job, is to take a leadership role in the community where you live and work.

> **QUOTE**
>
> The world is too dangerous to live in—not because of the people who do evil, but because of the people who sit and let it happen.
>
> Albert Einstein

Some companies have pet projects where most of their charitable dollars and work are directed. Many company websites have information about their corporate beliefs and values as they relate to community projects. Some companies focus their attention to elementary school children or international education or minority groups. Others participate in a wide range of projects. A favorite of many companies is Habitat for Humanity, where many employees show up on a site and help others construct a house for a deserving family. Often you see company employees dressed in matching T-shirts participating in a walk or race that benefits a particular charity. Study your company's website and see if you could become involved in a special project. Find out who is responsible for community service, and let this person know you want to participate.

We have found that students who participate in giving-back projects are deeply touched by the experience, and many continue working with favorite community projects when they leave college and go to work. If you can, you might want to consider giving some of your time to a community project while you are still in school. It looks great on your résumé, and the reward will most likely be greater for you than anything you can give to someone else.

We encourage you to become active in a philanthropic organization that will allow you to get involved in the community. If you move to a new community, this is a good way to meet people and to start building a network. Once you know what kinds of community projects your company promotes, identify the key person and let him or her know you want to be involved. Many times people have earned recognition in the community that impressed people in their companies and helped get them promoted in the corporation.

Study some of the websites that represent charities in your area. If you were to volunteer your time to one of these charities, which one would it be and why?

_____

_____

_____

_____

_____

SOLUTION 98 JOIN AND PARTICIPATE IN PROFESSIONAL ORGANIZATIONS

One of the best ways to learn and get recognition is to make a name for yourself in a professional organization. Amazingly, only a very small core of people use this excellent vehicle for gaining national recognition and as a stepping-stone within their corporation. This core of people with common interests tends to stick together and can become an outstanding network for each other.

Almost every profession has an organization, and often this organization has local, state, regional and national branches. Professional organization officers are always looking for people who will work and help promote the causes of the group. If you choose to associate with an organization, don't just be a joiner, someone who pays dues but never attends meetings and never does any work. This will earn you the wrong kind of recognition. If you join, go with the idea of becoming an active participant. Participating, no matter the level, will benefit you greatly.

QUOTE

If you think you're too small to have an impact, try going to sleep with a mosquito.

Anita Roddick

Bob Daemmrich/The Image Works

Identify the group you want to join and contact the local president or the membership director. Once you have joined, let it be known you want to be on a committee or you are willing to work on a special project. This is your time to shine. If you are placed on the membership committee, for example, and membership has been lagging, you can become a star by bringing in ten new active members. Membership is an organization's life blood, so anyone who can improve membership is well received. Another local committee that can earn positive recognition is the education or program committee. If the organization's programs have become stale and boring and you can breathe life into programs by using creativity and exciting speakers, you will gain positive recognition, and before you know it, you'll be nominated for an office.

Take time to attend state meetings and expand your professional network while you are there. Ask the state president to put you on a committee. Here again, if you do a great job, you will get positive recognition, and you'll be on your way. The ultimate goal is to hold a national office. You will need company support and encouragement for this because this type of office can be expensive because national travel is involved. Be sure you have the support of your supervisor in terms of time and financial commitments unless you are willing to give your personal time and money to this endeavor.

When you return from a conference, provide your supervisor with a written summary of all that you learned. Offer to present your new knowledge in a department meeting so you can share what you have learned. This, too, is recognition among your peers.

Here are some additional benefits of professional organizations:

- The opportunity to hear outstanding presenters
- The chance to build a national network in your field
- Time to meet leaders in your field, join a committee, and show what you can do
- The opportunity to travel to new destinations that offer personal growth
- New job possibilities as a result of people you meet and impress
- Credentials you can earn that give you more credibility in your current job or if you are interviewing for a new position
- Learning about new products if the organization has a trade show

POSITIVE HABITS

WORK

Find out which professional organizations are the most highly regarded in your company; select one, and become an active member.

- Taking home new ideas that will gain you recognition in your company

- Benefiting your colleagues with what you learn and share

Perhaps the most important benefit you get from professional organizations is the opportunity to be with like-minded people. In addition to a great opportunity to network and to learn, you will build a cadre of friends all over the country. Putting yourself in the presence of industry leaders can pay big dividends for anyone who wants to move up the ladder.

SOLUTION 99 EARN PROFESSIONAL CERTIFICATES AND LICENSES

Getty Images-Digital Vision

As we said earlier, earning a college degree doesn't end your need for education. Actually, a college degree should prepare you to keep learning and growing. One way of doing this is to earn professional certificates and licenses that are valued in your field and can enhance your résumé and make you more valuable and promotable. A professional certification is a designation that ensures a person is qualified to do a certain job or to use specific technology or software. Certificates are earned by taking a course and passing a test.

There has been a proliferation of certifications, especially in the technology fields. Some of these certificates lack the breadth and depth of knowledge to be valuable to you. Some certificate preparation will provide intense training on very difficult material, and you will end up with very little useful knowledge and a certificate that may not be respected in the industry. Typically, the certificates that are most respected are managed by a vendor of the respective technologies. The vendors have designed programs for people who use their equipment. Before you spend your money or your company's money, take time to find out which certificates are valued by the industry. Talk to more experienced employees who can offer you solid advice.

Certificates are more coveted in some industries than others. The project management industry, for example, recognizes certification as significantly important, whereas certificates in some fields might be appreciated but will not necessarily command as much respect or garner you a higher salary. The certified public accountant (CPA) designation in accounting is very difficult to attain but provides the holder a highly recognized and appreciated badge in the industry. Regardless of the value of a certificate in your industry, if you learn something useful by taking the training, it will most likely be worth your time and money.

Professional associations have made a big business by offering certifications in recent years. Some of these certifications are highly respected and others are less important. Again, do your homework before you spend your money and your time. Find out which certificates and licenses are respected and sought after in your field by asking employees who have extensive experience.

QUOTE

When you do nothing, you feel overwhelmed and powerless. But when you get involved, you feel the sense of hope and accomplishment that comes from knowing you are working to make things better.

Unknown

Questions you need to ask:

- Is the exam respected and valued by the industry?

- Will I learn valuable information that will help me advance and do my job better?

- How rigorous is the exam?

- What are the passing rates for people who have taken the exam? Does one's native language impact the passing rates?

- How many times can I take the test after the preparation if I do not pass the first time?

- Is this a written test? Is any part of it performance based?

- What does it cost to take the preparation and the test?

- How long will it take to complete the course?

- How often do I have to renew the certificate or license?

- What kind of degree or preparation must I have to qualify to take this preparation and test?

- Does the program require a certain number of years of experience?

To be successful today, you must be willing to pay the price for more skills and knowledge. Often your company will pay for advanced training, but you have to be willing to do the studying and the work.

BIGGEST INTERVIEW BLUNDER

Jason included a certification on his résumé that he did not earn. He also listed professional memberships that were not true. After Jason completed the interview, the interviewer checked out his claims and found he had been lying. Jason did not get the job and lost credibility in the industry.

SOLUTION 100   BE WILLING TO MOVE

"You have been transferred" or "You will have to relocate after your initial training" can be the most exciting news some people ever heard, or these messages can strike fear in the hearts of people who don't want to leave their family and friends. Moving around the country on a short notice doesn't bother some people in the least; in fact, they relish the opportunity. Other people, have never left home, haven't traveled very much, and can't stand the thought of not being able to have Sunday dinner at their mom's table with all their siblings and aunts and uncles gathered around.

We tend to say, "Get over it! If you don't move, your chances of moving up the ladder are greatly restricted. Look on this as a grand adventure." However, if you live in Richmond and moving to San Francisco is going to make you miserable, and you are absolutely positive of this, do yourself and the company a favor and turn this job down from the beginning. Typically, the more you are willing to move, the better your chances for success with a big international company. In today's world, you might even be asked to take an international assignment. There are certain top-level positions that one cannot hold without first having held an international assignment.

Although it is certainly possible to be successful and not move all over the country, in certain industries moving to any location, often frequently, is a given. You might be willing to move frequently and randomly until you get married and have a family. Some families decline moves when schoolchildren reach a certain age.

Robert Brenner/PhotoEdit Inc.

Another concern is when a professional couple is involved and one of them is transferred, causing the other one to have to give up his or her job. If this was a cherished job, it can be very hard on a marriage. Today, more and more companies are offering relocation assistance for the spouse in an effort to make the transition easier on their employees. If you are married, this is a discussion to have with your spouse *before* you take a job you know will require moving. Many marriages have ended because of this difficult decision. Still others end up with one spouse living in one state and the other living many miles away because neither spouse was willing to give up a job. This, too, can be very hard on a marriage. The time to decide how you will handle this situation is before it happens, not after.

Chances are you will be asked on an interview if you are willing to move. You need to be prepared to answer this question honestly. You might say, "Yes, I am willing to move anywhere in the South but I would not want to move to the West Coast." This might eliminate you from the competition if someone with the same qualifications says, "I'm willing to move anywhere. I want to live somewhere different."

Here are some tips on dealing with relocation:

- Prepare now by participating in a student exchange in another country for a few weeks.

- Travel as much as you can and become accustomed to different customs in other parts of the country.

- Get to know as many people as you can from other parts of the country and world.

- If you are transferred or asked to move, consider the cost of relocation. Ask these questions: Do you pay for relocation? Do you pay for travel, hotel, meals, and so on, for a family? If I can't sell my house, do you buy it? Will you pay closing costs on the other end where I move? Will you let my family fly to this new destination? How many times will you pay for my spouse and me to go to the new destination to look for a house? If the cost of living is much higher in the new city, will you provide a cost of living and housing supplement? Read the company's policy regarding relocation before you make a decision. The time to ask for additional perks and money is before you accept, not after you get to the new destination.

- Use an online cost-of-living calculator to determine the cost differentials from your current city to the new one.

- How do taxes on real estate compare in the new city with your current one?

- What about automobile taxes, utilities, regime or neighborhood organization fees, insurance?

- Can you afford to live the lifestyle you want in this city, or will you have to have a roommate, use public transportation, go to fewer movies? (Robinson, 2007).

- Does the weather satisfy you? Can you deal with a very cold climate or very hot, humid weather?

- How is the economy doing in this part of the country? Is there a chance you could move there and get laid off with few chances of getting rehired?

- If you like water skiing very much, is there a lake nearby? If you snow ski, does it snow? Does the city have cultural events that you like for your lifestyle?

- What about the schools? If you have young children, this is very important!

- If someone in your family has a unique medical need, can the medical profession in the new city provide the same excellent care?

- Do you have family needs that necessitate your being close to your parents or other people for whom you are responsible?

- If you have to live a long way from your work because of housing costs, are you willing to commute long distances? Will this erode your family's lifestyle?

- If you have to travel, is the airport close by? Do you have many options on airlines?

- If you want to go back to school, is there a university that offers majors in which you are interested?

- Drive through the neighborhood where you are thinking about moving. Ask people in the neighborhood what they think about the area. Are doctors and dentists nearby? Hospital? Schools? Do they feel safe in this neighborhood? Are there lots of children? Have the values appreciated well? What are the drawbacks to living in this city and neighborhood?

- As soon as you move and get settled, explore your new home; get involved and get your family engaged also so you can all adjust as soon as possible.

As you can see, making the decision to relocate is not a simple one and must involve all members of your immediate family *upfront*! If you decide to move, here are some things you need to do to make the transition easier:

- Complete change of address cards (inform newspapers, magazines, credit card companies, mortgage companies).

- Register your car in the new state and get a new tag. Also, you will most likely need to change your car insurance.

- Change your bank and select one in your new city.

GRADUATE QUOTE

The most important thing I learned when looking for a job was to always remain professional and treat that potential occupation as a business or career, not just a typical job. Having a positive outlook can open the doors to a successful and prosperous future.

MELISSA WYLIE, Graduate! Greenville Technical College, Greenville, SC Associate of Arts Degree, Marketing

CAREER: Administrative Assistant for District 1382 Greenville, SC, County School District

THINK ABOUT IT

How will moving several states away from your friends and family impact your life? Will you be able to adjust and make new friends?

Moving to a new city can be an exciting experience! It can also be nerve-wracking, especially if your family doesn't want to make the move. Even if everything goes well, moving is hard, and you will experience stress during the process, as will your family members, including the ones you leave behind. Planning carefully and getting buy-in upfront will save a lot of heartache and can make a move much more rewarding for all concerned.

CALCULATING THE MILES

An Exercise to Estimate Moving Costs

Go to Google and enter "online calculator for cost of living" to find several options to help you complete this exercise. Using an online calculator, determine the differences in living expenses comparing your hometown and a large city on the East or West Coast. Compare housing, transportation, insurance, taxes, food, utilities, and other important items. List the differences here:

_____

_____

_____

_____

_____

_____

_____

SOLUTION 101 LEARNING ABOUT THE GLOBAL COMMUNITY

Even if you never work anywhere but your hometown, you will be impacted by the global community. You could work in a factory owned by the Japanese or you might be a salesperson for a Swiss pharmaceutical company. You could even own your own Internet company and have customers from many different countries. Today we drive cars with parts, engines, and interiors that may be manufactured in other countries. Our clothes are made in many parts of the world. Many of our biggest conglomerates are international companies with divisions all over the world. Companies send employees to many global locations where they negotiate orders and buy huge quantities of products to be shipped back to the United States. You can, however, work in an international business position without living abroad. As you prepare to move into the workforce, you could easily be competing for jobs in the same global community as a Chinese or Indian counterpart. The world has become much smaller in terms of international competition. Consider this:

The number of North Americans who work for foreign employers and the number of foreign companies who have built plants in the United States is increasing. Evidence that the world is becoming more cosmopolitan can be seen

in the number of international businesses, such as Coca-Cola, McDonald's, Sony, and Honda, which are common around the world. The new economic bonanza is apparent in the universal appreciation of food such as sushi, fashion such as jeans, and music such as U.S. jazz and rock. (Chaney & Martin, 2007)

"Most job seekers today are unprepared and naive in approaching the international job market" (Krannich & Krannich, 1992). They make their decisions about working in a global community—if they even think about it—based on stereotypes, movies, myths, folklore, and the evening news. As stated earlier, you will work in a global community if you never leave your hometown and will need to learn everything you can about new and emerging ways of doing business.

We will only become more and more international in our thinking, ways of conducting business, and in interacting with people from many parts of the world. One of the best things you can do for yourself as you envision your career and the opportunities you want to seek is to learn everything you can about global cultures and ways of doing business.

If you are interested in working in another country or in doing a better job working with internationals in this country, there are certain steps you need to take:

- Learn everything you can about other people's customs and cultures.

- Learn a foreign language, which can be a major stepping-stone in business today.

- Study information that informs you about the meaning of certain gestures from one culture to another.

- Understand the significance of colors in different cultures.

- Make friends with people from different parts of the world.

- Open your mind to understanding and appreciating different customs and backgrounds.

- If you are working with people from a different culture, learn some of their common words and phrases.

> **QUOTE**
>
> The world is my country, all mankind are my brethren, and to do good is my religion.
>
> Thomas Paine

- Take courses and enroll in seminars related to international business.

- Develop a special skill or niche that will be valued in doing international business.

- Travel internationally if you have an opportunity. You might be able to participate in a student exchange. This one venture can change your life and your future opportunities.

Today American companies are sending employees to work all over the world. In many companies there is a constant flow of employees from one country to another. Business managers frequently have to lead a multicultural workforce here in the United States. Leaders are confronted with this type of question today: How do we deal with multinational workforces? How does the way we do business change from country to country? How do my company's core values translate in an international setting? What kind of training and preparation do we need to provide employees who accept international assignments? What kind of education do we need to provide internally to help a diverse workforce learn to appreciate each other and work better together? There is no doubt that mixing employees from all over the world presents special problems, as well as unique opportunities.

In many ways, a global workforce offers advantages such as the introduction of new ideas from one country to another, improvement of operations, a well-trained workforce, and international experiences for employees. Conversely, doing business in international arenas creates problems to overcome: the differences in cultures and customs, language barriers, managers who mispronounce common words, gestures that mean something in one country and something else in another country, and employees who try to do business with members of the international community in much the same way as they would at home.

One of the fastest ways to begin your ascent up the career ladder today is to become knowledgeable in the ways of the global business community. Some business experts recommend that you develop your own personal brand. You may be making excellent contributions and have a wonderful attitude, but if your outstanding attributes are not being recognized and do not bring you visibility, you need to work on marketing and promoting your brand. Your branding process includes:

- Developing your skill sets

- Marketing yourself within and outside the company

- Becoming known for certain abilities

- Promoting your brand through a highly developed network

- Helping colleagues succeed

- Taking on challenging jobs and performing them well

- Learning more about the global economy

Although you need to improve visibility for your personal brand, you must avoid coming across as a pompous, self-serving person who is only focused on personal needs and ambitions. It is just as important to help develop other people and to be a good colleague as it is to develop your own personal brand. People never forget someone who helped them when they needed it.

IF YOU WERE IN CHARGE

SOLVE THE PUZZLE

Xiang Cho is a highly valued computer programmer who has been given an assignment in the United States and works under your supervision. He seems to be having a very difficult time adjusting. If you were in charge, what would you do to help Xiang adjust and feel more comfortable with his colleagues?

MARKETING YOUR QUALITIES
An Exercise in Personal Branding

This exercise can be very helpful to you now, as well as when you accept your first job. Study the information in Figure 10.1 and then answer the questions that follow:

FIGURE 10.1 Building My Personal Brand

Within my company, I am known for at least two abilities.

I plan to develop several new abilities before the end of the year.

I have learned several new things in the last few weeks.

I am becoming known outside my company by participating in activities that provide visibility.

I am building a network of people inside and outside my company who can help me and to whom I can be helpful.

When I review my résumé now, it is considerably improved from a year ago.

I keep my résumé updated and am always aware of ways I can enhance my personal brand.

I am making myself highly marketable in case I need to be.

I am developing my overall understanding of the company where I work.

I am becoming more aware of global opportunities and the impact on my personal brand.

I am known as a team player and as a person who helps others succeed.

Answer the following questions as they relate to your personal brand as it is today:

1. **If you were working in your first career position today, what two abilities do you have that might make you stand out?**

   _____

   _____

   _____

2. **Based on what you have learned in this chapter, what two new abilities do you need to begin developing?**

   _____

   _____

   _____

3. **If someone asked you on an interview, "What skill sets can you bring to this job?" what would you say?**

   _____

   _____

   _____

(continued)

4. Who can you add to your personal network who might be able to help you grow professionally?

_____

_____

_____

5. What do you need to do now that you can add to your résumé and improve your chances of getting a good job?

_____

_____

_____

6. What have you learned from this exercise and the information in Figure 10.1 that you can use in building your brand when you go to a full-time job?

_____

_____

_____

PUTTING IT ALL TOGETHER

You are about to embark on a wonderful time of your life where you will have many opportunities to learn and to grow. If we could offer one prominent piece of advice, it would simply be to go into the workforce with gusto and be willing to take chances and keep learning everyday. Build your brand both internally and externally and help others build theirs at the same time. The world is changing rapidly; those who embrace change and never stop learning can have an amazing life.

REFERENCES

Bellm, D. (2007). "The Value of Professional Organizations." Retrieved from http://www.associatedcontent.com/article/134213/the_value_of_ professional_organizations.

Carr-Ruffino, N. (1993.) *The Promotable Woman.* Belmont, CA: Wadsworth.

Chaney, L. H., & Martin, J. S. (2007). *Intercultural Business Communication.* (4th ed.). Upper Saddle River, NJ: Pearson Prentice Hall.

Eby, L. T., Casper, W. J., Lockwood, A., Bordeaux, C., & Brinley, A. (2005). "Work and Family Research in IO/OB: Content Analysis and Review of the Literature." *Journal of Vocational Behavior* 66(1): 124–197.

Krannich, R., & Krannich, C. (1992). *The Complete Guide to International Jobs and Careers.* Manassas Park, VA: Impact Publications.

Nielson, T. R. (2008). *Career Trek.* Upper Saddle River, NJ: Pearson Prentice Hall.

Plog, S., & Sturman, M. C. (2005, May). "The Problems and Challenges of Working in International Settings: A Special Topic Issue of the *Cornell Quarterly.*" *Cornell Quarterly.* p. 116.

Positive Leadership: Improving Performance through Value-Centered Management. (2000). "Helping Workers Help the Community Pays Off in Many Different Ways". Chicago: Lawrence Regan Communications.

Robinson, K. (2007). *Career Tips for Road Trips: The Relocation Job Search.* Career Library. Retrieved April 20, 2008, from http://www.onlinerecruitersdirectory.com/article_details.php?id=2.

Wikipedia. (2007, August). "Lifelong Learning." http://en.wikipedia.org/wiki/Lifelong_learning.

INDEX